Praise for *The Job/Family Challenge*

"Researchers talk about the intersection between household and work, while workers live the 'juggling life' of balancing job and family. But *The Job/Family Challenge* bridges the gap by providing useful, practical advice along with guidelines for the way it ought to be. This book brims over with useful tips on subjects that range from how to manage discrimination to how to get the kids out on time in the morning. I can't imagine a working parent who won't turn to this guide for advice and information."

—Julianne Malveaux, Ph.D.
Economist/Columnist, First Vice President, National Association of Negro Business and Professional Women's Clubs

"A wise investment in human capital is the most productive investment any society or business can make. It's clear that if you want to attract and retain highly productive employees, you must be responsive to the needs of the workforce. This book makes a powerful case for a family-friendly workplace."

—Arnold Hiatt
Chairman of Stride Rite Foundation

"The integration of work and family is one of the greatest challenges facing American society today. Ellen Bravo's wonderully clear, extremely comprehensive and eminently practical guide provides a much-needed tool to all of us—employers, employees, families, and policymakers—who are working to address this critical issue."

—Marie C. Wilson
President, Ms. Foundation

"*The Job/Family Challenge* is a clear and helpful guide to juggling work and family demands for all working women and men. Every employer and employee should read this book to understand their rights and responsibilities and for tips on how to make the conflict between job and family easier."

—Gloria T. Johnson
President of the Coalition of Labor Union Women

"Ellen Bravo's *The Job/Family Challenge* is a comprehensive look at the complex aspects of making the workplace good for families and business. Using examples illustrating how individuals have made significant change occur in their lives and workplaces, Bravo provides important information on workers' rights and opportunities and builds a solid case for why we should *all* care about resolving this challenging dilemma."

—Barney Olmsted and Suzanne Smith
Co-directors, New Ways to Work, and co-authors of *Creating a Flexible Workplace: How to Select and Manage Alternative Work Options*

"In *The Job/Family Challenge*, Ellen Bravo offers a valuable tool to both workers and their unions in their struggle to bring family-friendly policies into the workplace. This easy-to-read guide is filled with historical insights as well as practical plans for the present. It's a 'must read' for anyone striving to master the work-and-family balancing act."

—John J. Sweeney
International President of Service Employees
International Union, AFL-CIO, CLC

"This book is an indispensable guide to work and family issues for women and men, workers and bosses, and policy wonks alike. Ellen Bravo combines many helpful stories from her own life and the thousands of 9to5 members with tons of reliable information about legal rights and the economics of implementing change at both the workplace and at home. This is the reference manual and how-to book we've all been waiting for."

—Heidi Hartmann
Executive Director, Institute for Women's Policy
Research

"This invaluable guide contains all the basic information that working women (and men, too) need to meet the challenges of balancing work and family. It shows readers real life evidence of how far we have to go to change the workplace to meet the changing needs of the workforce. It also gives concrete strategies to help us get there."

—Barbara Reisman
Executive Director, Child Care Action Campaign

"Loaded with helpful advice on everything from negotiating leave with your employer to creating less stressful family time, this book gives concrete solutions to many of the day-to-day issues faced by working parents, both at home and on the job. What a wonderful resource for working women—and men!"

—Judith L. Lichtman
President, Women's Legal Defense Fund

A 9to5 GUIDE

The
Job/Family
Challenge

Ellen Bravo

To The Women's Resource Center —
Together we can make
change happen!
Ellen Bravo
10-3-05

John Wiley & Sons, Inc.

New York • Chichester • Brisbane • Toronto • Singapore

Also by Ellen Bravo and 9to5:

The 9to5 Guide to Combating Sexual Harassment: Candid Advice from 9to5, the National Association of Working Women

This text is printed on acid-free paper.

Copyright © 1995 by Ellen Bravo
Published by John Wiley & Sons, Inc.

All rights reserved. Published simultaneously in Canada.

Reproduction or translation of any part of this work beyond that permitted by Section 107 or 108 of the 1976 United States Copyright Act without the permission of the copyright owner is unlawful. Requests for permission or further information should be addressed to the Permissions Department, John Wiley & Sons, Inc.

This publication is designed to provide accurate and authoritative information in regard to the subject matter covered. It is sold with the understanding that the publisher is not engaged in rendering professional services. If legal, accounting, medical, psychological, or any other expert assistance is required, the services of a competent professional person should be sought.

Library of Congress Cataloging-in-Publication Data:

Bravo, Ellen.
    The job/family challenge : a 9to5 guide / Ellen Bravo.
      p.   cm.
    Includes index.
    ISBN 0-471-04723-6 (paper : acid-free paper)
    1. Work and family—United States.   I. 9to5, National Association of Working Women (U.S.) II. Title.
HD4904.25.B72   1995
640'.43—dc20   94-45416

Printed in the United States of America

10 9 8 7 6 5 4 3 2 1

This book draws on 9to5's work with employers and employees across the country, including the thousands of people who call our toll-free hotline or send in entries to 9to5's annual National Boss Contest: The Good, the Bad, and the Downright Unbelievable. Over and over again, we hear from workers who feel forced to choose between their families and their jobs. I dedicate this book to the courage, creativity, and sheer determination of the thousands of people who have contacted and continue to contact us and are involved in the effort to build a more humane workplace. I dedicate it also to my husband, Larry Miller, for helping to create a new model, and to our sons, Nat and Craig, with the hope that being good fathers, sons, and partners will be easier for their generation than it was for ours.

Acknowledgments

To all the women and men who have shared their stories with me or others at 9to5 over the years, thank you. Your experience underlies every page of this book.

Thanks also to the many staff and friends of 9to5 who've assisted with this project: Maripat Blankenheim, Ellen Cassedy, Cindia Cameron, Linda Garcia, Sharon Hoahing, Sherri Jones, Kerryn Laumer, Alex Lazerow, Ruth Needleman, Barbara Quindel, Joanne Ricca, and Diana Roose. A special thanks to my editor, Judith McCarthy, and agent Diana Finch.

Contents

Introduction

Susan worked until the end of her pregnancy. She took three months off with pay and another three months without pay. At the end of her leave, Susan brought her new baby to the company's on-site child-care center.

Lydia's pregnancy was the happiest time of her life—until she was fired in her sixth month. Her boss claimed her sales lagged, even though she had just been rated among the top 5 percent in several categories.

James took a four-month paternity leave when his daughter was born. He hadn't planned on taking that much time, but his company mentor really encouraged it. Back on the job, his peer support group helped James juggle his new responsibilities.

When John's son was born, he used one week of vacation time and then returned to work. No male employee at the firm took longer than that for paternity leave.

While these people's experiences reflect the range of situations for working parents in the United States today, most American workers fall somewhere between the extremes. Still, for the average employee, a family-friendly workplace is about as real as the men and women on TV commercials—fictional folks with every hair in place and every muscle toned, moving effortlessly between job and family with plenty of time for themselves and each other. The reality for most people, as you probably know, is far more challenging.

Every pregnant woman who's had to worry about taking off enough time to care for her baby without jeopardizing her job knows about the job/family challenge. So does every father who's been pressured into taking the least amount of time possible to be with his spouse and new child. Parents of adopted children know how hard it can be to convince employers that their children need

1

them at home, yet they still need a job to come back to. Anyone who's had to rush to get the kids to day care while trying to make that crucial meeting knows the challenge—as does anyone whose child ever got sick on a workday, or whose elderly parent is no longer self-sufficient, or who has a personal health problem.

My own preoccupation with the job/family challenge started in 1963 at age nineteen. I remember sitting on the steps of a building at college, agonizing over how to choose between marriage and children on the one hand and a career on the other. A favorite professor of mine came by and asked me what was wrong. "I know three women who've done both," he said after hearing me out. "So can you." I decided I'd try to be one of the exceptions.

The years went by, and in 1989 I taught a class, "Women and Work," at the University of Wisconsin-Milwaukee. As the students introduced themselves the first night, every single one of the thirty-some women in the class expressed the anguish I'd felt twenty-six years earlier. Some were coming back to school after having kids; others were young women just starting out. The significant difference was that they didn't feel they had to choose between having a family and having a job. They assumed they *would* do both—but they couldn't imagine how. In some ways, little had changed!

As a wife and mother since 1977, I live the job/family challenge. I've experienced firsthand both inflexible and flexible schedules. I know what it means to be uninsured and to have to use vacation time when a child is sick. I also know how much a supportive employer can ease the stress of a family illness. And I know what a difference it makes to have a partner who shares the joys and the responsibilities of raising children and making a home. Our children were in day care since infancy, and, because it was good care combined with good parenting, they've thrived. Over the years, I've learned many practical steps for balancing care for my family with my job responsibilities.

After joining 9to5 in 1982, I learned why so little has changed—and what needs to be done. I became involved in grassroots efforts to make change happen, from fighting for flexibility at a huge corporation to working for state and federal family leave laws. I've written about this issue and debated it extensively. As the national Executive Director of 9to5, I was appointed in 1993 by Speaker of the House of Representatives Tom Foley to serve as one of twelve members on the federal Commission on Leave, established to study the impact of implementing the Family and Medical Leave Act and to make recommendations on where to go next.

WHAT 9to5 IS

The organization known as 9to5, National Association of Working Women, began in 1973 when a group of ten women workers gathered after a Boston seminar on workplace problems and began to trade stories. The group grew into a nationwide effort that garnered the attention of management and the trade-union movement—and even Hollywood. (In 1980, the movie *Nine to Five* was a box office hit—and was written about the issues raised by the organization.) In 1982, 9to5 helped create a sister organization, District 925 of the Service Employees International Union (SEIU), for those employees interested in being in a union. (SEIU, the fourth largest and fastest growing union in the United States, represents a wide variety of service workers, including office workers, hospital workers, and many others.)

Balancing job and family responsibilities has been a chief concern of 9to5 since its inception. Members from Wisconsin to Georgia to California successfully mobilized support for state family leave initiatives, and the organization was active in the eight-year fight for the federal Family and Medical Leave Act (FMLA), which was signed into law in 1993. Dozens of 9to5 members have given testimony before elected officials based on their personal experiences. We've researched many facets of the issue, including the impact of inadequate family policies on women struggling to move off welfare. Karen Nussbaum, 9to5's founder and longtime executive director, was appointed by President Clinton to head the Women's Bureau of the U.S. Department of Labor, in large part because of her role as an advocate for working families. 9to5's Job Problem Hotline (the phone number is printed at the back of the book) now receives more calls about conflicts between job and family than on any other issue.

THE JOB/FAMILY CHALLENGE—NOT FOR WOMEN ONLY

While 9to5's focus is on the concerns of working women, the job/family challenge is an even broader issue. If you're feeling the stress of competing claims on your time, you're far from alone. Ozzie and Harriet may have reruns on cable TV, but that type of family is fading from the neighborhood. Today only 8 percent of American households have dad as breadwinner, mom at home full time.[1] And this shift affects not only mothers but fathers, children, and business, too. How we succeed at balancing work and family will determine no less than the well-being of American society. The failure to make the workplace more livable for working families is costing billions of dollars in wasted productivity and tax dollars, lost time and talent, and needless rehiring and retraining expenses. The good news is that solutions exist and that they work. Decent wages and benefits, adequate and affordable leave, adjustable schedules, assistance with dependent care, job-sharing, cross-training, telecommuting, resource and referral services and support—all these practices help to resolve the job/family challenge. And employers who've implemented such policies find they pay off in improved productivity and lower rehiring costs. Yet the fact remains that only a minority of companies are adopting these practices as an integral part of how they organize work. If this approach is good for business, why the resistance?

WHY THE CHALLENGE PERSISTS

American culture still sees family as the responsibility of mothers or adult daughters. For a man, having both a job and a family means having a life. For women, wanting to have a job and a family means wanting to have it all—wanting too much, being unrealistic. Thanks to these assumptions, American women over the last decade or so have found themselves staggering under a new burden, the Superwoman Syndrome. Only Clark Kent had to be Superman, yet most working women would have to be Superwoman to manage. Some are rejecting that path: Recent years have seen a slight increase in the number of professional and managerial women who leave the workforce to be at home full time. This phenomenon has been described as a return to "family values." One could also argue that it's a result of the family having so little value in the workplace. (The vast majority of working women, of course, don't have a choice; they work because they have to.)

In reality, most people still work in places designed for employees with spouses at home full time, even though fewer and fewer people fit that description. The workforce is changing, and the workplace hasn't kept pace. Studies show that men are becoming more willing to take on family responsibilities. But even where men want to be good fathers, sons, and husbands, their intentions often collide with company demands. As fatherhood expert Joseph Pleck put it, "The message is really, 'Be more involved, but not to the point where it interferes with your job.'"[2]

Part of the reason for the job/family challenge is that 95 percent of top managers are men. And most of them—91 percent—have wives at home full time to care for family and household responsibilities. These executives simply aren't tuned in to the problem. The people who are tuned in generally don't make the policies. In most American businesses, those who do the work and experience the problems day in and day out have little role in decision making. In selecting upper-level managers, American corporations reward those who can meet, move, or travel at a moment's notice. Long hours on the job are a prerequisite for advancement. The managers who move up have little time to oversee the details of their own daily lives. No wonder, then, that most senior executives are men with wives who don't work outside the home.

Some employers pay lip service to job/family policies, but when they are implemented, they often turn out to be just for show, or just for managers, or just for those with exceptional supervisors. Policies are offered piecemeal, rather than as part of a wholesale examination of the way the company does business.

Many businesses assume they can't afford family-friendly policies because they look only at the short-term expenses. Often, they overestimate the cost of implementation, while drastically underestimating what it's costing *not* to implement.

Public policy has also been agonizingly slow to change, in part because most government policy makers are also men who have wives at home to handle the family responsibility. In addition, lawmakers have been subject to intense pressure from organized business groups that oppose any guaranteed benefits.

Workers are struggling fiercely to carve out solutions to the problem. But as a nation, we can't leave this issue to the ingenuity of individual mothers, the gumption of some fathers, and the generosity of individual managers. In order to rise to the challenge, we need a *coherent* approach to corporate and public policy.

The outlook is promising for many reasons. Women—and men—have higher expectations than in the past, and they're more likely to speak up about what they need. More managers and policy makers themselves are juggling work and family responsibilities, both for young children and elderly parents. And significant concrete evidence is now available to prove that what's good for families is also good for business. Still, change will come about only with organized efforts.

WHAT THIS BOOK WILL DO

If you are concerned with easing the conflict between your job and family responsibilities, this book is for you. That includes individual women and men at every level of the workforce who are struggling to cope with family and job demands—from executives to entry-level workers, from managers to support staff. Part I, The Job/Family Challenge, describes the extent of the job/family challenge today and how it came to be. Chapter 1 outlines the main issues of concern to families, while Chapter 2 gives a historical overview.

Part II, The Challenge on the Job—Your Rights and Opportunity, enumerates your rights under the law and your employer's policies. Chapter 3 helps you decipher the law as it applies to your situation. What laws exist to protect working families? How effective are they? What do they mean to you? The Pregnancy Disability Act and the Family and Medical Leave Act are explained in detail. Chapter 4 examines what to do if you feel your employer is breaking the law. In Chapter 5 you'll learn about family-friendly policies that have been proven to work and why we need more of these. Chapter 6 gives you step-by-step advice for taking action to bring about changes on your job. You may hear arguments against family policies at work. Chapter 7 lays out these arguments—and shows you how to combat them successfully. Chapter 8 provides nuts-and-bolts information on arranging your own family or medical leave—how to decide how much time you need and can afford and how to approach your employer with your proposal for the smoothest transition. You'll find specific advice for your needs, whether you are a pregnant woman, an expectant father, an adoptive parent, a member of a same-sex couple, an adult with elder-care responsibilities or someone in need of medical leave. Chapter 9 gives advice on negotiating a flexible schedule—flextime, reduced hours, job-sharing, or working from home.

Part III, The Challenge at Home—Helpful Advice and Personal Choices, addresses practical issues that can help you make your home life flow more smoothly. Chapter 10 gives sound advice on finding good, reliable child-care, whether you prefer on-site day care or an in-home provider, have a child with special needs, or have an older child who can stay home alone part of the day. You'll also find information on arranging good elder care and available services. Chapter 11 is full of tips for making your household as stress-free as possible by getting the whole family to share household tasks and by identifying trouble spots and working on those first. Chapter 12 presents typical scenarios that may arise and provides the best ways to prepare for these and handle them.

Part IV, Getting Support for the Family-Friendly Workplace, details how your employer, your manager, your union (if you have one), and your elected officials can help—and why they should. You'll also find several appendices of information that you should find helpful for arranging leave, negotiating with your employer, or simply getting more information.

Facing the job/family challenge will never be simple, but it can be livable and fulfilling. Anyone who wants to should be able to have a family *and* a job—and to feel good about both of them. Getting to that point will require change in how businesses do business, how society values family, and how families share the work at home.

I

The Job/Family Challenge

1

The Job/Family Challenge Today

"You mean I have to quit my job to spend time with my
newborn?" Andrea asks. "Don't be silly," her boss
responds. "You can quit. You can be fired. You can go
broke hiring baby-sitters. Or you can collapse from
exhaustion trying to do it all." Later, Andrea confides in a
friend: "We have options our mothers never dreamed of."

Conversation from a "Cathy" cartoon by Cathy
Guisewite.

The job/family challenge—if you have a job and children or have to
care for an elderly relative or a partner who's ill, you know what the
challenge is. It's the daily struggle to balance the often competing
demands of your work and home lives, without putting either one
at risk. Most of us can identify with the exhaustion of "trying to do
it all." While the *workforce* has changed drastically—more than our
mothers imagined—the *workplace* has not.

The most dramatic change in the workforce in recent years has
been the growing number of women, including mothers of young
children, employed outside the home. This transformation has
affected not only the workforce but the American family as well.
Yet if you're responsible for both a family and a job, you know that
most workplaces have changed very little to accommodate the
realities of their workers' lives.

These statistics show the extent of the changes:

• For the first time in history, most families don't have a wife/
mother at home full time. From 1950 to 1991, the number of
married women with paying jobs more than tripled. Wives now
account for nearly three-fifths of all employed women, up from

one-quarter in 1950. The dual-earner couple is now the norm among families with children.

• Not only are most wives working, so are the majority of married mothers. Theirs has been the largest increase of any group of women. And more moms are taking paid jobs *before* their children start school. In 1950, only 12 percent of women with children under the age of six were in the paid labor force. In 1990, that figure had skyrocketed to 57 percent—due in part to the increasing need of families for the wives' income[1] and to the growing number of families dependent on women's income alone.[2]

• Perhaps the most striking change has been the number of mothers of *infants* who work outside the home. In 1970, the number was so small that the Bureau of Labor Statistics didn't even track it; today, more than half of mothers of children under the age of one year are in the workforce.

Many businesses say they've responded to the changing workforce with "family policies" but mean only that they provide leave for new mothers. Yet workers' needs extend far beyond time off for birth. Almost half of the U.S. labor force has responsibilities for young children or elderly relatives. A surprising number of these caregivers are men. While women spend much more time than men giving direct care to elderly relatives, males make up 44 percent of those with elder-care responsibilities.[3] As the Families and Work Institute points out, "benefits, policies, and programs designed to help workers balance their work, personal, and family lives shouldn't be viewed as special assistance for a small group of workers, but as general assistance for virtually all workers."[4]

The daily struggles of working families mainly involve family leave, dependent care, and flexible work schedules. Take a look at how these affect your own job/family challenge and how the failure to address these issues is hurting business as well as families.

FAMILY LEAVE

Until 1993, the United States had no nationwide family leave policy. Leave was left up to states or, more often, individual companies. While all the Fortune 100 companies had maternity leave, most of these companies gave leave only to women during the time they were physically disabled by childbirth rather than offering both men and women time to care for a newborn. Only 28 percent gave postdisability or parenting leave to mothers; 22 percent to fathers; and 23 percent to adoptive parents.[5] And these large companies, employing only 5 percent of the nation's workers, were providing the most generous benefits. Small and middle-sized businesses tended to offer even less family leave.[6]

At that time, the only relevant law was the 1978 Pregnancy Discrimination Act, which said simply that companies couldn't treat pregnant women *differently* than other workers. Stories like these weren't uncommon:

> Brenda worked in the office of a downtown hotel. When she returned from her six-week maternity leave, she was told her job had been filled by someone else. Another position was waiting for her—but that one paid a dollar an hour less and was evening shift. Brenda had no car; the bus to her neighborhood stopped running before the evening shift ended. Brenda was forced to quit her job and go on welfare until she could find a job comparable to her old one.

> Denise was a plainclothes police officer in child abuse and neglect cases, a position she had worked hard to win. When her third child was born, Denise was entitled to take several months of unpaid leave in addition to her disability leave and vacation. She took only thirty unpaid days. When she returned to her job, however, Denise found that she would no longer be working in her specialty area; there was no requirement that she be returned to the same or equivalent job. She appealed the reassignment and was labeled a "troublemaker." Soon afterwards, Denise left the force. She went from earning $13 an hour to minimum wage.

The Family and Medical Leave Act

With passage of the Family and Medical Leave Act (FMLA), the federal government for the first time established the principle that having a family shouldn't cost you your job. The FMLA, which went into effect in August 1993, guarantees workers a twelve-week unpaid leave—with no risk to their job—to take care of a newborn or newly adopted child or a sick family member or to deal with a personal illness. The law was a victory for working families, but it has serious shortcomings.

Even with the FMLA, you may run into problems taking a family leave. Because the Act covers only firms with 50 or more employees, and only those who work at least 25 hours a week and have been on their job for at least a year, it leaves out 95 percent of all businesses and more than half of all workers. And some employers who are covered violate this law or the 1978 Pregnancy Discrimination Act. Enforcement agencies have been greatly weakened over the years, so little monitoring is done to see if businesses are complying. In 1993, pregnancy discrimination claims reached a six-year high, up 17 percent over the previous two years.[7] Donna's story is far from unusual:

> Donna Bovell worked at American Laboratories Associates in Fort Lauderdale, Florida. With good performance appraisals and two raises behind her, Donna's future with the company looked bright—until she told them she was pregnant. "Are you getting an abortion?" was her supervisor's response. A concerned co-worker warned Donna that her job was in danger as a result of the pregnancy. Since she'd done nothing wrong, Donna felt she couldn't lose her job. Then she discovered her personnel file was full of written complaints she'd never seen before. Donna was fired in May 1992, six months before her daughter was born. She still hasn't found another job. "We're a few feet from under," said Donna.[8]

Critics of the FMLA may say women have to be more accommodating in scheduling maternity leave. But some women find themselves out the door even when they go way beyond the call of duty:

> A sales rep had a phone installed in the maternity ward. She took literally no leave other than the time for delivery, and a few weeks later, she closed "the biggest deal of her career." Nevertheless, her boss claimed her performance had suffered and let her go.[9]

The number of pregnancy-related discrimination claims doesn't even tell the whole story. Many employees don't know their rights or lack funds to pursue a claim. Loretta was one of these:

> Like Donna, Loretta felt her firing was a result of pregnancy discrimination. Unlike many women, she knew her rights. She went to the Equal Employment Opportunity Commission and to an attorney. But funds were a problem. "You don't have money. You have doctor bills." Loretta dropped her charge.[10]

If you are covered by the FMLA, you may still find the amount of time for leave too limited:

> Linda had to go on maternity leave six weeks early because of a complication with her pregnancy. The time was applied to her FMLA leave, so she had only six weeks off after the delivery. "The law should give twelve weeks off [for birth]," said Linda, "regardless of how much time you may have taken off for other reasons. The pregnancy and postpartum should have separate leaves."

Even if you're allowed to take as much time as you need, most people can't afford to. One of the few things opponents and supporters of the FMLA agreed on was that many workers wouldn't be able to take leave if that time were unpaid. A special report issued by the Bureau of National Affairs in 1987 stated that passage of the FMLA would have "very limited practical effect: ... About 77 percent of women work in lower paying, nonprofessional jobs, and likely would not be able to take [10 to 18] weeks without pay."[11] Many parents who long to stay home with a new or sick child are wrenched back to work by the necessity to pay the bills and to put food on the table.

The Families and Work Institutes' 1991 study of four states with parental leave laws (Minnesota, Wisconsin, Oregon, and Rhode Island) showed women from low-income households take less time off after childbirth than women from middle- and upper-income households; poor women often take less than the medically advised minimum of six weeks.[12] According to Sheila Kammerman and Alfred Kahn, fewer than 40 percent of working women have enough income to allow them to take a six-week leave without severe financial penalty.[13] This can cause serious problems, as in Leila's case:

> Leila's boss allowed her to take off as long as she needed when her second baby was born. But because the leave was unpaid, Leila couldn't afford to stay home. She returned to work after one month. Six weeks later, Leila ruptured a disc in her back. Not only did she miss a considerable amount of time, she sustained an injury that will plague her for the rest of her life.

Some people refuse to make the tradeoff and find themselves out of a job at a time of greater demand on family finances. The costs of unemployment are high, both for workers and taxpayers. One study put the price tag at $607 million annually in lost earnings, plus an additional $108 million to taxpayers from increased public assistance.[14] Kerryn saw no other choice:

> When Patricia was diagnosed with terminal ovarian cancer, her daughter Kerryn promised Patricia she wouldn't have to go through the ordeal alone. Even if her employer had agreed to let her take a leave, Kerryn couldn't afford to be without income. So she wound up on welfare. Two years after her mother's death, Kerryn is still trying to find a permanent, full-time job with benefits.

What makes this situation even more serious is the importance of women's income to families. According to 1993 Census Bureau data, approximately 25 percent of American families live on $20,000 or less; they can't afford to have a parent out of work. Far from working for "pin money," women contribute one-third to one-half of the total income in dual-earner households and are the sole source of support in most female-headed households and in some families with two adults. Since median income for African-American and Latino families is significantly lower than that for whites, these families are even more dependent on women's income—and more at risk when that income is cut off.

Finally, those women who are entitled to leave and can afford to take it still have to contend with a corporate culture that sees them as deficient for missing any work. One MBA banker, whose image among colleagues changed drastically after a three-month maternity leave, gave this description of the attitude toward women like herself: "That's not what people expect from a dedicated, high-performing employee. They want your soul."[15]

Men and Leave

Most fathers do take some time off when their children are born—but not all, and not for long. Even in the four states with parental leave laws studied by the Families and Work Institute, not many more dads took leave to be with a new child. On average, the men missed one work week, and most used vacation rather than leave time to avoid loss of income. But pay wasn't the only thing holding them back. The Families and Work Institute reported that men are also affected by "persistent expectations in the workplace and in the larger society that men should—or at least will—give higher priority to their jobs than to parenting."[16] Lew's story is typical:

> Lew, who worked in the highly competitive field of broadcasting, opted to take his two-week vacation when his son was born. After one week, he got a call from his boss. "What are you doing, breast-feeding that baby yourself?" Lew was asked. "We could really use you here." Lew went back to the job—much to the chagrin of his wife.

In short, while the FMLA is a step in the right direction, the challenge of family leave is just as great if your company is too small to qualify, if you can't afford extended unpaid leave, if you're a man facing the still-prevalent notion that men don't have family responsibilities or if you're a woman shouldering a disproportionate share of the work.

CHILD CARE

Time off isn't the only form of help working families need, of course. Time and money for good, dependable child and elder care remain a big hurdle for many.

Most people are familiar with the image that sociologist Arlie Hochschild, author of *The Second Shift*, calls "the woman with the flying hair":[17] She strides confidently through a commercial, briefcase in one hand, baby in another. Her body leans forward; her hair flows out behind her (she's white). This woman is confident and happy. Her choices include generous leave, flextime, and an on-site child-care center.

"The woman with the flying hair" does exist. Unfortunately, however, she's the exception. Consider these statistics:

- Less than 1 percent of the nation's 6 million private firms offer on-site child-care facilities.[18]

- Only 10 percent of private firms with ten or more employees offer any child-care assistance; 55 percent of large companies offer assistance, but, rather than direct aid, it usually takes the form of allowing employees to earmark pretax dollars for child care—a program that saves the company money as well, since it pays fewer payroll taxes as a result.[19]

- Only 29 percent of American workers have flexible work schedules.[20]

- Twenty years ago, relatives cared for more than 60 percent of kids whose mothers were employed; by 1988, that figure was down to 40 percent, a trend that is expected to continue even as the need for child care goes up.[21]

Family support systems, once a mainstay for working parents, are less and less available. In the past, most people worked close to where they lived and had relatives nearby. Children were under the surveillance of a whole neighborhood. With a more mobile society and fewer neighbors at home, most working parents now face the challenge of job and family alone.

This reality presents a catch-22 for women on welfare. On the one hand, recipients are called lazy, dependent, and a bad example to their children for wanting to be with them full time. Yet the mother's moving into the workforce may literally jeopardize her children by forcing them into inadequate day care or by taking away medical insurance.

Parents' difficulties with child care are having a direct effect on business. According to the Families and Work Institute's *National Study on the Changing Workforce*, 26 percent of employed parents with children under age thirteen had experienced a breakdown in their usual child care arrangements in the preceding three months.

The Child Care Action Campaign estimates that such breakdowns cost American businesses $3 billion a year. A study by the Los Angeles Department of Water and Power showed that the company paid $1 million in wages over a one-year period to people who were absent because of child care problems.

Lack of help with elder care also takes a toll. An estimated 11 percent of all caregivers, most of them female, have lost a job because of difficulty balancing work responsibilities with caring for an elderly relative.

FLEXIBLE SCHEDULES

One of the greatest sources of stress for working families is lack of flexibility. A study conducted by Bank Street College for Merck, a pharmaceutical company, found that nearly one-third of respondents—the largest group—said the single change in the workplace that would most improve their work and family lives was a change in work schedules.[22] Consider Shawn's dilemma:

> When her son woke up with an ear infection, Shawn called the office to say she had to take him to the doctor. She wasn't allowed to make up the time because she hadn't notified her supervisor in advance. "Sorry," said Shawn, "my children just aren't considerate enough to warn me when they're coming down with something."

More companies are adding flexible scheduling, but we lack a precise picture. Many employers hire part-timers and call that flexibility. But the employees may *prefer* full-time work; 22.8 percent of part-time jobs are involuntary.[23] A 1990 study of 521 large corporations found an increase in flexible work arrangements; yet only 50 percent of these businesses offered flextime, and only 22 percent allowed job-sharing.[24] The majority of workers are in medium and small firms where flexibility is rare. Even in large companies, many workers complain about an increase in inflexibility—the use of mandatory overtime by their employers.[25]

THE STRAIN OF THE CHALLENGE

Families are feeling the strain. If you're facing the challenge, this news won't surprise you. One woman interviewed by Lifetime Cable TV in February 1994 described the feeling of "working undercover. . . . I had to hide the fact not that I had kids, but that they had an impact on my life. I was shocked at the lack of options."

A male lawyer put it this way: "[The way things are,] you can be a good father or you can be a good lawyer. You can't be both."

When the Families and Work Institute surveyed working families to see how they were managing, this is what they found:

- 42 percent say they feel "used up" by the end of the day.
- 66 percent say they don't spend enough time with their kids.
- What workers give up most is time for self; they want more flexibility, more time for personal and family life.
- A sizable proportion of workers, including men, say they would be willing to make substantial trade-offs to get flexible time, leave programs, and dependent-care assistance.

You should be able to have a family *and* a job—*and* keep your sanity in the bargain. Yet balancing work and family responsibilities was the number one issue women said they would raise to President Clinton in the 1994 "Working Women Count!" survey sponsored by the Women's Bureau.[26] This respondent's comment to the president was typical: "There are no breaks—the attitude is: have children and support them. How you do it is *your* problem!"

ARE COMPANIES ADDRESSING THE CHALLENGE?

Some argue that businesses are adopting family-friendly policies on their own, even if they're not obliged by law. Surveys do show that a high percentage of large businesses offered maternity leave even before the FMLA. But most of those firms also have policies providing short-term disability; since 1978, they have been required by law to treat pregnancy the same as any other short-term disability. Far from being generous to working mothers, these companies may simply have been complying with *another* law.

In 1990, Buck Consultants surveyed 253 U.S. corporations about parental leave. Only 27 percent had such programs in place. When the remainder were asked if they would offer parental leave without a mandate, 62 percent said they would not.[27]

Little Help for Most Needy

Though companies have been expanding job/family benefits and some have made great strides, a big disparity exists in benefits and support at large and small companies and at different wage levels. Those earning lower wages have much less access to health insurance, pension, flexible schedules, leave programs, and dependent-care assistance.[28] In short, parents who need the most help with their responsibilities for children are the least likely to receive that help at work.

Are Family-Friendly Policies Unfair?

Some critics think job/family programs unfairly benefit women with children over other workers. But the Families and Work Institute's study showed dependent care benefits are clearly as important to men as women—and good for business as well. Those with access to a range of family benefits were much more likely to commit to the success of the company, to work hard to achieve that success, and to be happier in the process.

These findings are not brand new.

• In 1980, a Gallup Poll for the White House Conference on Families showed 54 percent of those surveyed identified flexible hours, including-job sharing, as their first priority.

• A 1981 national study by General Mills, entitled "Families at Work: Strengths and Strains," reported "Part-time work with full benefits emerged as the benefit with the greatest breadth and depth of support."

• In 1983, *Better Homes and Gardens* did a readers' survey: 66 percent of 21,500 respondents wanted more flexible hours, 29 percent specifically mentioned job-sharing.

ARE FAMILIES ADDRESSING THE CHALLENGE?

Studies show that more men in dual-income families *say* they're doing an equal share, but their wives disagree. In *The Second Shift*, Arlie Hochschild reported that only 18 percent of husbands share equally; 61 percent of men do little or nothing.[29] Over the last two decades, women worked on household chores an average of 15 hours a week more than men. That comes to an extra month each year. University of Akron sociologist Patricia Ulbrich came up with an even more dismal picture when she analyzed data from a national study of 1,246 couples. Whether or not they're employed, American women average 32.3 hours of housework a week (not including child care), compared to 8.7 hours for men.[30]

"When I asked one man what he did to share the work of the home, he answered, 'I make all the pies,'" said Hochschild. "Another man grilled fish. Another baked bread. In their pies, their fish, and their bread, such men converted a single act into a substitute for a multitude of chores in the second shift—a token. [One guy] took care of the dog."[31]

The extra load is taking its toll on women, who are exhausted and frustrated—and angry. Columnist Donna Britt quoted one working mother's description of her weekend: "I got groceries, did at least sixteen loads of laundry, cleaned the grout, swept up plaster dust, put a coat of primer on a wall, changed the sheets, cleaned the basement, and changed the litter box. My husband took a nap. I can't talk about this . . ."[32]

All of these issues—more parents working, problems with leave, the expense and difficulty of dependent care, lack of flexible schedules, and outdated notions that men should not be concerned with family and housework—add up to the job/family challenge. But how did society get to this point? Is the challenge new? Chapter 2 will look at how working families in the United States have grappled with these same issues over time.

THE JOB/FAMILY CHALLENGE

Almost half the workforce has responsibilities for young or elderly relatives. Passage of the FMLA has helped, but leave is still difficult because:

- Most workers can't afford to take much unpaid leave.
- The corporate culture discourages most men from sharing family responsibilities.
- Smaller firms are not covered by the FMLA.

Parents' problems with child care are taking a toll on family life and on business.

Working families need flexible schedules—and most don't have them.

2

Is the Challenge New?

The job/family challenge seems new to many who associate it with the recent increase in the number of women in the workforce. Historically, most families solved the conflict between job and family by separating the two. Typically, men were the sole family breadwinner, while women left paid employment after marriage or childbirth. But this was not true for everyone. Some groups in the United States have always known the difficulties of balancing job and family. And in the early history of this country, most wives and mothers worked. For families with adequate resources, the arrangement was manageable. But for large numbers of families, the combination of responsibilities brought hardship, a low life expectancy for women, and a high rate of infant mortality.

THE EARLY YEARS

In the American colonies, pregnancy and childbirth offered no reprieve from women's day-to-day work. Women who labored as slaves, indentured servants, farm wives, pioneers, and workers in cottage industries depended on their extended family—or the community of slaves—to care for their children, or they simply incorporated childbirth and child care into their regular duties. Feeding and clothing young children were outside the responsibilities of most men; if a man's wife died or was too ill to tend to the children, he usually relied on another female relative for child care. Still, until the Revolutionary War, male colonists played a significant role in their children's upbringing.[1]

Certainly, wives and mothers in that period worked either in the house or outside it. In eighteenth-century Massachusetts, wives who refused to work obediently as well as economically gave their husbands grounds for divorce.[2] Historian Alice Clark's comment on seventeenth-century England was also true of American colonies: "The idea is seldom encountered that a man supports his wife; husband and wife were then mutually dependent and together supported the children."[3]

Native Americans

Mutual dependency of males and females characterized the native peoples in the "new world." Indian tribes varied in many respects—how they governed themselves, what food they hunted or raised, how they dealt with the Europeans who disrupted their lives. But like most people who live off the land, the women in these cultures worked hard alongside their men and in their special roles. Being part of a larger community may have made the work less onerous than for those who labored alone, but the work was constant. The children simply came along as women cared for the crops; child care was incorporated into daily homemaking tasks.

Slaves

In the days before labor-saving devices, the only women who were spared hard labor were those whose husbands accumulated enough wealth to buy or hire other women to do the work. Slave women who labored in homes and fields and raised their master's children had very little to say about the care of their own youngsters. A remarkable book, *Incidents in the Life of a Slave Girl, Written by Herself,* gives a glimpse into the painful choices slave mothers faced. In the following excerpt, Linda had just been ordered to work on one of her master's plantations because she refused to become his concubine. She left her son, who had been ill, with her grandmother and took her two-year-old daughter Ellen with her:

> Ellen broke down under the trials of her new life. Separated from me, with no one to look after her, she wandered about, and in a few days cried herself sick. One day, she sat under the window where I was at work, crying that weary cry which makes a mother's heart bleed. I was obliged to steel myself to bear it. After a while it ceased. I looked out, and she was gone. As it was near noon, I ventured to go down in search of her. The great house was raised two feet above the ground. I looked under it, and saw her about midway, fast asleep. I crept under and drew her out. As I held her in my arms, I thought how well it would be for her if she never waked up. . . .[4]

Linda soon sent her daughter back to her grandmother. After three weeks, Linda slipped away from the plantation at night and walked the six miles home to see her children. Again and again she "traversed those dreary twelve miles,"[5] brooding on how to find escape for herself and her children.

Indentured Servants

Indentured servants were a few steps above slaves. But while they were in service, females were forbidden from doing anything that might threaten or interrupt their labor. That meant no marriage without permission. Having a child by a man who wasn't willing or able to buy out the rest of her term could result in a sentence of two additional years of service—even if the child's father was the master himself. According to historian Alice Kessler-Harris, about one in every five women servants in seventeenth- and eighteenth-century Maryland got pregnant during service.[6] Many of them had to add care for the baby to their other duties.

Poor Women

The argument that women should stay home and take care of their children has never applied to poor women. Colonial and early industrial America viewed indigent women as a burden. The first attempt in the colonies to organize female labor under one roof was a spinning factory, opened in 1750 in Boston by the Society for Encouraging Industry and Employing the Poor. It followed a workhouse built twenty years earlier to support the large number of widows.[7] In 1779, some entrepreneurs in Beverly, Massachusetts, sought a factory permit to employ "otherwise useless, if not burdensome, women and children."[8]

Women who had a choice preferred to take work into their homes to better care for their families. Known as "given-out" or "putting-out" work, these jobs were extensions of the domestic tasks women had done for their own families. The production of cloth, clothing, hats, and food was carried out largely by women at home. Soon technological advances brought that work—and many women and children with it—into factories. The same developments that sent more and more women to work outside the home cemented home and family as women's special responsibility.

WORK FOR HIRE

The 1860 census estimated that 15 percent of all women were engaged in paid labor outside the home. Kessler-Harris put the

number at double that, when you add the women "who took in
boarders, worked with husbands at home or on farms, those
temporarily out of the work force as a result of childbirth or family
sickness, and those who simply would not admit to a census taker
that they engaged in any form of paid labor."[9]

The mothers who did work outside the home at that time tended
to be immigrant women who worked for the same reason they sent
their children into the mills: to supplement the family's income.
Some were the main breadwinners. The combination of high rates
of accidents and work-related illness in factories and lack of any
workers' compensation program—along with low wages—meant
that many men were unable to provide for their families.

Far from leaving the job when they had children, poor women
often kept working and relied on an older child or relative to watch
the babies. Some even took small children to the job—to wait or to
work themselves. Consider this report from the Massachusetts
Bureau of Labor Statistics on "The Working Girls of Boston":

> One of the most frightful features of the "sweating" system is the
> unchecked employment of very young children. In these districts it
> is no unusual sight to see children of five, six, or even four years,
> employed all day sewing on buttons, pulling out bastings, or carrying
> huge piles of work to and from the "sweater's" shop.[10]

Maternity leave was virtually nonexistent. Union organizer
Elizabeth Gurley Flynn described how pregnant women "worked
at the machines until a few hours before their babies were born.
Sometimes a baby came right there in the mill, between the
looms."[11]

The number of working women with families kept increasing. In
1909, more than a third of the women working in one New England
mill were married.[12] A Senate report published between 1910 and
1912 on the conditions of women and children wage earners found
that in Southern and Northern mill towns alike, "the so-called
normal family—father with wife and children dependent upon him
for support—is not found. . . ."[13] What did that mean for women?
Daily drudgery, often tragedy. Journalist Rheta Childe Dorr gives
this account of cotton mill workers in Fall River:[14]

> In the cotton mills whole families worked together, mostly the same
> tasks and always the same hours. All worked, but when the whistles
> blew and the toilers poured out of the mills and hurried to their
> homes, what happened? The women of the mills went on working.
> . . . Eleven o'clock at night seemed the conventional hour for

clothesline pulleys to begin creaking all over town. The men of the family were asleep by this time after an evening spent in smoking, drinking, talking union politics with cronies in barrooms or corner groceries, or placidly nodding at home over a newspaper, their stocking feet resting on a chair or a porch rail. Working men always seem to rest in their stocking feet. . . . I have heard women describing a period of unemployment say: "He ain't had his shoes on for two weeks."

I never heard of a working woman or the wife of a working man who kept her shoes off for two weeks. In Fall River a woman in the mills and at home worked an average of fourteen hours a day and had babies between times. The babies could not be taken to the mills, and as soon as the mothers were able to leave their beds, they relegated the care of the babies to some grandmother, herself a broken down mill-worker, or to the baby-farms in which the town abounded. Of course the babies fared ill under this system. . . . In summer, a reputable physician told me, [the mortality rate] sometimes reached the appalling rate of fifty percent of all births.

Night Shift

Some women handled the job/family challenge by choosing the night shift. A 1914 article describing a factory in Auburn, New York, reported that a large portion of the women were married. They worked from 7 P.M. to midnight, took half an hour for supper, then continued for another five hours, five nights a week. The company relied on women, said the author, not only because men were scarce but also because "it would be impossible to engage men at the same rates that are paid women and get the same efficiency."[15]

Some of the women were the sole support of their families; others had husbands who didn't earn enough. The women mainly preferred nights so they could be with their children during the days. The following comment is typical:

M.R.: "I am strong and healthy and I am glad to work and take care of my children. Else what would become of them? Don't stop the night work with troubling the foreman. They might shut down and then (pointing to the little girl) she will have nothing to eat and nothing to wear. I don't want to work days, as then my children are alone."[16]

When did the women sleep? According to the author of this study, they averaged four and a half hours of sleep a day. "Some slept one hour or two in the morning and for a time in the afternoon; others slept at intervals of about an hour each during the day."[17]

The night shift could pose an unbearable dilemma when children were sick. Ella Mae Wiggins, an organizer in the textile mills in Gastonia, North Carolina, recalled how she joined the union when four of her nine kids died of whooping cough:

> "I was working nights and nobody to do for them, only Myrtle. She's eleven and a sight of help. I asked the super to put me on day shift so I could tend 'em, but he refused. I don't know why. So I had to quit my job and then there wasn't any money for medicine, so they just died. I never could do anything for my children. Not even keep 'em alive, it seems. That's why I'm for the union. So's I can do better for them."[18]

Home Work

Other women stayed close to their children by performing work at home. Many took in boarders—perhaps the most common way to earn income and still take care of family responsibilities. A 1907 survey of working-class families in New York City showed one or more boarders in half of the houses surveyed. Sewing, cigarmaking, and laundry were other jobs done by women at home.

Yet home work had its own torment. Consider this 1913 description of artificial flower makers living in a tenement in New York City. The family consisted of a grandmother, father, mother, and four children aged one month and four, three, and two years.

> All except the father and the two babies make violets. The three-year-old girl picks apart the petals; her sister, aged four years, separates the stems, dipping an end of each into paste spread on a piece of board on the kitchen table and the mother and grandmother slip the petals up the stems. . . ."We must all work if we want to earn anything," the mother said.[19]

During the busy season, this family's combined income was $7 a week; they had no work from April to October. Previously, the mother worked in a candy factory. The wages were better, but she felt she couldn't go out to work after she was married. Others who did that had a relative living with them, usually a mother or mother-in-law, who watched the baby.

Farm Families

Among the most hard-working women were those who often didn't get counted: women who labored alongside their husbands on the farm. A 1914 report by the United States Department of Agriculture, *Social and Labor Needs of Farm Women*, gave a striking description of these women's lives.[20] The report grew out of a mass questionnaire to crop correspondents' wives asking how the USDA could better meet the needs of farm housewives.

> The routine work of the southern farm woman is about as follows: at this time of the year she is up at 5 a.m. preparing the breakfast, often building her own fire; milks the cows, cares for the milk—churns the cream by hand. Puts the house in order, gets the dinner, eats with the family at noon; leaves the house in disorder, goes to the cotton field and picks cotton all the afternoon, often dragging a weight of 60 pounds along the ground. At about sundown she goes to the farmhouse, puts the house in order, washes the dishes left over from the noon meal, prepares the supper—most of the time too tired to eat; gets the children to bed, and falls asleep herself. . . . Somehow she finds the time to do the washing and ironing, mending, knitting, and darning between times. If she is under 45 years of age, while all this is going on she is either enceine [pregnant] or nursing a baby. The result is she is weak and frail as a rule. There are a few well-to-do farmers in whose houses we find better conditions, but the above description applies to negroes, to white tenants and to the young farmers who are trying to build their homes.

Working by Choice

In the years following World War I, women from more affluent families entered the workforce—and more of them decided to stay there after they married. By 1930, more than 3 million of the 10 million women employed outside the home were married, an increase of more than 25 percent in a decade. Still, by the end of 1940, only one of every fifteen married women held a paying job, and most of these were still poor and black.

African-American Families

The only group besides immigrants with a high percentage of working mothers was African-Americans. As was the case with immigrants, low wages and job insecurity among males was a significant reason for this. Unlike immigrant women, African-American women were excluded from jobs in factories or offices or stores. In 1900 in New York City, 31.4 percent of married black women had jobs outside their homes, compared to only 4.2 percent of married white women. An astounding 90 percent of these women (compared to 40 percent of white females) worked as domestics taking care of other women's homes and children—with little time for their own.

Dick Gregory described this life in his autobiography:

> I wonder about my Momma sometimes, and all the other Negro mothers who got up at 6 a.m. to go to the white man's house with sacks over their shoes because it was so wet and cold. I wonder how they made it. They worked very hard for the man, they made his breakfast and they scrubbed his floors and they diapered his babies. They didn't have too much time for us.
>
> I wonder about my Momma, who walked out of a white woman's clean house at midnight and came back to her own where the lights had been out for three months, and the pipes were frozen and the wind came in through the cracks. She'd have to make deals with the rats: leave some food out for them so they wouldn't gnaw on the doors or bite the babies. The roaches, they were just like part of the family.
>
> I wonder how she felt telling those white kids she took care of to brush their teeth after they ate, to wash their hands after they peed. She could never tell her own kids because there wasn't soap or water back home.[21]

Gregory bitterly recalled the social worker who came to "poke around" their house looking for evidence that his Momma was cheating the welfare by working:

> [Momma] would have to follow that nasty bitch around those drafty three rooms, keeping her fingers crossed that the telephone hidden in the closet wouldn't ring. Welfare cases weren't supposed to have telephones. . . .[S]he couldn't explain that while she was out spoon-feeding somebody else's kids, she was worrying about her own kids, that she could rest her mind by picking up the telephone and calling us—to find out if we had bread for our baloney or baloney for our bread, to see if any of us had gotten run over by the streetcar while we played in the gutter, to make sure the house hadn't burnt down from the papers and magazines we stuffed in the stove when the coal ran out.[22]

WORLD WAR II AND WORKING FAMILIES

During World War II, women were suddenly encouraged to work because of labor shortages. Black women were finally allowed into factories that now needed their labor and that of other women as well. The proportion of females soared from 25 percent to 36 percent of all workers. This increase was greater than that of the preceding four decades; the number of employed wives doubled. At the end of the war, married women for the first time made up the majority of women workers.

Once again, as at other points in American history, debate took place over whether married (white) women should work. In 1946, for example, *Fortune* magazine ran a survey asking if "a married woman who has no children under 16 and whose husband makes enough to support her should or should not be allowed to take a job if she wants to." Only one-third of the men and two-fifths of the women who responded felt she should.[23]

If some women were more open to combining work and family, many employers were not. Certain states and municipalities fired women teachers, librarians, and social workers who married. During the Depression, the federal government limited its hiring to one person per family. Frances Perkins, Secretary of Labor under Franklin Delano Roosevelt and the first woman in a president's cabinet, had this comment on the policy:

> It's a well-known secret that married women just took off their wedding rings and pretended to be single. How else can you account for the actual increase in the numbers of married women working during the Depression? But we had no choice in the federal government but to limit one job per family. It was meant to discourage nepotism, but it discriminated against women.[24]

Other employers routinely either terminated women who became pregnant or required long leaves without pay and little or no guarantee of reemployment. Pregnant workers were often denied paid benefits available to other workers with a temporary disability. When New Jersey created a Temporary Disability Insurance fund in 1948, pregnancy was lumped with injuries that were "willfully self-inflicted or incurred in the perpetration of a high misdemeanor"[25]—and excluded from coverage. Some employers refused to provide health benefits for pregnant women workers, even while covering the pregnant wives of male employees. This pattern continued until the recent past.

THE DEVELOPMENT OF CHILD CARE

The more wives worked outside the home, the more families needed help taking care of their children. Historically, parents managed in a variety of ways: most by relying on extended-family members or by having each parent work a different shift. Neighbors who usually shared a bathroom often shared child care as well. Many women worked close to where they lived; if an emergency arose, they could get the message quickly and go home. Others had no choice: If there was no one to help, they left their children on their own.

Organized child care was not an option for the majority of parents, but it has existed in some form for more than a century. According to a study by the Women's Bureau in 1953, the first day nurseries were established by welfare groups in several large cities, beginning in 1854 at Nursery and Child's Hospital in New York City. By 1897, 175 nurseries existed, mainly in settlement houses. Then as now, poor women were pressured to work rather than stay home with their children. The day nurseries sprang up to create a place for those who had no network of relatives or neighbors who could watch their children while they were at work.[26]

Dr. Carolyn Zinsser described one such center, the Community Day Nursery, established in a small northeastern city in 1885 to "minister to the needs of poor working mothers."[27] One of the women Zinsser interviewed, Michelle, recalled how as a child she would pick up her younger brother from the Day Nursery when their mother went to work. She felt sorry for him and felt he was treated meanly; sometimes he would be shut up in the boiler room as a punishment. How had Michelle's mother reacted to this?

> Well, she was in a very desperate situation. My father was an alcoholic. He was abusive. She got him out of the house and she went back to work. She had been home in a bad situation for a bunch of years, so I think for her it was liberating and a relief. But she didn't like it, and she does have a lot of guilt associated with it. But you either sink or swim, and she chose to swim.[28]

The Nursery had been founded as a charitable institution, Zinsser learned, for women who were married or children whose mothers had died—the "deserving poor." Zinsser cited research describing the "two tiers" of early childhood programs in the United States during the nineteenth and twentieth centuries—one tier for the poor, driven by the desire to reduce welfare payments, with little attention to the needs of the child; the other for the more affluent, rooted in the educational system, aimed at expanding early learning.[29]

New Child-Care Programs

Some child-care centers were developed during World War I to serve the influx of working mothers. But because the increase was seen as temporary, centers were set up only on a local basis. Most working mothers at the time still relied on relatives or neighbors. The issue came up again during the job-creation programs of the Depression. Beginning in 1933, the Federal Emergency Relief Administration funded nursery schools. By 1938, more than 200,000 children of low-income families were cared for in these centers. Fewer children were eligible as the Depression ended. But according to the Women's Bureau, because so many people had seen the value of nursery schools, the public demand for them continued.[30]

During World War II, about half of all working women left their kids with relatives. Many others simply left them home alone. The number of accidents resulting from "door-key kids" became a national scandal.[31] As a result, temporary, emergency day-care centers were started for young children, mainly in cities and communities that grew up around new war production plants.

Finally by mid-1943, a federal child-care program was begun for employed mothers, helped by state agencies. The monies were first authorized by the 1941 Lanham Act, which provided funds for public works needed by defense industries. Child care was understood to be part of the infrastructure that had to be developed to make the war effort successful. In 1946, the federal money ran out. Some states continued funding the centers.

In 1955, the Women's Bureau reported renewed pressure from working women for community resources that would help "meet the needs of working women" by "various types of housekeeping services, meals on wheels, and properly licensed and supervised day care facilities for children."[32]

Unions and Family Policies

Today, there is more attention than ever to the need for child care, and unions often lead the fight for improvements. But this wasn't always the case. The following is the oral history of Stella Novicki, organizer for the CIO, as told to Alice and Staunton Lynd:

> "The women felt the union was a man's thing because once they got through the day's work they had another job. When they got home they had to take care of their one to fifteen children and the meals and the house and all the rest, and the men went to the tavern and to the meetings and to the racetrack and so forth. . . .
>
> "We talked about nurseries. In World War II we finally did get some because women were needed in greater quantities than ever before in the factories. But the union had so many things they had

to work for—the shorter work day, improved conditions—so many things that they couldn't worry about these things in relation to women."[33]

The Present

To many people, the horror stories of mothers forced to take their children to work or leave them home alone at an early age seem like a thing of the distant past—but they're not. Garment sweatshops still exist;[34] so do situations where mothers tend their children while picking crops. Some of the harshest conditions are experienced by migrant farm workers, whose union had to struggle even to have members' children attend school.

Even if you have access to a humane work environment, you probably understand the pain, frustration, and sacrifice that come along with trying to do your job well without putting your family at risk. While more workers than ever before are grappling with the challenge to take care of family responsibilities when there is no wife at home full time, there are answers. Parts II and III will cover how you can tackle the job/family challenge both on the job and at home.

THE JOB/FAMILY CHALLENGE THROUGH UNITED STATES HISTORY

Before industrialization, most women worked either in the house or outside it.

In the nineteenth century, immigrants and African-Americans were the two groups with high percentages of working mothers.

Women have traditionally born the brunt of household tasks even when working full time.

Child care was largely left to relatives, neighbors, or no one at all.

When women were needed in factories in World War II, child-care programs sprang up.

II

The Challenge on the Job—Your Rights and Opportunities

3

Knowing the Law

The United States is late in developing family policy. There was no national legislation concerning maternity leave until 1978 and nothing regarding parental leave until 1993. Among all industrialized nations, the United States stood alone with South Africa in this regard. Although the legislature and the courts were slow to act and the laws need strengthening, you do have hard-won rights. It's important that you know the law and how it applies to your situation.

THE LAW ON DISCRIMINATION—TITLE VII, THE PDA, AND THE ADA

The United States has a history of "protective" laws for women that, in effect, discriminated against working wives and mothers. Here are a few of the practices that led to antidiscrimination laws:

• In the nineteenth and early twentieth centuries, laws that limited the number of hours worked by women—but not men—resulted in employers excluding women from many higher-paying jobs.[1]

• During the Depression, as many as twenty-six states had bills prohibiting married women from paid work. One of them passed, along with six joint resolutions or governors' orders restricting employment of wives.[2]

• According to a 1931 survey, 77 percent of cities reported they didn't hire married women as teachers; 63 percent dismissed women if they married.[3] Many public utilities and large manufacturing companies prohibited married women from working as clericals.

• State policies commonly allowed employers to fire women who became pregnant. Teachers, for example, were typically forced to leave the classroom once their condition was known. Economist Barbara R. Bergmann described the motive of the school authorities as probably being a wish "to protect the innocence of the pregnant teacher's pupils and keep them from having to confront the indelicate result of their teacher's participation in a sexual act."[4] School boards defended the policy on the grounds of protecting the health and welfare of the pregnant woman and her baby.

• In addition to being forced out of work when they were not incapacitated, pregnant women weren't helped when they were incapacitated.[5] Disability policies routinely excluded pregnancy. Of the five states that passed Temporary Disability Insurance funds, only Hawaii treated pregnancy the same as other disabilities. The others either limited benefits or excluded them altogether.[6]

Title VII

Eventually, these practices were challenged in court. Plaintiffs based their charges on two grounds: the Fourteenth Amendment to the Constitution, which guarantees equal protection under the law, and Title VII of the 1964 Civil Rights Act, which prohibits discrimination on the basis of sex.

Title VII was added to civil rights legislation at the last minute by Representative Howard W. Smith (D-VA)—not to expand the bill, but to kill it. Boasted the 81-year-old congressman, "I have certainly tried to do everything that I could to hinder, delay, and dilapidate this bill."[7] Representative Smith was sure that the word *sex* would stop the Civil Rights Act cold. Fortunately, he was wrong.[8]

The first Title VII case to prevail in the Supreme Court was brought by Ida Mae Phillips, a single mother with seven children. Barely getting by as a waitress in Florida, Phillips saw an ad for a training program at the Martin Marietta Co. and applied. But her application wasn't accepted because she had three school-age children. *Men* with three school-age children were allowed to apply and were hired. Phillips sued.

"If I would win my case, it will mean that I would have a job, that I would have regular hours in order to plan things with my family," said Phillips. "It would mean more money to educate my children, to see that they had the better things in life."[9]

After losing in lower court, Phillips went to the NAACP Legal

Defense Fund, who took the case to the Supreme Court. They agreed that parents of school-age children should have the same rights regardless of sex.[10]

Unfortunately, the new law didn't specify that gender discrimination included discrimination based on pregnancy and childbirth. It would be another fourteen years before an official acknowledgment that pregnancy had something to do with sex.

Pregnancy Disability Act

During the 1960s, the Equal Employment Opportunity Commission (EEOC)—the federal agency charged with enforcing civil rights laws—told employers they could exclude pregnancy from disability benefits because pregnancy was "unique to the female sex."[11] The first formal proposal defining *pregnancy* and *childbirth* as job-related disabilities to be treated the same as other short-term disabilities came in 1970 from a group called the Citizens Advisory Council on the Status of Women (CACSW). This council grew out of the Commission on the Status of Women created by President Kennedy. In 1971, Women's Bureau Director Elizabeth Duncan Koontz argued that excluding pregnancy from disability benefits did amount to discrimination prohibited by Title VII and by the Fourteenth Amendment.[12] The EEOC adopted the CACSW proposal in its 1972 guidelines.

Thanks to those guidelines, many women in medium and large firms gained medical coverage and paid sick leave for the period of disability due to pregnancy. But many employers had no disability programs or even paid sick leave. And not all large or medium companies heeded the guidelines. The issue made its way to the Supreme Court.

Court Ruling In the early 1970s, the Court overturned two important obstacles for pregnant women. It ruled that employers couldn't tell a woman when to start maternity leave, nor deny her seniority once she returned.[13] But on the issue of disability, the Court agreed with employers that pregnancy can be treated differently.

In *General Electric v. Gilbert* (1976), the majority wrote, "There is no risk from which men are protected and women are not. Likewise, there is no risk from which women are protected and men are not."[14] The justices upheld the view that pregnancy is a unique and voluntary condition. Only a subclass, not all women, are affected, they said; therefore, treating pregnant people differently does not amount to sex discrimination.

In fact, conditions like vasectomies and prostate cancer, which affect only men, were covered under disability plans. Vasectomies are arguably more "voluntary" than many pregnancies. Still, this logic didn't win out in court.[15]

Federal Law   The Court may have thought pregnancy had nothing to do with sex, but Congress knew better. They passed the Pregnancy Discrimination Act (PDA) in 1978, after a coalition of unions, civil rights groups, and feminist organizations formed the Campaign to End Discrimination Against Pregnant Workers. The new law amended Title VII of the 1964 Civil Rights Act to make clear that the prohibition against sex discrimination includes pregnancy, childbirth, and related medical conditions. As a result, employers are required to treat disabilities arising from pregnancy and childbirth the same as they treat other short-term disabilities.

Antidiscrimination laws work only where women and men are being treated differently in the same arena. According to historian Dorothy McBride Stetson, the coalition won because they found a way to compare pregnancy and childbirth "to something that happened to men—namely, job-related disability."[16] The PDA is an equal standard, not a minimum standard. Employers can fail to provide disability to all—they just can't offer it in a discriminatory fashion. Consider these facts fifteen years after the PDA was passed:

- Most women worked for employers with no disability coverage.
- Many workers who were covered had no guarantee that they could return to the same or equivalent position after a disability leave.

Additional protection was needed.

State Laws   Passage of the PDA led to renewed debate over whether women should be given special treatment or equal treatment. Some states had passed maternity leave provisions on the basis that women couldn't be equal as workers if they didn't have leave as mothers. One such law was the Montana Maternity Leave Act (MMLA), which made it illegal for an employer to fire a woman because of pregnancy or to refuse to grant her a reasonable leave of absence. Given the many women not covered by disability policies, such a move made sense.

The MMLA was challenged after the PDA was passed. Both the state Supreme Court and a federal district court upheld the statute. Wrote the judge, "The MMLA would protect the right of husband and wife, man and woman alike, to procreate and raise a family without sacrificing the right of the wife to work and help support the family after her pregnancy."[17]

California enacted a similar law in 1978. Employers there were required to provide for pregnancy leave of up to four months. Although the leave was only for the period of physician-certified disability, this was more time than was permitted for other conditions.

In the legal battle that ensued (known as the Cal Fed case), women's groups took opposing positions. Some supported the statute on the grounds that female workers needed this leave in order to work like males—extend the disability period allowed to men, they argued, rather than taking it away from women. Others wanted the law overturned on the grounds that it discriminated against men and could be used to discriminate against women.[18]

The Supreme Court's ruling was similar to that in the Montana case. Said Justice Marshall in the majority opinion: "By 'taking pregnancy into account,' California's pregnancy disability statute allows women as well as men to have families without losing their jobs."[19] He distinguished the statute from the protective legislation of the past because it "does not reflect archaic or stereotypical notions about pregnancy and the abilities of pregnant workers." On the technical point made by lawyers for the employer, that Title VII preempted such state laws, the justices ruled that the PDA was intended to end discrimination against pregnant women, not prohibit additional benefits.

Many felt the best way to deal with this dilemma was federal legislation that would protect both men and women as parents, not just for the purpose of childbirth.

THE LAW ON FAMILY AND MEDICAL LEAVE—THE FMLA

Pat Schroeder first arrived on Capitol Hill with two small children in 1972, acutely aware of the conflict between job and family. Thirteen years later, she introduced the Parental and Disability Leave Act. The bill became the Family and Medical Leave Act (FMLA) in 1987, extending coverage to include care for a parent or handicapped child over age eighteen with a serious health condition.

Opposition from employer groups was fierce. Many arguments were made about cost, although a report by the General Accounting Office indicated costs would be modest.[20] In effect, as Susan Deller Ross put it, employers who opposed family leave were "fighting for the right to fire seriously ill workers and force parents back on the job within a few weeks after the birth of a child."[21] Eventually, most legislators found this position indefensible.

After being stopped by a senate filibuster in 1988, the FMLA won the necessary votes in 1991 and 1992, only to be vetoed by President Bush. Congress passed the bill again early in 1993; it was the first measure signed into law by President Clinton.

Provisions   The FMLA guarantees the following:

• Both male and female employees may take up to twelve weeks of unpaid leave a year for any combination of the following: birth, adoption, foster care, serious illness of a family member, or the employee's own illness.

• If you take a leave, you have the right to be reinstated to the same or equivalent position after you return to work.

• If your employer pays some or all of the cost for health benefits, those payments must be continued while you're on leave (you can be required to repay the premiums if you fail to return to work without a legitimate reason, but you can't be required to pay the costs up front and later be reimbursed).

• If you have to take leave to care for a sick family member or for a serious personal illness, you may take the time intermittently or on a reduced schedule if medically necessary (e.g., if your child needs physical therapy once a week during work hours, you may take FMLA leave for that purpose). In the case of birth, adoption, or foster care, leave must be taken all at once unless the employer agrees to another arrangement.

Eligibility   To be eligible for family leave, you have to:

• work for a public or private employer who has employed 50 or more people (full or part time) during at least 20 workweeks in the current or previous calendar year;

- have worked 12 months and at least 1,250 hours in the preceding 12 months for the same employer;
- be able to certify your need for leave.

Leave under the FMLA is not automatic.

- You may be denied leave or have your leave limited if you are a key employee (earning in the top 10 percent of salaries in your company) or work in a branch office of less than 50 people more than 75 miles from other company employees.
- If you and your spouse work for the same employer, you may be required to share the family care leave.
- If you have any paid leave, including vacation, available, your employer may require you to use it up as part of FMLA leave.

Limitations   Although the FMLA was an important victory, the law has several weaknesses:

- It covers too few people. Only 43 percent of women and 48 percent of men are estimated to be protected.[22]
- It covers too few situations. Especially problematic is the definition of *serious illness* in the regulations, which require an absence of at least three days from work or school, except for chronic conditions, and the definition of *family* in the legislation.
- It offers too little time, especially for someone experiencing problems with pregnancy or with a seriously ill child.
- Too few can afford to take the leave.

If women and men are to be able to fulfill the intention of the FMLA, these shortcomings will have to be remedied. But at least the principle has been established: Having a family shouldn't cost you your job. The Act makes it easier for women to be mothers and workers, and it sees that men, too, have dual roles. Rather than arguing that women should be treated the same as men, it declares that both men and women need help from government so that their responsibilities at work won't keep them from fulfilling their responsibilities with their family. And it acknowledges that the birth of a child is not the only acceptable reason for leave—that other family responsibilities, such as adoption or a family member's illness, are also legitimate concerns.

States and Leave

Most state parental leave laws were not as generous as the FMLA, so the federal law overrules them.[23] In some states, however, the statutes were more generous. Wisconsin, for example, allows employees to substitute any accrued paid time off for the unpaid leave and prohibits employers from forcing such substitution. Key employees are not exempt; husbands and wives working for the same employer do not have to share leave. The FMLA does not preempt more generous state provisions.

Americans with Disabilities Act

The Americans with Disabilities Act (ADA) was implemented in 1992 and applies to permanent rather than short-term disabilities. The ADA has two basic provisions:

• The employer *may not discriminate* on the basis of an employee's disability. An employer, for example, cannot pass over for promotion a qualified employee returning from a disability-related leave and give the promotion to a less qualified person who has no disability.

• The employer also has an *affirmative duty* to make reasonable accommodations for a person's disability provided that he or she can perform the essential functions of the job with or without accommodations and that the accommodation doesn't cause undue hardship for the employer.

If you need a leave or a reduced schedule because of a permanent disability, you may have additional rights beyond the FMLA. Tom's story indicates how ADA benefits can help:

> Tom had triple bypass surgery. As part of his treatment, he was told to cut back to half-time for a year. Working half-time could count as intermittent leave, but it required more time than is allowed under the FMLA. Tom requested the additional time not authorized under the FMLA as a reasonable accommodation according to the ADA. His supervisor agreed.

Now that you know the law, you need to know what you can do if your employer breaks it. Chapter 4 will give you the steps to take.

State Family Leave Provisions More Generous Than the Federal Law

Category	States	State Provisions	Federal Provision
Hours worked to be eligible	CT, DC, NJ, WI	At least 1,000 hours in preceding 12 months	At least 1,250 hours in preceding 12 months
	MN	Hours equal to one-half the full-time equivalent position in preceding 12 months	
	OR	At least 25 hours a week for 180 days (90 days for parental leave)	
Number of employees for employers to be covered	DC	20 or more	50 or more
	MN	21 or more	
	RI	10 or more if city, town, or municipal agency; all state agencies	
	VT	10 or more for parental leave; 15 or more for family leave	
Amount of leave	CA, CT, DC	16 weeks during 24-month period	12 weeks during 12-month period
	CA	Pregnancy disability up to 4 months for employees of firm with 5 or more employees	
Definition of family member	CT, NJ, OR, VT	Includes coverage of in-laws	Parent, child, or spouse
	DC	Includes person sharing mutual residence and committed relationship	
Key employee exemption	CT, ME, MN, OR, RI, WI	None	Exempts salaried employees if among highest paid 10% and if restoration would cause employer grievous harm
	NJ	Exempts highest paid 5% or 7 highest paid employees, whichever is greater	
Intermittent leave permitted	CA, VT, WI	For medical reasons, birth, or adoption	Only for medical leave
Accrued leave	OR, WI	Employee may use any accrued leave provided by employer, paid or unpaid	Employee may not substitute paid leave for any situation not covered by employer's leave plan

YOUR RIGHTS UNDER THE LAW

Sex discrimination was made illegal under the 1964 Civil Rights Act.

The Pregnancy Discrimination Act of 1978 declared that pregnant women could not be treated differently because of their condition.

In 1993, the Family and Medical Leave Act became law, recognizing the dual roles of both men and women. Its main benefits are up to twelve weeks a year of job-protected leave for birth, adoption, foster care, a family member's serious illness, or an employee's own illness.

The Americans with Disabilities Act of 1992 requires employers to make reasonable accommodations for persons with disabilities.

4

What If Your Employer Breaks the Law?

Chapter 3 outlined your rights under the law. But what happens if your employer violates the law? Many people are reluctant—for a variety of reasons—to confront their employers. This chapter will help you learn ways to do just that. You might find that it's easiest to deal with illegal acts at work through internal company channels. You can also file a complaint with an appropriate federal or state agency or a civil action in court. After detailing the various options, we'll look at examples of people who've pursued each.

OVERCOMING THE OBSTACLES TO SPEAKING UP

Despite the remedies available, many people take no action when their rights are trampled on at work. There are ways to overcome most of the obstacles:

1. Obstacle: *People don't know their rights*. Of those who call 9to5's Job Problem Hotline for information on these issues, the vast majority don't know what they are entitled to. Often, people hope they're protected by some law but don't know for sure what the law is called or even if it exists.

What to do: *Find out what your rights are*. The pertinent laws are the Pregnancy Discrimination Act (**PDA**), the Family and Medical Leave Act (**FMLA**), and the Americans with Disabilities Act (**ADA**) (see Chapter 3 for detailed information). Make sure that the company you work for is covered, that you are eligible, and that the treatment you've experienced is included in the provisions of the law. Read this book, consult a local library for other resources, or call a local social service agency or 9to5's national tollfree hotline (see Appendix A at the end of this book for information).

2. Obstacle: *Many companies have no clear channels for reporting problems.* The model of the large firm with detailed company handbooks and procedures masks the reality for millions of workers: no written guidelines, no clear statement of company policies.

What to do: *Investigate what company or union channels exist, and use them.* Most companies have someone responsible for personnel, even if there's no separate office. You may want to start there, or first go to your supervisor's supervisor. Be prepared to go as high as you need to until you find someone who'll listen. Whether or not your employer is covered under the FMLA, ask management to develop written procedures for requesting leave and to identify someone to handle appeals.

If the response you get is not satisfactory, *file a complaint with the appropriate state or federal agency.* Pay attention to agency deadlines (see relevant sections later in this chapter); you can always file a complaint while company action is pending; staff will wait to hear the outcome before proceeding with your case. The federal agency overseeing the FMLA is the Wage and Hour Division of the Department of Labor. Many states also have state family leave statutes enforced by a state agency. Get advice on whether the state or federal statute is better for your situation. The Equal Employment Opportunity Commission (EEOC) is the federal agency that enforces the PDA and the ADA. All but five states have state fair-employment statutes, most of which cover very small companies as well as those with fifteen or more employees. Under the FMLA, you also have the right to file a *civil action in state or federal court*. However, the remedies are limited (see 53), making litigation a difficult choice for most people. Broader remedies are provided for those who are successful in pregnancy and handicap discrimination suits. (See Appendix A for relevant addresses and phone numbers.)

3. Obstacle: *Those going through a birth, adoption, or family illness often feel vulnerable.* Both expenses and emotions may be running high, while energy is at an all-time low. These aren't the ideal circumstances for planning and taking action. As one woman put it, "Do I take care of the baby, do the laundry, look for a job, or fight a lawsuit?"

What to do: *Get support.* Standing up for yourself is a lot easier when you feel you're not alone. Talk to someone you know will be sympathetic—a co-worker or friend who's had a similar experience, a union steward or member of the union's Work and Family Committee or Women's Committee, a family member, and so on.

Create a safe way to express your anger with this person, and then gather your resources to take action.

4. Obstacle: *Even those who know their rights often fear repercussions* if they speak up.

As an immigrant, Cecilia didn't believe she'd be treated fairly by authorities and hid her pregnancy in order to get a job. She was hired because of her bilingual skills. When her manager realized she was pregnant, he let her go. The stated reason for her firing? "Customers don't like your accent," he told her.

Florence worked in a technical field with few openings. When her employer punished her for taking time off to be with her dying mother, Florence knew he was violating the Family and Medical Leave Act. But she also feared any action on her part would become known and would prevent her from getting another job.

What to do: *Fear of retaliation is understandable.* Even though the law prohibits such behavior, it's all too common; fighting to get your job back takes time and resources. Still, you may be able to prevent retaliation by keeping good *documentation*. Keep a log with all the pertinent details—who you talked to, what you asked for, their response. Have the manager responsible for the treatment *put it in writing*. If that person refuses to do so, write your own memo to the manager summing up the situation and citing the specific law or policy that is being violated. Keep a copy and be able to verify that the person received it. That memo might read as follows:

Dear Mr. Smith:

I met with you on Oct. 18 to request two weeks family leave to care for my father who recently suffered a stroke. At that time, you told me that the law applies only in cases of birth or adoption.

The next day I brought you a flyer with information about the FMLA, which states clearly that it includes time off to care for elderly parents. You told me it didn't matter because the department is too busy and can't accommodate a request without 30 days' notice. I pointed out that the 30 days' notice applies when it is practicable; obviously I had no way to know in advance that my father would become ill. Your reply was that you have a business to run and that you can't have people take off every time someone in their family has a problem.

I appreciate the needs of the business and have always worked hard to meet them. But the law recognizes that workers have family responsibilities, too. I want to be able to fulfill those without jeopardizing my job.

5. Obstacle: *Those who do go through the process don't always get satisfactory treatment or results.*

> [The EEOC] sent me a form. . . .I sent it back registered mail. When I called, they said they received it and would send me something in the mail. I never received anything. It's been seven months, and I've had no response. I feel helpless and unsupported. I work for a corporate giant, and they seem to do as they please.

What to do: If you're treated badly at a government agency, *lodge a complaint with the highest-ranking person* there. If necessary, go to the regional or district director. You should receive these names when you first go to the agency; ask for them if they're not provided.

6. Obstacle: *Even those who want to take action may lack the resources to do so.* You don't have to have a lawyer (see 51), but your employer almost surely will—and the imbalance can be intimidating.

What to do: Lack of resources is an objective constraint. Some lawyers offer a free consultation. Even for a fee, a consultation with an experienced lawyer is often worth the investment. You can learn what you're entitled to and how strong your case is, even if you aren't able to retain that person to take your case. Improvements are needed in the agency process so that you can count on meaningful and timely enforcement of the law (see Chapter 16).

THE AGENCY PROCESS

If you get no satisfactory resolution from your employer, you should file a complaint. Remember, you pay no charge to do this. Here's how it works for the various agencies:

Wage and Hour Division Process

If you believe that your employer has violated the FMLA, you can file a claim within two years of the date of the violation (three years if the violation is willful—that is, if the employer knowingly breaks the law).

Procedures You can lodge your complaint over the phone. Because of a lack of funds, some offices are understaffed, so if you get a busy signal, keep trying to call, go in person, or send a letter if you can't go to the office. Be sure to mention in your visit or letter that you had trouble getting through by phone. Staff are authorized to return a call to your home after their work hours if necessary.

Anonymity   The Wage and Hour Division is the one federal department that will accept a complaint anonymously. This works only in a case in which the violation is occurring to several employees across the board. If your employer has failed to post a notice of the FMLA or to include information on company policies in an official employee handbook, you can report this to the Division, and they'll take action to correct it without mentioning who made the complaint. If, however, you're concerned about your individual situation, you will have to give your name in order for the agency to lodge a formal complaint on your behalf.

The Wage and Hour Form   The form you'll have to fill out is a simple one. It asks for your name, address, and phone; the name of your employer; the kind of business; information such as the number of employees (to show whether the company is covered); and the period of your employment (when you started work there, whether you're still working). On the back of the form are lines to write a statement about the nature of your FMLA complaint. You don't need to bring many records. If medical certification is an issue, it would be helpful to bring a copy.

When It's Urgent   Sometimes you don't have time to wait for a decision; you need leave immediately and you don't want to lose your job. If that's the case, let the staff know and ask for an expedited procedure. Dean Speer, Director of the Division of Policy and Analysis at the Wage and Hour Division, advises people in this situation to go ahead and take the leave if they've met all the eligibility tests and given proper notice and to negotiate with the company when they're able to come back. For those who want the matter settled before they take leave, Wage and Hour policy is to try to handle emergencies as quickly as possible.

Do You Need an Attorney?   You don't need an attorney to file with the Wage and Hour Division. According to Speer, if the complainant hires an attorney, the agency generally won't pursue the complaint, on the grounds that the attorney will file a civil action. Speer encourages complainants to retain counsel only if the situation is not resolved to their satisfaction at the agency.

Labor lawyers don't agree. Milwaukee attorney Patricia Meunier says an attorney can help a claimant get the department to move the investigation along and make sure that any settlement reflects the full damages allowable. She argues the Department of Labor should change its policy on this.

Meunier advises people with a family- or medical-leave problem to consult an attorney to see what, if any, claim they have and what relief they're entitled to. She describes a case in which a woman whose child was born with a handicap asked for two weeks' leave beyond the six weeks she'd originally requested in order to find a child-care provider who could deal with the baby's disability. Instead of getting the leave, the woman was fired. This woman has three claims, says Meunier, based on pregnancy discrimination, disability discrimination, and a violation of the FMLA.

For those whose damages would be limited to getting reinstated or a few weeks' pay, however, Meunier advises going through the agency process.

If you do consult an attorney, be sure to choose someone who specializes in employment discrimination and has a track record of representing employees who bring a charge against an employer. Your local Bar Association (the professional organization for lawyers) can make a referral, as can the National Association for Employment Attorneys. You can also ask a local women's or civil rights or labor group for suggestions. Look for such a group in the phone book under Social Services or Labor.

Some attorneys offer a free consultation. (In a number of cities, 9to5 works with cooperating attorneys; all 9to5 members are entitled to a free legal consultation if one of these attorneys practices in their area.) Ask for an estimate of the total cost. Is there a printed fee schedule? A sliding fee scale? Get a clear idea of the expected payment plan and how you will be kept informed of any additional charges that may arise. Some attorneys may take a discrimination case on contingency (you pay only if you win). Since the damages are so small in FMLA cases, however, most attorneys will want payment ahead of time.

Conciliation According to Speer, the majority of complaints are dealt with in less than 30 days. In most situations, he says, employers have simply misunderstood the law. "We pick up the telephone and call the employer. We tell them we've got a problem. This is what the law says, this is what you did, we have to straighten it out." If the employer doesn't agree, the agency converts the conciliation attempt to an investigation. That process usually takes 90 to 120 days.

Remedies   If the employer is found to have violated the FMLA, you're entitled to your job back if you've been fired and to any wages, benefits, or other direct monetary losses plus interest. Unless the employer is found to have acted in good faith, you're entitled to double damages (twice the actual amount of lost compensation or expenses). You can also be awarded reasonable attorney fees and court costs for having had to file the action. Relief in civil action may include pay in lieu of reinstatement if you don't want to go back to the job because of the way you were treated or if you're unable to go back because of a medical condition; but this issue has not yet been decided by the court. The FMLA statute itself mentions only back pay, reinstatement, and damages. However, in cases involving other employment statutes that are similarly worded, courts have interpreted the power to award reinstatement to include what's known as "front pay" if reinstatement is not an option.

If You Don't Get Satisfaction   If you feel that your complaint is not handled properly by the Wage and Hour Division, you should talk to the local district director. If that person is the source of the problem, call the regional administrator.

The EEOC Process

If you feel you've been discriminated against because of pregnancy or disability, you may also file under the PDA or ADA, both enforced by the EEOC.

Eligibility   The EEOC's jurisdiction extends to companies that employ at least fifteen people. If the firm you work for is smaller than that, you can file with your state or local antidiscrimination agency (all but five states—Alabama, Arkansas, Georgia, Louisiana, and Mississippi—have an antidiscrimination agency; thirty-six states include all employers or those with at least two employees). You can find the agency by looking in the phone book under "state and local government."

Federal guidelines require that you file within 180 days of the most recent incident of discrimination. Some states allow 300 days.

Procedures   You don't need to make an appointment to lodge a complaint with the EEOC, unless you have to see someone outside normal office hours. You may bring a friend along for support. If you can't get to the office nearest you (listed in the phone book under United States or Federal Government), you can ask that the forms be mailed to you.

You will first be given a form with precharge instructions to see if you believe an agency investigation will find proof that you were subject to discrimination. If you answer yes, you'll be asked to fill out an intake questionnaire.

This questionnaire is quite detailed. Among other things, it asks what reason the employer gave for the treatment you describe and who could serve as witnesses. You can name witnesses later on in the investigation, too. Be sure to check with these people ahead of time to determine what kind of information they can give and to alert them to the fact that the EEOC may be contacting them.

The Charge Form   Assuming that you meet the criteria regarding jurisdiction and time limits, you'll be able to file a charge. The charge form asks only for your name, address, and phone; the company's correct name and other identifying information; what kind of discrimination you experienced; and the date of the most recent incident. There is also space for you to write whatever particulars you want to include. Some offices provide assistance in filling out the form; others don't have adequate staffing to do so. You will now be referred to as "the charging party."

Notification   The EEOC's guidelines require the complaint be sent to the employer within 10 days. Also included is a questionnaire about the allegations, with a request for a response within thirty days. (The agency can grant extensions.) It's illegal for the employer to retaliate against a complainant. Report any retaliatory behavior to the EEOC immediately.

Fact-Finding Conference   In some cases, the agency may hold a fact-finding conference in which both parties tell their side of the story and try to reach an agreement. This conference is not the same as a hearing. There is no administrative law judge and no cross-examination. EEOC investigators are not attorneys and are less strict than a judge would be about what kind of evidence may be considered. Verbal accounts of what other people said are admissible.

Investigation   If you don't reach an agreement at the fact-finding conference, the EEOC is supposed to do a full investigation of the evidence on both sides. The more evidence the charging party has, the stronger her or his case. Witnesses may speak to an investigator anonymously, as long as the proceedings stay within the agency. If the case goes to court, their names will be disclosed.

When It's Urgent   In urgent cases, where the EEOC staff believe that irreparable harm could occur, a mechanism called "expedited processing" can speed up the process. In these rare cases, the agency immediately gets an attorney involved. The attorney works with the investigator to schedule interviews and issue a questionnaire to management with very short time frames in order to reach a determination quickly and to get the case into court.

Do You Need an Attorney?   As with the Wage and Hour Division, you don't need an attorney to file a complaint. But thanks to the Civil Rights Act of 1991, individuals whose civil rights are violated may be entitled to compensatory and punitive damages. You may want to consult an attorney to find out what remedies you're eligible for. (See the information on attorneys in the preceding section on the Wage and Hour Division.)

Many agencies are encouraging complainants to enter into Alternative Dispute Resolution (ADR) as a way to settle complaints without lengthy and possibly expensive proceedings. An attorney can help you decide whether to take this route and what kind of settlement to aim for.

Determination   After the investigation is completed, the EEOC makes a determination of whether there is "reasonable cause" or "no reasonable cause" to believe that discrimination took place. If the finding is "no reasonable cause," the investigator will notify both the charging party and the employer. The charging party may request a review of the finding by the district director or deputy director. The staff will also give the charging party a *Right to Sue* letter, which allows her or him to bring a private lawsuit in court. A complaint must be filed in court within 90 days after a Right to Sue letter is issued.

The charging party may ask for a Right to Sue letter 180 days (or more) after the EEOC process begins, regardless of how far along the process is and whether any determination has been made.

Conciliation If the EEOC finds "reasonable cause," the staff attempts to get the employer to agree to eliminate the discrimination and provide appropriate remedies. This stage is known as *conciliation*. If the employer refuses or offers a settlement that you deem unsatisfactory, the agency may choose to take the case to court for you. Given the lack of funds and huge backlog of cases, the EEOC litigates only rarely. If the agency does not litigate your case, you'll receive a Right to Sue letter.

If a case starts in the EEOC and winds up in court, the judge may or may not admit the agency finding into the record. *An EEOC finding of "no reasonable cause," in other words, does not mean that the charging party will lose in court.* Many attorneys advise complainants to request a Right to Sue letter and to proceed with a court action *before* the EEOC has made any determination.

Remedies Thanks to the 1991 Civil Rights Act, victims of sex discrimination are now entitled to damages for pain and suffering, known as *compensatory damages*; if the employer's behavior was particularly outrageous, the victim may also be awarded *punitive damages*. (Before 1991, damages under Title VII were limited to back pay if victims lost their jobs. They weren't even entitled to reimbursement for medical expenses. Now they can recover these costs.) The victim can also be awarded reasonable attorney's fees. Under federal law, damages for sex discrimination claims have a cap, from $50,000 for small firms to $300,000 for the largest. Statutes in some states, such as California, do not put a limit on damages. Most states, however, allow no damages at all.

GOING TO COURT

If you decide to go to court, be prepared for a lengthy process. Getting a trial date usually takes from several months to several years. Unlike the agency process, a trial is very difficult to pursue without an attorney.

Procedure

In order to prepare their case, lawyers go through a process of *discovery* to obtain documents and other relevant information about your case from the other side. They also question under oath, or *depose*, relevant parties and witnesses. You can expect to be deposed by an attorney for the employer. Your lawyer should prepare you for the kinds of questions you'll be asked. Often, this process feels hostile and even degrading. The lawyer for the company may well try to paint you as irresponsible, incompetent or untruthful. The better prepared you are, the more you'll be able to stay focused on the facts. The lawyers write up their positions in *briefs*.

At various points in the process, the attorneys may try to reach a settlement (sometimes at the urging of the judge). Be sure to discuss carefully with your lawyer the kind of settlement that would be acceptable. Most cases under the Civil Rights Act are heard by a jury. (You can also ask for a jury in an FMLA-related case.) Or the case could be heard by a judge. If no settlement is reached, the jury or judge decides whether or not discrimination occurred and, if so, what damages would be appropriate.

PEOPLE WHO FOUGHT AND WON

The following case studies illustrate different ways people have handled violations. Every case is unique, but these will help you to see that you can stand up for your rights and win.

Using Internal Channels

Ray works at a large medical center and is a union delegate for 1199, which represents hospital and nursing home workers. When the FMLA first took effect, Ray worried that workers at the medical center would be disciplined for taking leave allowed by the law. Like many employers, the center has an absence-control policy that counts every day missed as an "occasion." Employees are penalized after a certain number of occasions, regardless of the reason. In many departments, no notice of the law was posted, and every absence was being counted as an occasion, even when it should have qualified as family or medical leave.

"This is the best law that's been passed for workers," Ray said. "Management said they knew nothing about it; personnel didn't know much either. So we educated ourselves."

First, Ray made sure the workers knew their rights. He made copies of a union handout on the law and passed them out on every floor of the hospital. Then he made personal visits to managers of departments where notifications of the FMLA hadn't been posted. He also insisted that all departments hold meetings to inform workers about their rights.

The channels worked. Ray was able to stop the violations and get uniform compliance with the law.

Filing a Charge

Candy was eligible for eight weeks' disability leave when her son was born by cesarean section in July 1993. Knowing the FMLA was going into effect in August, Candy began calling her employer, the local school board, to ask if she'd be able to take any additional time off. She was told she could take child-care leave, but only if she took a total of twelve weeks beyond her maternity leave.

"I couldn't afford to take that much time," Candy said, who wanted only four extra weeks. When she mentioned the new law, the personnel staff said they had no copy of it. Their attorney had advised them that current policy was valid. Candy then called 9to5, who referred her to the Wage and Hour Division. After DOL staff called the head of personnel, explained the new law, and said Candy could file suit if they didn't uphold the law, the policy quickly changed.

"I got a call saying I must have misunderstood them," Candy said. Although she was able to take the extra leave, Candy was not allowed to use her sick time for that purpose; she had accumulated 100 sick days during her 14 years of teaching. Still, winning the leave meant she could continue to breast-feed, which Candy feels contributed to her son's good health.

Candy attended a new mothers' class at a community college with several teachers whose babies were born before the new law took effect. "When they heard I filed a complaint, they were real excited for me," said Candy. "They realized in the future they could push for things, too. I've never really taken a political stance or anything. But it was sort of neat to do it and win."

Going to Court

Sherry had worked at a restaurant for about eighteen months when she learned she was pregnant. She told the office manager right away. When asked if she planned to keep on working, Sherry pointed out that she'd just bought a home and needed to work as long as possible.

At first, the owner was supportive. But as soon as the pregnancy started to show, he began making comments such as, "You're getting a little big there. Suck in your stomach." He kept asking Sherry when she was leaving.

"I can't tell you how many times I came home bawling," Sherry said. "I got physically sick. I had a new house, was going to have a new baby, and I had no idea how to manage. This was my first pregnancy. I was supposed to be so happy, and it was terrible." Soon the owner began cutting Sherry's hours. He moved her to serving at parties, which caused a significant drop in income. The comments about sucking in her stomach increased. Then the owner told Sherry she had to go. "People could bump into you," he told her. When she said she could continue, he agreed—but never put her on the schedule.

Sherry hired an attorney. She was eventually called back to work, then fired for poor appearance and poor attitude. After a positive determination at the state agency, the case is pending in federal court.

"My point was not to get money," Sherry said. "If you asked me, I would rather have him lose something that means something—lose his job or lose a restaurant or go to jail. He took away something so important for me. If this ever happened to anyone else, I would definitely tell them to fight for it."

WHAT TO DO IF YOUR RIGHTS ARE VIOLATED

Know your rights under the law and your company's policies.

Get support wherever possible.

Document your situation and make a paper trail.

Identify company channels (and union channels if available) and use them.

File a charge with a federal or state agency if you need to.

You don't need an attorney to file a charge, but you may want to consult one to see what you're entitled to.

You can make a general complaint to the Wage and Hour Division anonymously.

5

Family-Friendly Policies That Work— and Why We Need More of Them

You don't need a crystal ball to describe a family-friendly workplace. The kinds of policies we need already exist. This chapter shows you what they look like and how they make it easier for workers to do their job well without sacrificing their families.

The origins of the model programs vary widely. Some exist because a company's top management includes one or more visionaries. Others came into being because of the hard work of employees, often through collective bargaining. Some were instituted in response to a crisis. Still others were the result of a CEO bumping into the reality of the job/family conflict in private life. As the president of a small bank put it, "I did not think about alternative work schedules until my own daughter-in-law was working and she had a child."[1]

Many of the best programs grew up in Fortune 500 companies that have strong resources and a reputation for progressive practices. Government units have often been an incubator for family-friendly policies, particularly child care and flexible schedules. But models also come from small business owners, from individuals who are more open to innovation or simply more in tune with what employees need and how that need affects the bottom line.

What follows is a sampling of exemplary policies. It is meant to show you the variety of programs that exist and what impact they have. The list is neither exhaustive nor meant to name the best in each category. (For more examples, see Chapter 15.)

FLEXIBLE SCHEDULES

Flexibility can mean many different things: flexible scheduling, reduced hours without penalties in benefits or assignments, job-sharing, and alternatives to downsizing. Consider these examples:

Flexible Scheduling

Duke Power Company, Charlotte, North Carolina When Sharon Allred Decker was assigned to make the telephone call-in center more customer-friendly, she saw she had to start with the employees. "As I treat my team, that's how they're going to treat the customer," Decker said. "We needed to recognize that people have lives."[2] Workers hated swing shifts, Decker learned; she did away with the practice. She also dropped the requirement that staff had to get supervisor approval before swapping shifts. "They're adults," said Decker. "They know they're responsible for someone being here." As a result of the changes, turnover at the telephone call-in center at Duke Power is down to 12 percent, as compared to the 40 percent figure for such jobs nationwide. And three-fourths of those who leave Decker's center transfer within the company. The changes also hit home with Decker herself. Employees pointed out that she was working too hard, not practicing what she preached. She began to spend more time with her two young boys.

Xerox, Dallas, Texas Jim Edwards, a manager known for his "WMB" ("We mean business") motto, had banned flexible hours in his department. Then, in February 1993, at the annual employee meeting, he announced that the 300 assembled workers could set their own hours, starting immediately. "This is high risk to me," he told the stunned audience. "But I am willing to take that risk."[3] What had caused Edwards's turnaround? Ford Foundation–funded researchers had found that a high proportion of single-parent and dual-earner couples in the company were feeling stress because of rigid schedules. After Edwards's speech, nearly half the workers chose compressed work weeks, meaning fewer work days with more hours each day. Middle managers started meeting weekly to share problems and solutions. Ten months into the experiment, absences had fallen by one-third. Teamwork improved. Worker surveys showed morale was up. Follow-up interviews with Ford researchers showed "employees feel they have more control over their work and . . . are dealing better with their customers," said Lottye Bailyn, an MIT management professor leading the research.

Engelhard Corporation, Huntsville, Alabama When Joseph Steinreich took charge of the chemical company's two plants in 1981, he was given six months to turn them around or see them closed. The plants had a 150 percent turnover rate, along with high rates of product waste, serious injuries, absenteeism, and drinking. Steinreich focused on employee problems at work and home, instituting an Employee Assistance Program with an on-site psychologist available by beeper. Steinreich also let workers vote on adjusting and distributing overtime, lunch, and break schedules. The majority voted for a compressed work week: four 10-hour days starting at 5 A.M. and ending at 3 P.M. Absenteeism dropped from an average of 20 days to 3 days a year; both turnover and product waste decreased to less than 1 percent. There were no serious injuries.[4]

Berkshire Medical Center, Pittsfield, Massachusetts Along with a variety of schedules, the center offers a "bank of hours" for all paid leave. Any sick leave or other paid time off, such as holidays, can be banked and used for any legitimate family leave purpose. Management also identified certain jobs that can be done from home and pays employees by the project. Marianne Kelly, benefits coordinator, says the more flexible management is, the more motivated are employees.[5]

Harris Bank, Chicago, Illinois Kimetha Walther Firpo, vice president and work-and-life program coordinator at Harris, designed a three-page form for employees requesting an alternative work schedule. Employees must explain in writing how their requested schedule would help the company and must propose how their work should be evaluated. The form gets employees to think through their role in helping the company meet its objectives, and the process gives workers more stake in the goals. Of ninety-three requests made from September 1993 to January 1994, only three were turned down.[6]

Reduced Hours with Full Benefits

CIGNA Corporation, Philadelphia, Pennsylvania This insurance company offers full health, dental, and life insurance as well as savings benefits to employees who work seventeen or more hours a week. Part-timers also receive prorated holiday and vacation benefits. "In designing a work/family program, we asked three questions," said Susan Thomas, Director of Employment Policies and Programs at CIGNA. "Are we competitive? Are we meeting employee needs? Are we making the best use of available resources? We saw [benefits for part-timers] as part of the package to help us meet these three objectives."[7]

BayBank, Massachusetts Its "work-style" program allows reduced schedules with full benefits to suit individual life-styles. According to New Ways to Work, a nonprofit organization that helps employers and employees design flexible schedules, the program was developed to attract higher-skilled employees for part-time, entry-level positions but has since been expanded to full-time employees who want to cut back on work hours.[8]

Mattel, Inc., Segundo, California This toy maker closes every Friday afternoon so employees can have more time with their kids. Originally, early Fridays were a summer phenomenon, but the results were so successful that the company decided to continue the benefit year-round. A spokeswoman says that helps "get people to be more productive during the rest of the week.[9] Employees receive the same pay, but also put in an extra half hour the other four days.

Part-Time without Penalty in Assignments

Illinois State Attorney's Office After having two kids of her own, Renee Goldfarb's mission was to craft a flexible workplace for others. Some twenty-seven attorneys at the Criminal Appeals Division here have taken advantage of the opportunity she offered them to work part-time. The part-timers spend three days in the office and read cases outside. Because of their years of experience, many part-time attorneys work on major cases—they're considered the best for the job.[10]

Flexibility as an Alternative to Downsizing

University of California–Berkeley Here's a solution that helps everyone in tough fiscal times. Rather than laying people off, the university offers a Time Reduction Incentive Plan (TRIP) to non-academic staff who agree to reduce hours in exchange for benefits. These include extra paid leave upon completion of TRIP (ranging from 40 to 96 hours), and service credit toward retirement benefits as though the employee had been full-time. Managers are urged to approve employee requests for reduced time wherever feasible.[11]

Rhino Foods, Burlington, Vermont This specialty dessert manufacturer needed to downsize during slow seasons but didn't want to lay off any of its fifty-five employees. Workers came up with twenty-five ideas, including a pool of workers who do temporary jobs for other companies. Rather than paying a higher unemployment rate—and forcing workers to get by on unemployment benefits—the employer pays the difference between the worker's normal salary and the pay from the temporary job. If the other company pays more, employees keep the difference while they are at that site.[12]

Charles Schwab & Company, New York, New York Instead of laying off employees after the 1987 stock market crash, this brokerage firm introduced a variety of voluntary reduced-work-time options: partially paid sabbaticals, reduced work weeks, and job-sharing. Jim Wiggett, Sr., Vice President for Human Resources, estimates that nearly all of Schwab's employees participated in this program, saving the company $3.5 million.[13]

AT&T, New York, New York The union representing workers at the telecommunications company, Communications Workers of America (CWA), was concerned about positions being filled by temps and contract labor while permanent employees were being laid off. The company wanted to maintain flexibility. So the company and union agreed to pilot a program to address both concerns. Workers in a new job classification, Administrative Intern, would float from one job to another as required but stay no longer than six months in any one position. The workers are AT&T employees, with all the rights and benefits of other union members.

Job-Sharing

Marshfield Clinic, Marshfield, Wisconsin When a medical technologist gave birth, she felt she needed to spend most of her time at home but wanted to stay involved in her field by working one day a week. Another technologist was willing to work four days a week and job-share, provided she continued to receive full benefits. Clinic management approved the arrangement, which has worked well for two years.

PRENATAL CARE

Haggar Apparel Company, Dallas, Texas   After learning that 95 percent of its female workforce wasn't seeking prenatal care because of expense, this employer offered full reimbursement for all prenatal expenses, as long as the employee came under a physician's care during the first trimester. Anne Hunt, Haggar's health and wellness coordinator, said, "Health claims dropped from $2.3 million in 1991 to $1.8 million in 1992, a savings of more than a half-million dollars. And this savings was realized even though the total number of births increased."[14]

SUPPORT FOR ADOPTION

Trammel Crow Company, Dallas, Texas   Adoptive parents, male and female, may take four weeks of paid leave after three years of service at this real estate investment trust.

Ben and Jerry's, Waterbury, Vermont   The ice cream maker reimburses adoption expenses up to the amount of normal hospital costs associated with childbirth.

Time, Inc., New York, New York, and Hallmark Cards, Kansas City, Missouri   These employers both offer up to $5,000 for adoption costs.

Wendy's International, Dublin, Ohio   Parents are reimbursed up to $4,000 per adoption, with an additional $2,000 for adoption of special needs children.

LEAVE

Model policies include paid leave, extended unpaid leave with benefits and a job guarantee, and leave-sharing.

Paid Leave

Lotus Development Corporation, Cambridge, Massachusetts The computer firm provides one month of paid parenting leave for men and women, birth or adoptive parents, with another eight weeks of unpaid leave. Pregnant women are also entitled to disability pay for the period of disability. Workers may use paid sick and personal time for short-term care of sick family members.

Atlantic Richfield Company (ARCO), Los Angeles, California
This employer allows paid time off for participation in manager-approved community activities such as Habitat for Humanity. Salaried employees may also take up to six paid days of leave per year to care for sick family members. This time, which does not accrue, is in addition to personal illness days, which are carried over from year to year.

Extended Unpaid Leave

IBM, Armonk, New York Known as a leader in this area, IBM allows up to three years' unpaid leave, with a guarantee of a job upon return, and company-paid benefits for the entire period. The leave is approved on a year-by-year basis. If business needs require it, the employee might have to return part-time in the second and third years.

Beloit School District, Beloit, Wisconsin Teachers and other school personnel are allowed to take up to two years' unpaid family-care leave, with an additional two years at reduced time. "Communities need strong families," said Ernest Blandon, who directs Human Resources for the school district. "The kids get better teachers, we get better employees."[15]

Johnson & Johnson, New Brunswick, New Jersey Its one-year unpaid leave can be used to care for a new child or for an ill dependent.

Leave-Sharing

Pacific Presbyterian Medical Center, San Francisco, California Employees may donate unused paid time off to other employees who need leave to care for a personal illness or for a sick family member.

City of Milwaukee, Wisconsin When a paramedic developed an incurable brain tumor, her co-workers demanded and won the right to donate up to one week of their own sick time to her. The leave-sharing allowed the woman to stay on the payroll and, thus, covered by health insurance until her death.

DOMESTIC PARTNERS

Beth Israel Medical Center, New York, New York Medical coverage applies to domestic partners, including same-sex couples. The two adults involved must sign a statement affirming that they are in a committed partnership, are each other's sole domestic partner, share the common necessities of life, and are responsible for each other's welfare.

CHILD CARE

In addition to on-site centers, innovative support for child care includes emergency on-site child care, full or partial reimbursement for child-care expenses, funds to support care providers, and programs for school-age children.

On-Site Child Care

Huntsville Electronics Plant, Huntsville, Alabama When the United Auto Workers and Chrysler Corporation found serious child care problems at this electronics plant, they worked together to start a center that operates nearly round the clock, from 5:00 A.M. to 1:00 A.M. The center, which began in December 1992, serves 100 children each shift.

SAS Institute, Cary, North Carolina The child-care center they operate for 300 kids is a fully paid benefit of employment.

Emergency On-Site Child Care

Time Warner, Inc. When the babysitter is ill, employees based in New York City can use the company's short-term backup care center at no charge. The center, established as a pilot program, can serve up to thirty children from age six months to twelve years.

United States Hosiery Corporation, Lincolnton, North Carolina A Get Well Room in this child care center, sponsored by a consortium of businesses, is stocked with toys to encourage quiet play. For no charge, employees of any of the sponsoring companies can bring children to the Get Well Room, which has a separate bathroom, kitchen, entrance, and ventilation system.

Arthur Andersen, Chicago, Illinois During tax season, this employer provides on-site child care on Saturdays.

Full or Partial Reimbursement of Child-Care Expenses

Joseph Alfandra & Company, Inc., Rockville, Maryland In 1989, this real estate development and construction company began offering subsidies for child care to its fifty-five employees. The subsidies, which vary according to income, pay up to 50 percent of actual costs up to a maximum of $60 a week.

NationsBank, Bethesda, Maryland Their Child Care Plus program pays a maximum of $70 a week per employee's child. Rather than waiting for reimbursement, employees can submit child-care expenses in advance for the upcoming month and get a check made out to the child-care provider.

Ding-a-Ling, Fort Lauderdale, Florida Since 95 percent of the 100 employees at this family-owned answering and beeper service are female, owner Herman Shooster was aware of the role that child-care problems played in high turnover. He decided it was economical to authorize child-care subsidies of up to $30 per week for licensed child-care expenses. In 1990, Shooster spent $25,000 and helped seventeen employees. In addition to lowering absenteeism and turnover, Shooster was able to attract new employees and new clients.[16]

Support for Care Providers

AT&T As a result of contract negotiations with its unions, Communications Workers of America (CWA) and International Brotherhood of Electrical Workers (IBEW), AT&T in 1990 agreed to create a Family Care Development Fund. Management committed $10 million for a three-year period for child-care and elder-care initiatives. They later extended that commitment and increased it by 50 percent. Work/Family Directions helps AT&T direct funding to specific programs in communities where the company has a large presence.

Steelcase, Inc., Grand Rapids, Michigan One of the first to establish a network linking family day-care providers, this furniture manufacturer gives extensive support. Providers can receive funds for a wide range of expenses, including training, health and safety inspections, vacation and sick days with substitutes provided, conference registration fees, reimbursement for an annual physical, supplies, and home improvements.

The American Business Collaboration for Quality Dependent Care (ABC) In September 1992, this joint effort was announced by dozens of the nation's employers to fund a broad range of family services in order to improve the quality and supply of child care and elder care nationwide. As of 1994, the collaboration included 146 companies and a combined investment by them of $26.1 million.

School-Age Child Care

Corning Inc., Corning, New York This employer provides full-day care on-site for children of school age on business days when schools are closed, as well as summer care programs for 180 kids. Named by the children in the program, Kids Adventure Club has grown to include preschool and afterschool programs in eight local elementary schools.

SUPPORT FOR ELDER CARE

IBM In 1988, IBM was the first Unites States company to launch a nationwide elder care information and referral service to employees in more than 200 locations.

AT&T The Family Care Development Fund helps expand eldercare services, as well as child care. A $40,000 grant, for example, to increase the number of slots and expand the hours of care at an adult day-care program in Reynoldsburg, Ohio, helped twenty AT&T families in the area.

ARCO This is one of many companies that make available a tollfree hotline offering names and numbers for specific elder-care services. Advice can include anything from how to prepare a living will to how to pay for nursing care. Participating companies pay $5 to $8 per employee. "For every time they call us," said one consultant, "they save about fifteen hours of [their own] time. We conservatively believe at least 80 percent of that is time saved at work."[17]

Stride Rite, Cambridge, Massachusetts The first company known to offer an on-site child-care center, Stride Rite also pioneered an intergenerational center that cares for both young children and elderly dependents of employees. In 1989, the company started the center as a joint venture with Lesley College and Somerville/Cambridge (Massachusetts) Elder Services. Chairman and CEO Arnold Hiatt said, "Besides the fact that it's given our company a sense of family, . . . we can demonstrate the *economics* of day care."[18] Hiatt figures two day-care centers save him $22,000 per employee by helping retain quality people. The intergenerational center has separate areas for children and elders, along with common space for activities like baking, woodworking, and storytelling.

Procter & Gamble Company, Cincinnati, Ohio   This personal-care products company was the first private employer in the United States to offer long-term-care insurance. Benefits, which can be used by an employee or his or her spouse, parent, or parent-in-law, include $21,000 a year for eligible nursing home care—$10,950 a year for in-home nursing care.

Philip Morris, New York, New York   Managers saw employees juggling elder-care responsibilities. "Adult children trying to do everything are getting overwhelmed and run down," said Kathy Lampe, manager of the employee assistance program there.[19] So in 1986, the company joined American Express, J.P. Morgan & Company, and the New York City Department for Aging to start Partnership for Eldercare, a nonprofit company hired by businesses to advise workers about ways to care for elderly relatives. The service has contracts with ten companies and serves nearly 700 people a year, according to Barbara B. Lepis, director. At least 30 percent care for a relative who lives at a distance; in New York City, many employees live more than an hour away from the elderly relative they care for.

ENCOURAGING FATHERS AS PARENTS

LA Department of Water and Power, Los Angeles, California
This organization, which is 78 percent male, encourages men to get involved in parenting through the "Doting Dads" program. Policies include a four-month unpaid paternity leave, father mentorship program, child-care referral, breast-feeding classes for both mothers and fathers, peer support groups, "Tips for Dads" hotline, lunchtime workshops, beepers for expectant dads, and four "Daddy and Me" excursions a year. Beverly King, the Human

Resources director who created the program, said it earned back $2.50 for every dollar spent, mainly in increased productivity and in decreased absenteeism and turnover. According to Yolie Flores Aguilar, Work/Family manager at the department: "We wanted to encourage fathers to be strong role models in the family. We realized dads have different issues from moms, so we specifically targeted them for separate programs."[20]

Apple Computer, Cupertino, California A senior manager at the computer company took paternity leave to be home with his two older kids and his newborn. "For people to see a director do this sort of thing dispels some of the myths about the fanaticism of commitment that you have to have," the manager said. "In a volatile organization like ours, where there have been layoffs in the not-too-distant past, there's got to be concern about job security. This says taking a leave doesn't compromise your commitment to the organization."[21]

Supreme Court Justice Ruth Bader Ginsburg The judge agreed to let one of her law clerks work a flexible schedule so he could take care of his children in the morning and early afternoon while his wife worked. Said Ginsburg, "This is my dream of the way the world should be. . . . Other men might be fearful they won't succeed . . . or will be thought of as less than a man if family is of prime importance. More than anything else, I believe the acceptance of full parental responsibility by men will make things genuinely equal for women."[22]

Advancing Those Who Take Leave

Peabody & Arnold, Boston, Massachusetts This law firm made several lawyers partners after they'd put in 1,800 hours instead of the usual 2,100. The lawyers had reduced their schedules in order to spend more time with their families. The firm also offers seminars called "Families First."

Ohio State University, Columbus, Ohio Faculty can claim an extra year to meet requirements for tenure if the family has a new child during the propationary period. For two or more children, faculty can claim an additional two years.

ENCOURAGING MANAGERS TO BE MORE SENSITIVE

DuPont, Wilmington, Delaware   Faith Wohl became DuPont's director of work-force partnering in 1989. Families and Work Institute estimates 200 companies have such a position, most created in the past four years. Wohl's accomplishments include getting men covered by the family leave policy, winning flexible schedules, and helping reclassify part-time employees who were contract workers with no benefits or job security as permanent employees with benefits. In one plant in Troy, Michigan, workers formed a work-family committee. Their grassroots efforts won flexible schedules, part-time jobs, and a work-at-home program.

CIGNA Corporation   Along with other training materials, the company developed a video entitled "The Expectant Manager" to help answer managers' questions about supervising pregnant employees. To emphasize employee concerns, the producers invited this author, as Executive Director of 9to5, to be one of the featured experts, along with CIGNA manager Susan Thomas and clinical OB nurse specialist and author Connie Marshall.

NCR, Dayton, Ohio   CEO Jerre L. Stead ties 25 percent of managers' pay to how well they help workers meet personal objectives (measured by employee satisfaction surveys), including balancing work and family. He said this figure will go up.[23]

The United States Coast Guard   Officer evaluation now includes a category to measure "work-life sensitivity/expertise." An officer can receive one of three ratings: failed to recognize importance of Work-Life (one example would be "contributed to imbalance"); knowledge of Work-Life principles, issues, and resources; or superior in-depth knowledge of Work-Life program.[24]

Prudential Insurance Co. of America, Newark, New Jersey
Estelle Holzer, the company's work-family manager, says if a manager refuses to follow the company's work-family guidelines, she can give that person a "black mark" in his or her personnel files, hurting chances for promotion or pay raises. "The message can get across real fast," said Holzer.[25]

WHY EXISTING POLICIES ARE NOT ENOUGH

All of the examples given sound great—and they are—but most workers with families still face serious problems. Here is 9to5's list of top ten reasons we need more—and better—family-friendly policies.

1. Many companies simply have no family-friendly policies. Most people can't afford to take much time off without pay. Yet according to a 1990 Labor Department survey of companies with fewer than 100 employees, only 50 percent of employees are covered by short-term disability plans. Fewer than 20 percent of all employees at that time received unpaid maternity leave. The 1993 Family and Medical Leave Act has increased the number, but 95 percent of businesses are exempt from that law because of their size. Many of those companies without family-friendly policies make no bones about it. As a *Wall Street Journal* reporter put it, "It's against the way companies do business."[26]

John Goodwin, a human resources manager at a large midwestern energy company and former director of the Society for Human Resource Management, makes this argument against job/family policies: "The role of business with regard to employees is to treat them with dignity and particularly with respect—to respect your people as individuals who have the intelligence and the ability to solve their problems." Family-friendly programs, maintains Goodwin, make employees "dependent." "The structure of a job," says Goodwin, "should be determined only by this: What does it take to get the job done effectively? Period. If it happens to take something that people are unwilling to give, then they're not qualified for the job."[27]

Contrary to Goodwin's assertions, all the intelligence in the world can't solve the problem of children getting sick at inconvenient times. A parent who's "unwilling" to send an ill child to school or to work a 60-hour week may, in fact, be highly qualified and able to do an effective job. Making a workplace family-friendly means letting go of the old ways of doing business, not letting go of quality.

The traditional mind-set isn't the only reason for companies' failure to adopt job/family policies. A *Wall Street Journal* survey found that 77 percent of employers questioned believe the policies are too costly. Many face opposition from managers who see such policies as disruptive and hard to administer or who are simply resistant to change. Some employers think older or childless workers will resent policies designed to help working parents. And others feel no pressure to change.

"It's still a buyer's market," said Barbara Provus, a Chicago-based executive recruiter. "The good jobs and the good companies can still get whoever they want." [28]

2. Some companies have policies just for show or just for managers, rather than all workers. Before passage of the FMLA, Hofman-LaRoche, a pharmaceutical firm based in Nutley, New Jersey, boasted of its twelve-week family leave policy. In reality, the company was required by New Jersey law to offer twelve weeks—and made that time available only to its New Jersey employees. Those working for the company outside the state got an eight-week unpaid leave, for childbirth or adoption only.[29]

A San Francisco law firm asked consultant Linda Marks to put together a family leave policy, but without implementation plans. They wanted the policy for recruiting purposes only.[30]

Firms that do have policies don't necessarily offer them to all employees.

Sandy attended a meeting of women lawyers discussing family-friendly policies. As the women listed all their needs, one of the attorneys advised the group to be circumspect in discussing the matter with support staff. "They'll want the same benefits for themselves," she warned.

Unfortunately, disparity in disability and leave policies for managers and nonmanagers is not uncommon—or illegal. But it can cause big problems. The experience of Sprint, a telecommunications company, is a good example.

In 1992, *Working Mother* magazine included Sprint on the list of the top 100 places for women to work. But the company was dropped from the list the following year as a result of protests from employees. The magazine had commended Sprint for a broad array of family-friendly benefits, including flextime, job-sharing, work-at-home, and adoption aid. But long-distance operators were excluded from many of these programs.

"We don't understand why we don't get these benefits," said Laura Cordingly, a Jacksonville, Florida, customer agent. The only flextime option Cordingly has is one opportunity within a three-month period to arrive fifteen minutes late, provided she stays fifteen minutes later at the end of her shift.[31] Gloria Melton, another Florida operator, described how she and her friends "wondered exactly which Sprint company they were talking about. The only thing we could figure out was that those [pro-working-mother] policies were for management."[32]

Sprint is not unique in making benefits available to managers but not to line staff. The law prohibiting discrimination applies only to people in certain protected categories. The boss can't give out perks based on race, sex, age, religion, national origin, or color. But if the boss is uniformly stingy or more generous to managers than to nonmanagers, the law has nothing to say about it except in the areas of pension and health insurance.

Treatment of nursing mothers is one area where managerial women often have special treatment that should be available to everyone. According to Rona Cohen, lactation expert for a breast-pump manufacturer, "There is still a tendency to feel that breast-feeding is for the privileged in the corporate office, for the high-level individual."[33]

Consider the case of Theresa Riegel, a floater on the production line at Chrysler. Riegel asked to lengthen her fifteen-minute break in order to express her breast milk. The company refused her request on the grounds that such treatment would be unequal to that of other assembly line workers and would be tantamount to extended unpaid leave. Riegel sued for discrimination. Her lawyer called the company's action "elitist," saying managers were "closing their doors or going into nice executive bathrooms" to express their milk. The case was resolved when a lactation expert helped Riegel learn to pump more quickly and the company agreed to equip a room for her to use.

3. Some firms have policies on paper but discourage employees from using them. A survey at Corning found that employees judged 40 percent of senior managers to be unsupportive of job/family issues. "Here we had all these policies, but people were afraid to use them because they thought their careers were at risk," said Sonia S. Werner, work/life balance consultant at Corning. While 75 percent of workers at the company have two-income families, 90 percent of senior managers have wives who do not work outside the home.[34]

Some career consultants warn women that using family-friendly policies will hurt their career. Listen to Ellen Klein, a partner in the New York executive recruitment firm of Scott-Bennett, Inc.: "You may be perceived as less serious; you will most likely move on to a slower track. Women should know that when they make that choice."[35]

Or consider the views of this male attorney, who had raved about his firm's part-time policy at a hearing of the American Bar Association's Commission on Women in the Profession. "[When] asked privately whether he had worked with any of the part-time attorneys, he responded that he hadn't—and wouldn't. When pressed to explain his position, he admitted that he would not consider working with them because he did not want to work with anyone who didn't work as hard as he did."[36]

As long as managers measure employee performance through "face time"—time actually spent in the workplace—those with family responsibilities will clearly be at a disadvantage. A 1994 study found that women executives with relatively brief interruptions in their careers—an average of just 8.8 months—earned seventeen percent less than women with no gap in employment.[37]

4. There's still a stigma against men using leave. Since 1987, Campbell Soup Co. has offered both male and female workers a three-month unpaid family-care leave with full medical benefits. Campbell spokesman John DiEleuterio told a reporter that, as of August 1993, 95 percent of eligible women—and not a single man—had used the leave.[38]

James Levine, director of the Fatherhood Project for the Families and Work Institute in New York, thinks the corporate culture in most firms discourages men from using leave, even if it's available. In 1986, Catalyst polled personnel directors and CEOs at 1,500 of the nation's largest companies on the amount of paternity leave they thought it reasonable for men to take. Of 298 respondents, 63 percent responded "none." Even among executives who'd been offering paternity leave, 41 percent said no time at all. The second highest response was "two weeks or less."

Only 1 to 2 percent of firms offer paid paternity leave, and, even there, most men don't participate because of the stigma and the fear that their careers will suffer. This fear isn't paranoia; they've seen other men punished for taking time off.

"I'd heard about one guy who had taken the leave," said a San Francisco attorney. "Suddenly he was off the partnership track. All the male associates knew it would be career suicide." After one male operator at AT&T took a two-month leave, his supervisor warned that it "might affect" his raise.[39]

When Levine interviewed fathers, he heard countless stories in which supervisors told fathers that the rules permitted them family leave but advised them to use vacation time instead. The message, according to Levine, is this: "Real men—upwardly mobile men—don't take leave."[40]

The problem is compounded by the lack of role models. "If an upper-level [male] manager would take the leave," said an operator at AT&T, "everybody else would get the message that it's okay to do it."[41]

Even families who embrace the idea of men sharing parenting have to grapple with cold economic facts: Most men earn more than their wives. Many families can't afford to have dad take unpaid leave—and in most companies, that's all that's offered.

5. Some companies offer flexibility but not on equitable terms. More companies are offering part-time employment. But no law requires employers to pay the same hourly rate to part-time and full-time employees performing the same tasks. On the average, part-timers earn only 60 percent of the hourly pay of full-time workers. Benefits may also be unequal. Only 16 percent of part-time workers receive employer-provided health coverage; only 11 percent are enrolled in employer-sponsored pension plans. Many part-timers receive no sick or holiday pay.

Some workers worry about how they'll be perceived if they ask for part-time work.

Amy and her family decided the best solution for them was for Amy to work part time. She'd looked for part-time jobs in her field, copyediting. "People treat you like you're not serious," says Amy, who is highly skilled. "The pay is terrible. If you ask for a copyediting job part-time, they think of you as a data entry clerk and pay you at that scale." Finally, Amy went to work as a self-employed caterer. "At least I know I won't get fired if my kids get sick."

6. Economic conditions may make family-friendly policies hard to use. Some companies don't intentionally deny benefits to nonmanagement workers, but income may limit access. Milwaukee-based Marquette Electronics, for instance, was one of the first companies to set up an on-site child care center. Yet some production workers don't use the center because they can't afford the fees.

Many workers can't take advantage of the unpaid leave they won under the Family and Medical Leave Act. After the law went into effect August 5, 1993, an official at Weyerhaeuser told the *Wall Street Journal*, "Employees . . . can't afford to take unpaid leave, so it's not a major problem."[42]

Employers who offer a dependent care assistance program (DCAP)—the use of pretax dollars to pay a caregiver—are often surprised that more workers don't take advantage of it. In fact, 95 percent of employees don't use DCAP because of its IRS reporting requirements, which include listing the caregiver's social security number.[43] The caregivers many people can afford to hire to watch their children don't report their income on tax forms and don't want to be identified to the IRS—either because they feel they can't afford the taxes on their income, or because they are undocumented workers who fear being deported.

Economics affect how people use policies for other reasons as well. In a time of downsizing, many employees are afraid that taking advantage of leave will mark them as less desirable when cuts have to be made.

7. At most places, leave is up to the discretion of the individual manager. The power of individual managers is probably the biggest reason for the discrepancy between what the employer may authorize and what actually happens. US West, for example, has many model policies on paper, and some great examples of their use. When Shirley Ellison's husband had brain surgery, her manager allowed her to work from home. Yet at the same company, the union had to fight to help a single mother keep her job after she stayed home with a sick child. "There are a lot of mixed messages," said one union representative.[44]

Some managers continue to have unrealistic expectations about workloads. One manager acknowledges that when she looks at time sheets on a monthly basis, "I'm really looking for them to work 40, 50 hours and up. If they aren't, I wonder about that employee, and we may have a problem."[45]

"[Managers'] attitudes about 'power hours' and success may be the greatest single barrier to women's achieving equality in the workplace," according to Susan Bacon Dynerman and Lynn O'Rourke, authors of *The Best Jobs in America for Parents Who Want Careers and Time for Children, Too*. "If success means a 70- or 80-hour workweek, it's difficult to imagine many parents who can sustain that level of commitment over the course of a career without an extraordinary support system at home."[46]

Many executives simply don't understand the issue. When Faith Wohl was Work-Family Manager at DuPont, she met with substantial resistance from managers. One finance department executive told her, "I don't believe your statistics on dual-income families being the norm." *He* didn't know any man in his neighborhood, church, or circle of friends who had a working wife. "This is why we face such a challenge," said Wohl. "The top people responsible for policy aren't affected by this. They live in a totally different realm."[47]

Unfortunately, managers who don't understand the issue have responsibility for large numbers of women and men who struggle to take good care of their families without risking their jobs. Consider the high-placed government official helping to push through mandatory work programs for welfare mothers. He told a single mother on his staff that his own wife was quitting her job in order to spend more time with their children, ages two and eight. "This guy was putting millions of poor women to work without regard for the well-being of their children," the staffer noted. "Yet he wanted his own wife at home."

8. An employee may need consideration other than time off.

When her 18-year-old daughter was killed by a drunk driver, Patricia was able to take eight days off work. But management had no understanding of the grief process. "First they expected me to be over it," Patricia said. "When they saw I wasn't, they looked to me to educate them about grieving. I wanted them to get it—but I wanted someone else to help them understand."

Bereavement is one area where managers may lack insight. Few companies offer training in skills such as how to manage an employee who's experienced a crisis. Counselors point out that grief takes several stages; the employee won't be "over it" for quite some time. He or she may need a reduced work schedule or flexible hours; but, above all, the person needs some acknowledgment that this is a difficult period. Referral to a grief therapist or support group would be helpful.

9. Some otherwise reasonable policies penalize parents.
Understandably, managers want to control personal calls during working hours. Yet strict "no personal calls allowed" policies can be disastrous for working parents with latchkey kids. Likewise, some employers want anyone who can get to work during a snowstorm to show up as scheduled. But where does this leave parents of young children whose schools have been closed?

10. Other countries surpass the United States.   Paid time off for vacations, sick leave, personal days, and holidays declined 15 percent in this country during the 1980s. That means American workers are putting in an extra month of work a year.[48] Citizens in the European community average between twenty-five and thirty days' paid vacation; Americans have less than half as much.

Other countries—including some with poorer economies—do much better than the United States in providing child care. Mexico, for instance, pays for childbirth and offers twelve weeks of paid leave, which can be extended with unpaid leave for up to one year. Nursing mothers receive two daily breaks for breast-feeding. Employers are required to provide day care or pay a payroll tax. The system isn't foolproof; many employees fall through the cracks. Yet considering how much poorer Mexico is than the United States, these programs say a lot about the difference in national commitment to working families.[49]

In France, parents pay on a sliding scale for children ages three months to three years to go to day-care centers (crèches) and family day-care providers; preschools for children two and a half to five years of age are free. Ninety-nine percent of three-, four-, and five-year-olds attend preschools or crèches. That number has grown as research demonstrated that children who'd been in organized care perform better in the first years of elementary school than children who spent those years at home or with nannies. Health care delivery is an integral part of child care in France, and licensing requirements are much higher than in the United States. In addition to having to pass medical and psychological exams, child-care providers are eligible for monthly training sessions. Their homes are also inspected for safety. Efforts are underway to make the job of child care workers more respectable and lucrative.[50]

Clearly, American business can and must do much better. In the next chapter, we'll look at what you can do to get your company to adopt family-friendly policies.

PROVEN FAMILY-FRIENDLY POLICIES

Employers who offer flexibility say it increases motivation—and productivity.

Some companies use reduced schedules as an alternative to downsizing.

Employer support includes several forms of paid leave—for adoptive as well as birth parents, for participating in community activities, and for long-term care.

An increasing number of employers are offering leave for domestic partners.

Both large and small companies can help take the bite out of child care expenses.

Support for dependent care can include funds to increase the supply and quality of providers.

Even some traditional organizations are holding managers accountable for job/family issues.

Ten Top Reasons Why We Need More—and Better—Policies

1. Many employers simply have no policies.
2. Others have them just for show, or just for managers.
3. Many have policies but discourage employees from using them.
4. Corporate culture still stigmatizes men for taking leave.
5. Flexible schedules often pay less per hour and earn no benefits.
6. Many workers can't afford to take advantage of certain policies.
7. Management discretion can lead to large disparities within the same company.
8. Employees may need considerations other than time off.
9. Some policies penalize parents.
10. The United States is hardly Number One when it comes to helping working families.

6

How You Can Win Family-Friendly Policies at Work

On National Secretaries' Day 1994, I led a workshop on balancing work and family for more than fifty women at Alverno College in Milwaukee. After we discussed what support we need at work and at home, I asked the participants to divide into small groups to discuss how to bring about change; each group was to decide whether to focus on employer or family. Without exception, all the women chose the home front.

I learned several things from this exercise. The women were desperate for help from their families and felt as if they had some control there. They had little confidence in the willingness of their employers to change. And they had a hard time imagining themselves as agents of change at their workplaces.

I offer these ideas for mobilizing support and proposing change, along with real-life case studies, to encourage you to work with others to win family-friendly policies on the job. To be successful, you must gather support, know whom to ask and how, and follow up on your requests. (This chapter assumes you are not in a union. If you are, see Chapter 15 for how to get your union to help.)

MOBILIZE SUPPORT

These suggestions will help you organize others in your workplace to support your efforts.

Know What You Want

In thinking about proposing policies where few or none exist, it's fine to start with your own immediate needs. Whether your main concern is a flexible schedule or time off or help with dependent care, figure out what would give you the most relief. But remember, your needs will change. Suppose you're preparing for a new child, and your concern is parental leave. In the near future, you may need reduced hours or a more flexible schedule. Even if your parents are in good health, someone in your family may become ill at any time. So make sure that the goals you aim for are broad enough to cover your own multiple needs—and those of your co-workers.

Approach Others Who Have the Same Needs, and Form a Group

You have the best chance of winning what you want by working for a policy that the majority of people will ask for—and benefit from. Look for what will unite rather than divide the staff, for example, people with no children resent being seen as having no needs. Share what you and your co-workers have in common, and frame your request to reflect that broader need.

In forming a group, start by talking to people who feel the same way you do and who are likely to want to do something about it. This may be a very small number to begin with, but, as Margaret Mead put it, "Never doubt that a small group of committed citizens can change the world. Indeed, it's the only thing that ever has."

This core group (even if it's only two or three people) should make lists of other people who are likely to be sympathetic and should decide who'll approach each of them. Try to approach people at all levels of the organization if possible. Remember that some people won't be willing to sign on until you get a strong enough group going. There'll be others who will give you a hard time; stay away from them for the time being. Your job isn't to get unanimity, but to demonstrate a strong basis of support.

You want as many allies as possible. Does the company have a women's committee? a diversity task force? any grouping of people of color? a gay/lesbian group? a quality of worklife committee? If not, look for informal networks. Be sure these allies have a say in determining what to ask for. Also, look for people who have some experience in being changemakers within the organization, and learn from their experience.

Sometimes, management tries to keep employee groups divided by pitting their issues against each other ("If we expand family leave, we won't be able to develop our community hiring program"). Remember, the policies you're advocating aren't a favor or a handout—they're what you need, and they're good for the company's bottom line. The policies should be judged on their own merits because they'll more than pay for themselves. Chances are the other programs or policies in question are also good for working parents and should be seen as *complementing* what you want, rather than competing.

If your employer already has a number of job/family policies but not the one you want, your job may be much easier. Even so, being one of a group (which can mean two or three people) approaching management puts you in a stronger position to indicate that the problem isn't unique to you.

Do Your Homework

Your group needs to have as much information as possible. First, you want to have a good idea of your company's resources and current situation. It doesn't make sense to ask for something requiring a lot of up-front expenses, such as an on-site child-care center, if the company is downsizing.

Then, you want to know what benchmark policies exist in comparable organizations. Use this book (Chapter 5 will be particularly helpful) and other resources (see the list in Appendix A) to gather facts and figures about how the policies you seek will help the company's bottom line.

If possible, do some informal surveying among employees to make a case that the need exists.

Find Out Whom to Approach and How

Here you have two tasks: to ascertain who has the power to make decisions and who has the experience and vision to advocate for you. In some instances, this may be the same person, but often it's not. The manager who's most understanding may have no direct decision-making power in this area. But she or he may be someone who has influence and is willing to use it. This person may also have valuable advice about whom you need to approach and what method and arguments would be most persuasive.

It's helpful to know, for example, whether the decision-maker has any personal experience with balancing work and family. The more aware that person is of the challenges, the more open he or she may be to suggestions for change. When Susan Thomas,

Director of Employment Policies and Programs for CIGNA Corporation, researched what policies the company should have in place, she went to firms that were considered leaders in this area. Wherever she went, she heard things like, "The chairman's daughter had a child-care problem." Said Thomas, "It wasn't the size of the industry, or profitability, or geography, or anything else. The only common element [among the best practice companies] was someone on top understood why this was important."[1]

PROPOSE THE CHANGE

Once your group is together and informed, you're ready to begin. Keys here are deciding what is most important, being prepared, and then asking.

Decide on Priorities and Bottom Lines

Especially if you're successful in bringing diverse groups together, you'll have multiple issues. Brainstorm all possible issues and then prioritize. Focus on policies like leave and flexible schedules that can apply to everyone. Be sure to frame these in as generous a way as possible; for instance, even if parents of young children are the driving force, ask that the policy—resource and referral, education, subsidies—apply to any form of dependent care, including elder care.

If the company has not taken any initiative in family-friendly policies, your initial request may be for an assessment. Make sure this is tied to a timeline for following study with action steps.

As you list your priorities, decide on fall-back proposals and bottom lines: What's the least acceptable option you can all live with?

Prepare to Make Your Case

You want to demonstrate the need, the impact of the current situation on the company's bottom line, and the way in which the policy you're advocating for can help. You also want to show that the employees are committed to winning the change they need.

Brainstorm the best arguments to support your case. If you've done any surveys, write up the results. Document examples within the company of the issue you're calling attention to and the effect it has on key areas such as turnover, absenteeism, and productivity. Include information on the benchmark practices you've researched in comparable organizations.

Once you've prepared your case, rehearse. Anticipate the comments and questions you may hear from managers and be ready to respond. (Chapter 7 will help you by laying out the most frequently heard criticisms—and by giving you ammunition for arguing against them.) It's very empowering to hear arguments you've anticipated and to know that you're able to answer them. Have actual rehearsals and assign roles to different members of your group. Discussions will still be spontaneous, but each of you can become familiar with a particular set of issues. The more the group relies on all its members rather than on one spokesperson, the more you'll bring home the point that yours is a broadly felt need and a broad-based movement for change.

Ask

Top management won't always say yes—but they'll never say yes if you don't ask. Arrange a meeting with the people you need to persuade. You may want to write up a proposal first and ask for a meeting to discuss it. Or you may want to talk first and then sum up your request in writing. Try to find out which style works best for the person you need to talk to. You may have several meetings with individual executives. Ask anyone who seems supportive to make that support known to other managers.

If any research or assessment needs to be done as a result of the discussions with management, see if people from your group can volunteer to help. You'll have input, and you'll show your willingness to share responsibility for coming up with a plan appropriate to the company's specific situation.

What if You Get Nowhere?

Some employers won't budge. You'll have to evaluate how to respond in this event. Analyze your strengths. Is there any pressure you can bring to bear? Will it help to wait a while and try again later? Or is the policy you worked for something you must have in order to stay on the job? What are the risks and opportunities in going to the Board of Directors or to the media? You should appraise the situation as a group. Some people may choose to move on and hope the loss of talented, trained staff will hit home. Others may dig in for a longer haul.

FOLLOW UP

Since you have gotten the ball rolling, keep up the momentum. Don't let the issue die. Follow up and keep your group active.

Follow Up in Writing

After the meeting, write a letter of thanks that sums up your understanding of what was discussed and agreed upon. Use this opportunity to reiterate your key points and to underscore your conviction that the policy will be a win/win situation for the employer and employees. Be sure to ask for a response by a certain date. And mention any assignments your group has agreed to do.

Keep the Group Informed

You may involve more people than will be able to participate in these discussions. Be sure to keep everyone informed on how things are going. Regular brief communication will spread ownership for the plan and will help build critical backing among employees should you need it.

Follow Through

Do any volunteer tasks as thoroughly and promptly as possible. But don't get set up with tasks beyond your capability. The employer has a lot more resources than you do. Make sure you're given the resources you need to get your part of the job done.

CELEBRATE

Count any progress as a victory. Celebrate with your group on anything you win or even the steps you make toward winning. The first time one 9to5 member met with management, she and her co-workers went out afterwards to cheer themselves for making it through the meeting. "I can't believe I didn't throw up!" she rejoiced. Their request was turned down—but they continued to organize support and were successful the following year.

PEOPLE WHO MADE CHANGE

I offer these three cases studies—each resulting in a different kind of change—to show you that it is possible for an individual to change company policy for the better.

Winning Domestic Partnership Benefits for Same-Sex Couples

About six months after starting at Silicon Graphics in Silicon Valley, California, Ann Mei Chang and a few other employees decided to form a gay and lesbian employee network. In addition to giving each other support, their goal was to win two company policy changes: to expand the nondiscrimination policy to include sexual orientation and to gain benefits for domestic partners.

Even though Silicon Graphics was a progressive company, many of whose managers already gave support to employees with a partner of the same sex, formal policies of this sort were seen as a big step. As one supportive personnel manager told Ann Mei, "This makes you sound like you're on the radical fringe."

Ann Mei and her colleagues spent a year and a half educating personnel and other executives about gay and lesbian issues. According to Ann Mei, the managers felt they were already very positive and there were no problems. In a series of face-to-face meetings, the group was able to raise awareness of various departments in which homophobic behavior was common.

Education also took place at several events in the cafeteria, celebrating occasions like Gay Pride Day with lavender balloons and informational brochures. The president and CEO sent a memo to all employees announcing the celebration and affirming the company's support for gay and lesbian employees. In December of 1991, management added sexual orientation to the company's nondiscrimination and harassment policies.

Soon after this victory, Ann Mei's network began to work on domestic-partner benefits. Again, they went to talk to executives and to people in personnel. This time, the stumbling block was finances. While the executives understood that the cost of adding benefits for same-sex couples was minimal because of the relatively small number, extending the policy to unmarried heterosexual partners would be far more expensive.

The gay and lesbian network said the ideal solution would be benefits for both same-sex and opposite-sex partners. But if the company couldn't do both, they argued, at least add same-sex couples as a step in the right direction, since gays and lesbians don't have the option to marry. Members of the network talked to co-workers in heterosexual domestic-partner relations to make sure they would support the move.

"They were pretty supportive because they understood the distinction," said Ann Mei. "While they wanted benefits, too, they understood that they did have the right to marry if they wanted to."

This reasoning won out, and the policy was instituted in August 1992. The company already had an affidavit that married couples have to sign in order to get benefits; management added a line saying the couple would marry if they were legally able to.

Ann Mei offers this advice: "I think the most important thing is to make the goal educating people rather than winning any particular policy. The nondiscrimination policy was a much smaller thing than the domestic-partner benefit, but it took much longer. The process of educating we did during that time was what won the other policy so quickly.

"Take the time to really educate execs and the HR department, people who work at the company," says Ann Mei. "That improves the overall environment of the workplace, which is less quantifiable but most important."

Winning a Policy More Generous Than the FMLA

Since 1985, the Denison University chapter of 9to5 has worked to increase the role of support staff in university decision making. When the governance system was revamped in 1991, the chapter was able to get support-staff representation on the Personnel Committee, among others. Thus, they were in a good position to voice support-staff concerns when the Personnel Committee began discussing how to implement the new Family and Medical Leave Act.

Denison 9to5 President Flo Hortz sent all members an overview of issues that the chapter had been hearing from support staff and called two meetings to discuss these. Issues included not having to use vacation time before taking family leave; being able to use sick time to care for sick children; extending leave to part-time employees on a prorated basis; and allowing spouses who both work for the university to be eligible individually for up to twelve weeks leave, rather than having to share the time. In addition, there was a request that same-sex partners be counted as family, both for purposes of leave and for health benefits.

Mary Phillips, the 9to5 member who served as support-staff rep to the Personnel Committee, raised these issues. The Committee agreed that staff could take leave and still reserve one week of vacation and could use up to eight days of personal days or holidays to care for sick family members. They also agreed that couples working for the university could be treated as individuals for leave purposes. Prorated leave for part-timers won approval. The Committee is currently reviewing all university policies with regard to domestic partners.

Mary found very little resistance to her arguments. This was partially due to the support of the new vice president of management and finance, who had a young child at home and a wife who worked in the Admissions Office. Denison 9to5 also had support from faculty members, more than 100 of whom had signed on as Friends of 9to5. The established presence of a workplace group that was in a position to gather and voice concerns of staff and that had won support from other groups over time contributed to winning a more generous leave policy.

Winning a More Family-Friendly Leave Policy

Kavita Ramdas is a program officer in the Community Initiatives Program of the MacArthur Foundation. As she approached her maternity leave, Kavita discovered that the foundation had an inadequate parental leave policy. Pregnancy was covered under the short-term disability plan, which required that the employee use up any accrued sick days before receiving disability payments. All employees were also eligible for up to ten days of paid and twelve months of unpaid family leave to care for a newborn or newly adopted child or a sick family member or to treat a personal illness.

To encourage reexamination of the policy, Kavita wrote a memo outlining the shortcomings of the current policy framework. She pointed out that it favored birth over adoption and women over men, that it didn't respond to the need of an infant for continuous care for the first eight to twelve weeks of life, and that it forced new mothers to exhaust all their sick leave, creating a serious flexibility problem once they returned to work.

Kavita then summed up emerging trends in the foundation and nonprofit sector, providing an appendix with sample policies. The policies she highlighted treat pregnancy and childbirth as positive choices rather than disabilities; offer longer paid leave (eight weeks) for both male and female employees, birth or adoptive parents; and have no linkage to sick leave other than to allow for tacking it on to a parental leave.

The next section of the memo urged consideration of a new policy framework that embraced these principles. Kavita raised several questions that would need to be addressed, including whether to give weight to the physical toll of childbearing, how to address the existing family leave policy, and how to assess the financial implications of the recommended policy shift.

The memo concluded with recognition of the MacArthur Foundation's leading role in the field of philanthropy and social change. It listed examples of steps already taken to meet the challenges of the future and concluded with the hope that the memo would be viewed within that broader change context.

After follow-up discussions, foundation management made an immediate change; they ended the requirement that employees use all their sick leave before being eligible for disability payments. Recently, the foundation added an adoption assistance program, in which adoptive parents can be reimbursed for costs associated with adoption, including legal fees, up to a maximum of $3,000. The specific examples, sample policies, clearly stated recommendations, and thoughtful questions Kavita supplied helped generate the change.

Says Kavita, "It really is possible, given a somewhat supportive work environment, for an individual to try to make change. Before I put this memo through, I was talking to someone who works for a large consulting firm. [That person] said, 'Why would you want to take this on as an individual? Wouldn't it compromise your status within the company and make life more difficult for you? I'm not sure it's the best thing for you to do.' I disagreed. I feel like I've had enough history within the institution and that this is an institution that has committed itself to social change.

"Each one of us has to take responsibility for pushing that agenda. You can't just wait and hope that the management will change unless the people who work for that institution feel strongly enough to participate in that change process."

YOU CAN MAKE A DIFFERENCE

Sometimes one person *can* make a difference; more often what tips the balance is a group working together. In each of the given examples, the people involved knew what they needed and understood that, because they were affected by the absence of some policy, they were the best people to articulate a new direction. They knew how to make their case and, in the process, to change awareness throughout the organization. They understood that change is a process that takes time and persistence but that it can be done. Like you, they wanted to make it easier to have a family *and* a job. Like them, you can help create change at work by using these tips and remembering this advice: You don't always win when you stand up for yourself, but you never win if you don't.

TIPS FOR WINNING FAMILY-FRIENDLY POLICIES AT WORK

Mobilize support

- Know what you want and who else needs it.
- Organize support among co-workers and managers.
- Do your homework; know best practices and how they help the achieve business goals.
- Get advice on whom to ask and how.

Propose the change

- Decide on priorities and bottom lines.
- Prepare your case.
- Ask.

Follow up

- Follow up in writing.
- Keep the group informed.
- Follow through.
- Celebrate any victory, large or small.

7

How to Answer the Arguments against Business Support for Job/Family Policies

In advocating for the changes you need, you may run into resistance. This chapter gives you ammunition for answering the critics.

WHY COMPANIES SHOULD BECOME FAMILY-FRIENDLY

Here are some excellent reasons—backed up by research and examples—for your company to institute family-friendly policies.

The Numbers

Some of the reasons for becoming a family-friendly company have to do with simple demographics. A workplace designed for employees with wives at home will make less and less sense in the twenty-first century. In 1993, women accounted for 69 percent of the total growth in the labor force. After the year 2000, two-thirds of new entrants to the workforce will be female.

Competitiveness

Many employers cite competitiveness as a driving force for taking up the job/family challenge. Adopting family-friendly policies frees workers to use their full potential on the job rather than worrying about things like child care. As Jerre L. Stead, the CEO of NCR Corporation, commented: "The only sustainable competitive advantage a company has is its employees."[1]

Job/family policies don't just look good, they help the bottom line. Consider these examples:

• As part of instituting family leave programs in 1990, Continental Corporation eliminated the concept of *occurrences* (discipline for missing more than a certain number of days). Managers balked but the policy paid off. Voluntary turnover was halved to less than 5 percent and productivity increased by 15 percent.[2]

• According to a study by the National Council of Jewish Women, "Accommodating Pregnancy in the Workplace," pregnant women in firms that provided more flexibility and support during the pregnancy and allowed for reasonable leave missed fewer days, were sick less often, worked longer into their pregnancies, and were more likely to work extra hours.[3]

• Aetna Life and Casualty was losing hundreds of women workers who didn't return to the company after giving birth. New family leave policies improved the return rate from 67 percent to 91 percent—and saved $1 million in not having to train new employees.[4]

• Michael A. Snipes, compensation and benefits director of Allstate Insurance Co., concluded: "[T]he bottom line is [that work/family programs] save us money. It may run as high as $60,000 to train someone [new] for sales and $30,000 for claims adjusters. We want to retain employees."[5]

• Stride Rite put the customer-service unit of the Sperry Topsider division on flexible schedules. Nearly thirty hours were added to the work week, yet costs went up only 3 percent. Clerical workers found they could do their tasks faster in the evening, when fewer people were working, thanks to fewer interruptions and greater access to office machinery.[6]

Studies Confirm Savings

Three studies at major corporations show that family-friendly policies boost morale and productivity.

• An evaluation of family-friendly policies at Johnson & Johnson found that absenteeism among employees using the policies was, on average, 50 percent less than that of the workforce as a whole. Of those surveyed, 58 percent said such policies were "very important" in their decision to stay at Johnson & Johnson; and, among employees who were actually using the benefits, the figure was an even higher 71 percent.[7]

• A study for AT&T showed that the average cost of giving new parents up to one year unpaid leave was 32 percent of their annual salary, compared to 150 percent to replace that employee. Sixty percent of employees were back to work within three months; all but 10 percent returned within six months.[8]

• University of Chicago researchers studied job/family policies at Fel-Pro, an Illinois-based firm that manufactures automotive parts. They found high-benefit users have the highest performance evaluations and the lowest intentions of leaving the company. Sixty-six percent of workers said they would not prefer more profit-sharing to fewer benefits. "[W]orkers perform best when they use and appreciate workplace supports," said researchers.[9]

• The New York-based research group Catalyst conducted a study on flexibility entitled, "Flexible Work Arrangements II: Succeeding with Part-Time Options." Researchers interviewed personnel managers from seventy companies, more than a third of which had 100 or more employees working flexible schedules. The major reason given for offering flexibility was to retain valued, experienced employees. All participants in the Catayst study were women; they unanimously agreed they would have left their jobs had their needs not been accommodated. Most said they worked more efficiently on part-time schedules.[10]

Ellen Galinsky, co-president of the Families and Work Institute, helped conduct the studies with Johnson & Johnson and AT&T. "The research is pretty clear," says Galinsky. "There's a cost to not providing work and family assistance."[11]

Cost of Implementation Is Low

If the savings for family-friendly firms are great, the cost of implementing family leave programs is not.

Most firms spread the work of the employee on leave to other employees. Blue Cross of Western Pennsylvania uses cross-trained workers whose work is monitored to make sure they're not unduly burdened. Consolidated Natural Gas in Pittsburgh actually describes the duties of workers on leave as "developmental opportunities" for others.[12]

In 1991, Families and Work Institute conducted a study of four states with parental leave laws—Oregon, Rhode Island, Minnesota, and Wisconsin. More than 90 percent of employers surveyed said they had no difficulty with implementation. The majority of employers with actual experience administering new leave policies experienced no increased cost.

SPECIFIC ARGUMENTS AND HOW TO ANSWER THEM

At 9to5, we've heard all the arguments, or excuses, managers and employers come up with to turn down requests for family-friendly policies. Here we list the most frequent and provide you with ways to combat the arguments.

Arguments Regarding Leave

1. The business of business is business, not the personal lives of workers. Workers can and should separate most aspects of their personal lives from work. But certain situations affect one's ability to do the job. That's when personal lives become the business of business. No employer can afford to ignore the *benefits* to the organization of helping workers meet family needs. Management at the Los Angeles Department of Water and Power, for example, estimate they save $2.50 for every dollar spent on family programs by improving productivity and infant and maternal health and by lowering absenteeism and turnover.

2. Don't have kids unless you can afford them. The American business world would be in a pickle if only the wealthy were allowed to reproduce—they would lose a talented workforce, not to mention the all-important consumers. Fewer and fewer parents can afford to raise children on only one income without jeopardizing the family's well-being. Most women, like most men, work because they have to. Having a family costs a lot; it shouldn't also cost you your job.

3. We already offer leave for vacation and disabilities. We can't afford to give time off for all these frivolous reasons as well. Already more than half of all mothers of infants under the age of one are in the workforce. By the year 2000, 75 percent of mothers of children under the age of six will be employed, and women will make up an estimated 63 percent of new entrants to the workforce. If women had not entered the workforce in record numbers since the 1970s, family income would have declined 15 percent in the last fifteen years. But this leaves more women—and men—with dual roles to struggle with.

Along with these figures, consider that more than 12 percent of today's population is age sixty-five or older, with the percentage expected to grow in coming years. Having to manage work and care for young or elderly dependents is becoming a necessity—not a frill—for most Americans.

It's true that family leave is inconvenient for those who have to pick up the slack. Worklife would be easier if no one was ever absent. But because illness and the need for relaxation are facts of life, business has adjusted. Increasingly, the nation is adjusting to time off for family responsibilities as well as illness.

4. If you give employees the option of taking leave, they'll abuse it. Of course, some employees may try to take advantage of available leave, but the United States now has a body of experience on this issue, thanks to the companies and states where some sort of parental leave has been instituted. Studies show people take *less* leave than allowed, sometimes at great personal risk.

5. Family leave is just the first step. Next thing you know we'll have to pay for twenty weeks of vacation. Proponents of family policies are not trying to push employers into unrealistic changes. This is a call for a minimum standard—a *floor*, not a ceiling, nor a cellar. *Minimum* does not mean optimal or even good, but the standard must be *realistic* and *survivable*.

The minimum parental leave has to take into account the needs of the child and the needs of the parent. Allowing only six weeks for childbirth, for example, addresses the minimum medical recovery time necessary for a new mother—but not the needs of the newborn infant or other emotional needs of both parents. Adoption agencies frequently require one parent to be at home for six months to bond with the child.

The minimum also has to include time off for sick dependents—both children and elderly parents. According to a 1990 report, 11 to 13 percent of caregivers of elderly parents quit their jobs because of the pressure of balancing their caregiving responsibilities with work.[13] Allowing them some time off would save the employer rehiring and retraining costs.

Provisions for family leave can include tax breaks for small businesses that really cannot afford any increases in cost, however small. But the legislation ultimately should not exclude up to one-third of all employees (as it does now) because they happen to work in a smaller firm. Nor should it tell certain people (as it does now) they will not be able to exercise their right to family leave because they are "key" to the business. The FMLA needs to be expanded, but individual companies can change their policies now—and reap the advantages of less turnover and absenteeism as well as healthier, more motivated employees.

6. Leave policies are not fair to people who don't have children; businesses run the risk of discrimination suits. Not every employee is a parent, but most of us have parents who may fall ill and need help at some time. And all of us face the possibility of a personal illness that could force us to miss time at work. Far from discriminating, policies that help people balance work and family responsibilities should make every employee feel more secure.

The Families and Work Institute's *National Study of the Changing Workforce* showed 85 percent of respondents disagree or strongly disagree with the statement, "If I had to work extra hours occasionally to accommodate the personal or family needs of co-workers, I would feel resentful."

7. We just hire and promote the best qualified for the job; family status has nothing to do with it. If the job's qualifications include being able to travel, move, or work long hours, family status has everything to do with it. Many women who've spent time at home raising children find themselves dismissed from consideration for jobs because they "haven't worked"—with no recognition of the skills they demonstrated during those unpaid work years. To create genuinely equal opportunity, we have to remove artificial barriers and make sure talent, creativity, and accomplishments determine hiring and advancement.

Arguments Regarding Government Mandates

8. We don't mind helping exemplary employees, but we have to have the discretion to decide who gets what. The exemplary employee should be favored in the way of pay, promotions, and the like. But everybody needs the right to take time off for a sick family member. If an employee is performing badly or causing problems at work, the employer should deal with that directly—not by denying time for family responsibilities, but by describing the problem, setting goals for improvement, and evaluating progress toward those goals.

9. Employee mandates for family leave interfere with protected negotiations between employer and employees. Requesting leave is very different from having the power to negotiate for that leave. Most workers don't negotiate policies or benefits with their employers. Fewer than one in five employees is in a union; 86 percent of all women workers have no collective bargaining agreement.

Workers who are covered by collective bargaining can negotiate more substantial benefits than those mandated by a minimum government standard. But even those workers need a floor from which to proceed. Family leave should be seen as a minimum labor standard.

10. Government mandates deny employees flexibility and take away freedom. The *minimum required* by law is never the same as the *maximum allowed*. Firms still have enormous flexibility in offering, or negotiating, more generous leave.

Until passage of the Pregnancy Discrimination Act (PDA) in 1978, many firms routinely fired women for being pregnant or denied them paid medical benefits or the right to return to work. During the debate over the FMLA, the U.S. Chamber of Commerce quoted the high percentage of large- and medium-sized businesses offering maternity leave. But they were actually citing companies *complying with the mandate* of the PDA.

Not all business owners oppose family leave. Robert Weisenberg, co-owner of Effective Management Systems of Milwaukee, testified in favor of state and national legislation. Although Weisenberg described himself as "sympathetic to the argument that we should carefully restrict those areas in which government controls the day-to-day operations of a business," he sees family leave legislation as falling within "that limited category of basic employee rights that must be guaranteed for everyone."[14]

Similarly, Al Bergerson from Eastman Kodak made this statement in 1990 in support of family leave legislation: "Generally, we don't favor mandates. . . .On the other hand, we recognize that not all employers are doing this—there is a societal issue that needs to be addressed, and the mandate may be the best way to ensure that society's needs are met."[15]

11. These kinds of leave programs will destroy small businesses. Representatives of small business argue that they simply can't afford to replace certain key employees. And they can't—which is why a reasonable family leave policy makes good business sense, so that key employees will return to the company. Refusing an employee leave is exactly what forces business to replace workers on a permanent basis.

One study estimates the cost of hiring and training a new

employee to amount to 93 percent of the first year's salary. The cost is less to small business, but still significant. A 1990 study commissioned by the U.S. Small Business Administration (SBA) found that the costs of terminating an employee due to illness, disability, pregnancy, or childbirth ranged from $1,131 to $3,152, compared to the average costs of granting leave—$0.97 to $97.78 per week. The study concluded that family leave might actually save businesses money.[16]

The cost of implementing unpaid family leave, in fact, is not much at all, according to a report by the Government Accounting Office. The study said that many employers cope with family leave the same way they deal with vacations, by shifting workloads or hiring less expensive temporary employees. While there is some loss in productivity, employers save on recruiting costs by retaining experienced and trained people. Maintaining benefits is an expense, but employers also save by not paying the employee's salary during leave.

There is hard evidence showing that family leave does not hurt small business. In a 1987 report, 9to5 compared seven states with parental leave policies, most of them in effect since the 1970s, with the seven states ranked by Grant Thornton, Inc., an international accounting and management consulting firm, as having the highest pro-business climate. Both groups of states experienced employment growth, but the rates of growth (measured through a multiregression analysis) were *21 percent higher* in parental leave states. (See resource list in Appendix A for how to order this report.)

Another study by Families and Work Institute looked at representative samples of employers in Minnesota, where the threshold of coverage for the state parental leave bill is firms employing twenty-one or more, and Oregon, where the threshold is twenty-five as opposed to the federal threshold of fifty. Researchers found that smaller firms had no more difficulty and experienced no greater cost complying with the law than larger employers.[17]

Some small businesses and nonprofit organizations may need help if several employees are on leave at the same time. A system of tax incentives or direct subsidies for such organizations should be considered.

12. Family policies will lead to discrimination and hurt the very people you're trying to help. Some business owners argue that, as a result of family leave, they will choose to hire a man or a 45-year-old woman rather than a young woman with children. To choose personnel by gender, however, is against the law. And the 45-year-old may well need leave to care for an elderly parent or a spouse or for a personal illness. In reality, employers benefit from helping all employees balance job and family responsibilities.

Arguments Regarding Flexible Schedules

13. Managing flexible schedules would be a nightmare. Supervisors wouldn't be able to monitor their employee's work. People would come and go at all hours. Most employers who offer flexible schedules have a set of core hours when all employees are present. Good scheduling techniques keep the process orderly and ensure adequate coverage at all times. Few managers are able to look over their employee's shoulders every minute of the day—and those that do aren't likely to improve the company's productivity or quality. Successful companies are learning that the best managers rely on motivating employees and involving them in setting clear objectives and evaluation methods.

14. If you let one employee work part-time, everyone will want to. Because a reduced schedule means a cut in pay and often in benefits, most employees can't afford to make the switch. But even if a significant number did choose part-time work, most studies report an increase in productivity when flexible work arrangements are properly implemented.[18]

ANSWERING THE CRITICS

The workforce of the twenty-first century will require a family-friendly workplace.

Case studies and research all reach the same conclusion: Family-friendly policies are good for the bottom line.

Costs of implementing these programs are generally low.

8

Steps for Arranging a Successful Family or Medical Leave

When you enter the workplace each day, you don't leave behind the person who began the morning by feeding a child or checking in with an elderly parent. Sometimes, those responsibilities require time off or changes in your work schedule. The next two chapters are designed to help you determine what you need in the way of leave and scheduling, and how to ask for it. We'll start with asking for leave. Whether or not you're protected by the FMLA, knowing the best way to go about arranging leave can help smooth the process.

STEPS TO TAKE FOR BIRTH, ADOPTION, OR FOSTER CARE LEAVE

Step One: Figure out how much leave you need and can afford.   Deciding how much leave to ask your employer for means serious thinking about your circumstances. Ask yourself these questions:

• *If you could wave a magic wand, how long would you and/or your partner be at home on leave?* Some new parents would ideally take leave for several years. Others are eager to get back to work. The experts agree that at least three to six months of leave are desirable to allow adequate bonding between a parent and a new child. Many infants do fine with a shorter time; others benefit from more. What matters most is *good* care. Whether a parent spends all day or a few hours with the child, the more intact and fulfilled the parent feels, the better the child will fare. However, some children have special needs. An older adoptive child or foster child may need more time to feel at home in a new family.

• *What kind of help will you get?* Women need time to recover physically from birth. Both first-time parents need time to learn the basics of rearing a child. If a second or third child joins the family, in addition to the new baby and the mother, the older sibling needs some special attention. Bringing an older adoptive or foster child into your home adds another dynamic. All this is much easier with a partner or relative to help. Be realistic about the time it will take to get the household running well. (More concrete tips follow for pregnant women, for men, and for same-sex partners.)

• *How much time off can you afford?* You need to make a budget, weighing available income against expenses. Will any of your leave be paid? Check with your employer on whether you qualify for disability pay or can (or have to) use vacation time, personal time, or accumulated sick time. Do you have any other sources of income—savings, help from family? Then look at the expense side. Calculate any additional costs due to a new child or medical bills. Subtract child-care fees, commuting costs, lunches, and any other work-related expenses. Take a close look at regular monthly costs and see if you can cut back. This exercise should give you a good idea of how many weeks you can manage to be out of work.

• *Can you or your partner go on a reduced work schedule once you go back to work?* Assess whether your employer or supervisor allows part-time work in your position and on what terms. Reduced scheduling doesn't have to harm a person's job future—but in practice it often does. Weigh the risks and the reduced income against the advantage of having more time with your family. You may want to negotiate reduced hours for a limited period of time to help you make the transition, with an evaluation built in. Once you can see the impact on your family and your work, you can decide whether you want to continue that schedule; your supervisor will also have the benefit of measuring how the new arrangement works in practice. (See Chapter 9 for more information on arranging a flexible schedule.)

• *How much leave is your employer—and your partner's, if appropriate—likely to offer?* What are the precedents at your company? Is your company covered under the FMLA? (See Chapter 3 for specifics on this law.)

• *What kind of dependent care are you able to arrange?* If you have a new baby, you should know that many centers have only a limited number of slots for infants younger than four or six months. Some family care providers don't accept very small infants or have restrictions on the number they can accommodate. Don't wait until the birth or adoption to make these arrangements, as they'll affect your decision about how much leave to request. (For more on choosing a child-care provider, see Chapter 10.)

• *Is working at home for a while an option?* Think this through carefully before making the request. Infants require a lot of attention—you would still need to have child care or reduced hours. Also, if you want to negotiate work at home (or telecommuting), be clear on who pays for equipment and added utility costs. And weigh the effects being away from the workplace may have on your job. (For more on arranging a flexible schedule, see Chapter 9.)

Answering these questions as early as you can before your leave can help you assess your personal priorities and your company's realities.

Step Two: Decide on your ideal plan, an acceptable compromise, and your bottom line. Sum up the basic information to see what your options are. Gather information on company policies and practices and refer to any precedent you can. Filling out a worksheet like the sample on the next page may help.

Step Three: Once you have a sense of priorities, approach your supervisor with your plan. Make your best case—show how your work can be done while you're gone. It may well be your supervisor's job, not yours, to figure out how to manage coverage while you're on leave; but it is to your advantage to demonstrate your willingness to train your replacement, to leave your work in such a way that someone else can carry on with it, and to answer questions that may arise if your situation permits.

Spell out your availability while on leave. Some supervisors act as if the new parent is "on call." It's helpful to describe yourself as "off duty" and to make no promises until you see how things go with the baby.

Step Four: Follow up in writing. After meeting with your supervisor, sum up in writing what has been agreed upon. You can do this as a thank you note, along these lines:

Sample Worksheet

[Second Child Born to James (drafter) and Jane (secretary)]

Goals:	For someone to be home with the baby for at least 4 months (16 weeks); special attention to older child (age 3)
Recovery time for new mother:	6 weeks
How much help:	Jane's sister for 1 week after Jane comes home from the hospital
What can afford:	2 months at reduced pay
What's allowed:	Jane: 6 weeks disability, 6 weeks unpaid; also 3 weeks vacation
	James: Not covered by FMLA (firm has fewer than 50 employees); 3 weeks vacation
Company precedents:	Jane: Some managers require employees to substitute all vacation time before taking unpaid leave. Jane knows of managers who have not required this.
	James: Women and men at the company have been allowed unpaid time off, but James knows no man who has requested leave for more than 2 weeks.
Dependent care:	Family provider, can start any time; 3-year-old is in day care.
Ideal Plan:	Jane: Weeks 1–10: 6 weeks paid leave and 4 weeks unpaid. Weeks 15–16: Vacation.
	James: 3 days vacation when baby is born, 7 days after Jane's sister leaves. Weeks 11–14: Unpaid leave.
Compromise:	If James can't take more than 2 weeks unpaid leave, Jane takes 2 more weeks.
Bottom Line:	16 weeks with at least one parent home; both parents involved; each saves at least one week vacation for later in the year.

Thank You Note

Dear Sue:

Thanks for meeting with me about my parental leave. My understanding of our agreement is as follows:

I will work as long as I'm physically able. Following the birth of my child, if all goes well, I will take eight weeks paid leave (six weeks of disability and two weeks of vacation) and another eight weeks unpaid. Until my child's first birthday, I will reduce my schedule to 25 hours a week, working from 8 A.M. to 3 P.M. Monday through Wednesday and from 8 A.M. to 4 P.M. on Thursday, with an hour each day for lunch. My pay and benefits will remain at the same rate and be prorated accordingly. When I return from leave, we'll adjust my objectives to this new schedule. After eight months, we'll evaluate whether I'll stay on this schedule or return to full time.

I appreciate the company's support for my family responsibilities. As you know, I'm committed to continuing to perform at the highest level. Your backing means a lot to me.

Step Five: Help train your replacement. Before you go on leave, spend time with the person who'll fill in for you. Many companies have found that cross-training is a good idea, and not just in cases of parental leave. One never knows what could happen, even to nonpregnant nonparents, to cause one person to have to take over the job of another.

Step Six: Prepare for your return before you leave. Make sure you know what the expectations will be regarding schedule and workload when you return. This should include hours, responsibilities outside of work, and travel. If your schedule changes upon your return, anticipate what impact those changes may have on other staff. Analyze what tasks are needed to make the accommodation possible, and volunteer to help.

Remember, the key to a successful balancing act is to prepare for and limit the unexpected—by making provisions, by anticipating, by fighting for flexibility.

Those six steps are advice for anyone asking for leave. Now read on to get more suggestions specific to *your* situation.

IF YOU'RE A PREGNANT WOMAN

If you take care of yourself and if you have a low-risk pregnancy, you can work as much and as long as you want during the pregnancy, according to a National Institutes of Health study.[1] However, depending on the nature of your job duties and the particularities of your pregnancy, you might not want to work right up until the day you go into labor. Each case is different; you have to be realistic about your own situation.

Pregnant women sometimes feel they're treated differently. Some women report being denied plum assignments or being left out of important meetings because their manager assumes they won't be as committed. Not uncommonly, a supervisor might feel "a once-assertive woman executive will ease up on the job [after she becomes pregnant]."[2]

Other women report the opposite problem—being loaded down with more numerous and more difficult assignments as a way of being forced out of their job, or being suddenly held to a standard that never existed before. Michelle was such a case:

> Michelle worked for a company that distributes videos and compact discs. After her doctor wrote a note saying she couldn't lift more than 25 pounds, Michelle was suspended. So were seven other pregnant women when they submitted similar notes. Company officials said they had informed workers upon hiring that they must be able to lift up to 50 pounds. The women had never heard of this rule until they were suspended. "Rarely do you have to lift that much," another worker told a Dateline NBC reporter.[3] "I was pregnant in 1988, and it worked out fine."

Still others face management's assumption that they won't want to return to work. Though 85 percent of pregnant women do come back to their jobs after maternity leave, many supervisors expect women to quit after they have babies.[4] Diana's case was blatant:

> In her sixth month of pregnancy, Diana was amazed to see a job posting of her position. When she confronted her manager about it, he acknowledged that he'd simply assumed she wouldn't be returning. "How on earth will you manage, my dear?" he asked her.

Those employers covered by the FMLA have a guarantee that the job they return to will be equivalent to the one they left. But more than half the workforce is not covered by the FMLA due to company size or hours worked.

If you're pregnant, here are a number of steps to take to help protect your job:

- Keep records of your good work performance. In addition to holding on to any written evaluations or notes of praise, you can keep a daily log or can send occasional memos to verify assignments or issues when appropriate.

- If you see you're being left out, talk to your manager about the problem and encourage discussion about it.

- Have a meeting with your supervisor to talk about your plans for leave and for returning to work. Sum up the discussion in writing. Be clear about the assignment you will be returning to.

- Work with others to discuss policies and corporate culture—attitudes toward pregnant women and new parents—before you're pregnant as well as once you are expecting.

- Identify allies and ask for their support in winning the policies you need.

- Get others to see how these issues may affect them. Work for policies to cover all manner of family leaves, not just pregnancy.

- If you're in a union, keep in close touch with your steward if you detect any discriminatory treatment.

Some things you DON'T have to do:

- Don't feel obliged to inform your supervisor as soon as you know you're pregnant. Weigh the situation and decide when's the best time. Use your judgment; if your manager is supportive, she or he will appreciate your cooperativeness.

- Don't agree to be on call while you're on leave. You can check in from time to time if you choose, but you should be free of job responsibilities. The baby will need your attention.

- Don't see your pregnancy as something to apologize for. It may be inconvenient for some at work, but it's natural. People can adjust. It would be much more inconvenient (and costly) if you were to leave your job. Some career advisors tell pregnant women to act as if they have no special needs. If, for example, you have to go to the bathroom a lot, according to this line of thinking, you should try to tie the trip to a visit to the supply room.[5] This is nonsense. You don't have to advertise any physical limitations, but there's no need to cover them up.

- While you can assure your employer that you have satisfactory child-care arrangements, you are under no obligation to answer specific questions about those arrangements—any more than you are required to describe your plans for birth control. An appropriate response to such a question might be this: "If you're asking about my reliability, let me assure you I will continue to be entirely dependable."

IF YOU'RE AN EXPECTANT FATHER

In most workplaces, the presumption will be that you don't want a lot of time off. Challenge this notion before you need leave for yourself.

Rather than being cautious about your own intentions to spend time with a new child, speak up about the importance of men becoming more involved family members. Help organize programs and discussions on the subject. Sometimes your very visibility on this issue can serve as protection against a manager who's behind the times. At the very least, it may inspire other men to take time off—or at least to expand their thinking on the subject. That was Keith's experience:

> Keith Epstein is an investigative reporter with the *Cleveland Plain Dealer's* Washington bureau. When he returned from a two-month getaway in the northern Cascade Mountains, his friends and associates couldn't believe he'd just wanted to be with his family. Surely he was working on a secret project, they insisted. Privately, a number of men in prestigious jobs acknowledged that they wished they'd done the same when their kids were still young.[6]

When requesting a leave, affirm your commitment to your job, and draw on any stated principle of the organization regarding work and family. Urge management to walk their talk. Point to any arrangements that have been made for female employees, and ask if they can justify treating male employees differently. Look for other men to support you and to take leave as well—the more men utilize their rights, the more difficult it will be to punish those who do.

In your letter summarizing whatever arrangements are made, spell out any concerns you have about how you'll be viewed upon your return. You won't always prevent trouble by naming it, but you will make it harder for old stereotypes to prevail. And you'll also strengthen your case if you need to take action later on.

IF YOU'RE AN ADOPTIVE PARENT

Before the FMLA, most employers had shorter leave policies for adoption than for birth. Now, the FMLA applies the same standard to birth, adoptions, and foster care. Yet many adoption agencies require one parent to be home for up to six months. This can lead to serious conflicts, as Chris and his family found:

> With his adoption at age 12, Chris had his first real family. He knew they needed time to get acquainted. But his new mom had to put the kids to bed at eight each night to go to work. "She wants to take time off to help the family get used to each other," Chris said, "but she can't. If she does take some time off, she will lose her job."

Many support groups exist to help adoptive parents. Use these networks to help educate your employer about adoption agency requirements and the needs of adoptive families. And, even if the employer isn't covered by the FMLA, the fact that the law includes adoption and foster care may help convince some employers to expand their policy as well.

IF YOU'RE A SAME-SEX COUPLE

Many gay and lesbian parents face a painful double bind: If you ask for leave to adopt a child or to support your partner, you may well have to disclose that you are gay—and, for good reason, you may fear that will jeopardize your job. Even managers who are reasonably supportive of same-sex partners are often prejudiced about gays raising children. Here are some things to consider:

• Only you and your partner can weigh the risks and decide how open to be. Obviously, it's better if you're able to tell the truth. Know the law: Most states do not include sexual orientation as a protected category in antidiscrimination statutes; neither does the federal government (although such legislation is now pending). Where legal protection does exists, refer to it if you need to. (The states that prohibit discrimination on the basis of sexual orientation are California, Connecticut, Hawaii, Massachusetts, Minnesota, New Jersey, Vermont, and Wisconsin.)

• As is true for any other group, work for policies before you need them. See who might be allies. If you're a union member, ask the union to make domestic-partner coverage a bargaining issue. This, of course, is broader than same-sex partners—which is why it's a good way to gain additional support.

• You may want to seek advice from an attorney. A local lesbian/ gay rights organization should be able to make referrals.

Many gay and lesbian couples who are open about their sexual orientation but not protected by domestic-partner coverage or by state law are able to negotiate leave by appealing to basic fairness. If your company grants leave to adoptive parents (and all companies covered by the FMLA must do so), then that same leave should be granted to an adoptive parent in a lesbian or gay relationship.[7]

Lesbians and gays have a monumental task to win equality in the workplace. If you're not gay, don't wait until someone who is gay asks for your support. Be sure as you work for family-friendly policies that you include *all* families. Children who are raised by a couple who happen to be of the same sex need time with their parents just as any other child does.

STEPS TO TAKE FOR HEALTH LEAVE

One of the most important aspects of the FMLA is its recognition that birth and adoption aren't the only times workers need leave. At some point, most of us also have to care for a sick family member or to recover from a personal illness. Arranging a leave for this purpose is complicated for several reasons. First, you may have little or no advance notice. Training a backup employee may be difficult or impossible. You may have no idea how long you'll need to be out. And unlike welcoming a new family member, dealing with illness is usually painful, with little joy to balance the stress and extra expense.

Step One: Line up a support person right away, either at work or outside. Let this person make sure you've taken care of all the details, such as getting any medical documentation you'll need for the job.

Step Two: Learn company policy regarding notice, communication while on leave, certification, and so forth. Use the recommended channels.

Step Three: Know your rights. Many companies have "absence control policies" stating that employees may miss only a limited number of days, beyond which any absence is unexcused regardless of the reason or documentation. Such a policy violates the FMLA. If you're allowed to take the time off, you shouldn't—and can't—be disciplined for doing so. (For what to do if your employer violates the law, see Chapter 4.)

Special Situations

• If you're gay or lesbian, you may have a particularly hard time getting time off to care for a sick child or partner. If the supervisor denies your request, ask if they would deny it for a heterosexual employee, and challenge the bias.

• If your employer isn't covered by the FMLA and doesn't offer time off to care for a sick parent or other family member, make your case clearly. Show that the time you spend helping immediately after the injury or illness may very well shorten the time—and expense—of the patient's recovery. Explain that you want to give your full attention to the job and that being able to take some time off then will help you do this when you return. As in every other case, work to win this policy before you need it.

Arranging time off to care for a family member is a big part of solving the job/family challenge, but you may find you need ongoing flexibility. Chapter 9 will help you decide what you need and how to ask for it.

STEPS FOR ARRANGING A SUCCESSFUL LEAVE

1. Figure out what leave/schedule you want and can afford.
2. Decide on your ideal plan, an acceptable compromise, and your bottom line.
3. Approach your supervisor.
4. Follow up in writing.
5. Help train your replacement.
6. Prepare for your return before you leave.

Special tips:

• Take steps to guard against pregnancy discrimination.
• Men who take the leave to which they're entitled help change the corporate culture.
• Lesbian and gay parents deserve support and rights equal to those of other parents.

9

Steps for Arranging a Flexible Schedule

You may want to rearrange your schedule to accommodate your family responsibilities or a change in your own health. Even in a family-friendly company, you have to take the initiative to figure out what you want and how your job will get done if your schedule changes. Here are some suggestions for how to proceed.

STEPS FOR ANYONE CONSIDERING A FLEXIBLE SCHEDULE

The basic steps you need to take are similar to those for arranging leave. But you'll need to analyze the alternatives more and to make a specific case about how the company's objectives can be met under the proposed arrangement.

Step One: Figure out what you want and how much room you have to maneuver. Because flexibility can take so many forms, you need to start by taking a good look at your own situation. Ask yourself these questions:

• *What's my goal?* You may want more time with your family every day; if so, reduced hours (for a short or long period of time), job-sharing, or working out of your home may suit your needs. If you want to be available at certain times of the day, such as early morning or after school, changing your start or end time could provide a solution. Many people want more time on certain occasions, perhaps for a child's sports events or for a class; they need a schedule with flexible start and end times. A compressed work week helps cut down on travel and frees up a block of time.

Examining your goals may show you that what you really want is a more reasonable work load within a full-time schedule. That realization could lead not to changing schedules, but rather to changing positions within the company or changing managers—

or finding a new job. (I'm not going to address here the matter of starting your own business, which for some people is a way to have more flexibility; see the resource list in Appendix A for readings and organizations that can help.)

• *What can I afford?* You may prefer a reduced schedule but need full-time income. In that case, another form of schedule change might still provide some relief. If you are considering reduced hours, check on your child-care costs. Part-time hours are not always available, and the cost may not go down by the same proportion.

• *What are the opportunities and risks at work?* You'll want to examine how your choice might affect your future with your employer. Find out whether there's any precedent at the company, particularly under your supervisor. Any concerns can be part of your negotiations.

• *What will the impact be on my actual job?* Can you meet the objectives of the job in the framework you want? Will you have enough communication with clients? with co-workers? with your manager? If not, can you work out a reasonable alternative to the ways your job is currently organized, such as delegating some duties to other staff?

• *What can my spouse or partner do?* If you have a partner, each of you should look at opportunities and risks. Is it possible for both of you to reduce hours slightly without losing benefits? Could first one and then the other cut back for a given period of time?

Step Two: Decide on your ideal plan, an acceptable compromise, and your bottom line. Use a worksheet similar to the sample given to come up with your ideal plan. First map out your goals and the flexible arrangements that might help you meet those goals. Then look at the advantages and drawbacks to each. Finally, list any risks or opportunities within the organization for someone taking this step. The exercise should also help you determine an acceptable compromise and your bottom line.

Step Three: Find precedents. Do some research for examples of other people in similar jobs who've successfully managed on a schedule like the one you're proposing. Arrange a meeting with someone in the personnel office to see what company practice has been. If you're in a union, ask the steward to find out what precedents exist—and enlist the union's help in arguing for you. In the event that no one has worked out such a schedule at your

Sample Worksheet

GOAL	More time with family at no less than 60% present wage, life and dental insurance, retention of promotion opportunities		
Possibilities	1. Part-time	2. Job-share	3. Work at home
Advantages	• with family more • stay involved on job	• with family more • stay involved on job	• with family more • keep full-time wage and benefits • save commuting time and costs
Disadvantages	• less money • fewer benefits(?)	• less money • fewer benefits(?) • need to find partner	• distractions • higher utility costs (heat, lighting, etc.)
Risks	• hurt advance- ment possibilities	• blurs credit	• no network
Opportunities	• use attention to excel	• share ideas, burdens	• use attention to excel
DECISION	• Job-sharing helps me meet my goal if I can negotiate for a 3/5 share (3 days a week) at the same hourly rate, full dental and life insurance, prorated sick days, holidays, and vacation, and with assurances about not being ruled out for advancement. • I won't accept a lower hourly rate or loss of all benefits, but I will accept a job-share of only half time (2½ days a week—no less) and prorated life and dental benefits, with those assurances about advancement opportunities.		

company, check on comparable organizations. (See resource list in Appendix A for where to go for help.)

Step Four: Approach your supervisor. No matter what type of flexible schedule you propose, you'll need to demonstrate how your job duties will be accomplished, how the work will be evaluated, and how the change fits with the goals and objectives of the company. (Later in this chapter, you'll find sections on each type of flexible schedule, with a list of some bargaining points.) You may need more than one meeting to work out the details. Since you're negotiating for an ongoing change, rather than a one-time leave, you need to build in an evaluation component. Get agreement on both when your work will be evaluated and what criteria will be used. The first evaluation should be scheduled to allow you enough time to work out the wrinkles and demonstrate results, but it should be soon enough to answer concerns your supervisor might have.

Step Five: Follow up in writing. It's important to have a detailed record of the points on which you and your supervisor agree in order to avoid conflict down the road. Your memo can be written as a thank you letter or as a more formal document such as this:

Memorandum of Understanding

Mary Jones and John Smith will share the job of Senior Assistant to the Marketing Manager beginning May 1. Mary will work all day Mondays and Tuesdays and Wednesday mornings until 1 p.m. John will work Wednesday afternoons beginning at noon and all day Thursdays and Fridays. Both job-sharers will handle customer contact and daily office responsibilities while they are on duty. Each will be responsible for an equal number of accounts, but they will be familiar with each other's accounts in order to answer questions if necessary.

The job-sharers will communicate via a daily log on the computer and a meeting every Wednesday at noon. At that time, they will divide up new accounts and exchange other information and ideas. Whenever possible, Mary and John will provide backup for each other in case of illness or family emergency.

In order to ensure continued quality, the job sharers and their manager will review this arrangement after one month and every six months thereafter. Based on feedback from clients and from others in the department, each employee will be evaluated individually and as a team member.

Mary and John will each draw 50 percent of their full-time salary. Mary will receive full health and dental insurance. John will receive full dental and life insurance. Both will maintain full seniority and be eligible for vacation, sick days, pension, and holidays on a prorated basis. If a holiday falls on a day when one or the other employee is scheduled to work a full day, they will both have the holiday and arrange to split another day that week, so four days are worked, two each.

Those steps should be helpful no matter which scheduling option you're considering. In the following sections, we'll look at six types of flexible schedules. For each, we'll consider how it works, the advantages and disadvantages, what you'd have to demonstrate to your supervisor, what you need to negotiate, and the bargaining points you can use.

PART-TIME EMPLOYMENT

How It Works

Part-time means you work reduced hours for a period of time, either limited or undefined. Pay and benefits can be prorated—if you work *half-time*, for example, you receive *half* your pay and *half* the premium toward your benefits. Some employers pay a lower rate (part-time employees, on the average, earn just 60 percent of the hourly rate of full-timers[1]); typically employers offer part-timers fewer or no benefits. Others pay full benefits for anyone working at least twenty hours.

Considerations

Advantages

- Having more time outside work.
- Staying on top of developments in your field and being visible in the company.
- Having flexibility if needed at work or at home.

Disadvantages

- Losing some income and (often) benefits.
- Having to find a way to assign the rest of your job duties.
- Being viewed as less committed by co-workers.

What You Need to Demonstrate

- What work will be accomplished in the number of hours you work.
- How the rest of the work can be handled.
- How work will be evaluated.
- How your plan fits the goals and objectives of the business.

What You Need to Negotiate

- Pay (should be prorated at the same hourly rate).
- Benefits (full benefits, or the same benefits full-timers receive prorated, or some benefits at the full rate).
- Hours, days.
- Evaluating the arrangement.
- Impact on your future with the company.

Bargaining Points

- The company retains trained and skilled employees.
- You'll be even more productive because your schedule will help you feel less stressed, better able to concentrate. (Evidence supports this view. In 1963, for example, the Boston Department of Public Welfare permitted 50 half-time caseworkers to fill the equivalent of 25 full-time positions. An evaluation by an outside consultant after two years found that the half-time workers were, on the average, 89 percent as productive as full-time employees—in half the time, they produced nearly nine-tenths of the work. The turnover rate for the half-time workers was 14 percent, compared to the average of 40 percent for full-time caseworkers.[2])

JOB-SHARING

How It Works

You and another person share the responsibilities of one position. Some job-sharers split up each day, overlapping at lunch; others split up the week. Some work three days each in order to have more overlap. You and your job-sharer do not have to work the same number of hours. One could come in two days a week, for instance, while the other is on the job for three days. Depending on the position, you either divide up duties or do roughly the same tasks. The division of labor is more straightforward with certain jobs, like receptionist, bank teller, or retail clerk. It may be more challenging for someone who has ongoing contact with a limited number of customers or clients.

Considerations

Advantages

- Having more time outside work for your family (or education, starting a business, a hobby, etc.).
- Having someone to share ideas, responsibilities.
- Having someone to take over in an emergency.

Disadvantages

- Having to find a partner.
- Possibly not liking how the partner completes what you've started.

- Having to share credit that rightfully belongs to you.
- Having less pay, possibly losing benefits.
- Possibly being on a slower promotional track.

What You Need to Demonstrate
- How the work will get done.
- How you and your job-sharer will communicate.
- How job-sharer will handle partner's sick days.
- What will happen if one job-sharer wants to go full-time.
- How job-sharers' work will be evaluated. (What if one's performance is average, the other excellent?)

What You Need to Negotiate
- Pay (same hourly rate).
- Benefits (full benefits, or the same benefits full-timers receive prorated, or some benefits at the full rate).
- Division of labor.
- How to evaluate performance of each job-sharer, as well as the overall accomplishments of the team.
- Impact on your future with the company.

Bargaining Points
- Job-sharing means two employees bring creativity to the job and can exchange ideas for continuous improvement.
- The employer should have little, if any, additional expense.

FLEXIBLE START/END TIMES

How It Works

The employer sets core hours when all employees have to be on the job, with varying start and end times (e.g., you work from 6:30 A.M. to 3:30 P.M., with an hour for lunch; Bruce starts at 9:30 A.M. and gets off at 6:30 P.M., with an hour for lunch; Danielle works from 8:00 A.M. until 4:30 P.M., with a half hour for lunch—you and your co-workers are all in the department from 9:30 A.M. to 3:30 P.M., the core hours).

Considerations

Advantages

- Having more time with your family when you need to be there.
- Keeping your full pay and benefits.
- Having less stress rushing to work.
- Possibly avoiding heavy traffic.

Disadvantages

- Still working full-time (the change may not free up enough time).
- Having to be a self-starter or needing clearly defined tasks.
- Possibly having to give up a car pool.

What You Need to Demonstrate

- How the work will get done.
- How hours will be monitored.
- Whether shifts will change from week to week or stay the same.

What You Need to Negotiate

- Core hours.
- Definition of tasks during times when supervisor is not there.
- Evaluation.

Bargaining Points

- There's little or no expense for the company.
- Studies show morale and productivity improve with flexibility; employees can get more done during times when fewer co-workers are present.

FLEXIBLE COMP TIME

How It Works

If you need a few hours off, you can make up the time.

Considerations

Advantages

- Having more time with your family when you need to be there.
- Keeping your full pay and benefits.

Disadvantages
- Possibly not freeing up enough time.
- Unpredictable schedule (you may have to negotiate each time you want off).

What You Need to Demonstrate
- How the work will get done while you're out.
- How hours will be monitored.
- How your supervisor will be notified.
- How soon the work has to be made up.

What You Need to Negotiate
- Grounds for taking off.
- Core hours, if necessary.
- Definition of tasks during times when supervisor is not there.
- Evaluation.

Bargaining Points
- The company has no extra expense.
- This is one of the easiest ways for the employer to help you meet family responsibilities without giving up anything at work.
- You're on your regular schedule most of the time.

COMPRESSED WORK WEEK

How It Works

You spend more time working each day for fewer days a week. Usually, the schedule is four 10-hour days, but it could be some other combination, such as three 12-hour days, or a two-week pay period with five 9-hour days the first week and four the second week.

Considerations

Advantages
- Having more time with your family.
- Keeping your full pay and benefits.

- Having more blocks of time off.
- Possibly saving some commuting time and costs.

Disadvantages
- Possible difficulty of long days.

What You Need to Demonstrate
- How the work will get done.
- How productivity will go up, not down, from compressed time.
- How supervision will work.

What You Need to Negotiate
- Who will work on which days?
- How to coordinate schedules.
- Definition of tasks during times when supervisor is not there.
- Evaluation.

Bargaining Points
- Companies that have implemented compressed work weeks report increased productivity and morale, decreased absenteeism.
- The employer incurs little, if any, extra expense.

WORKING AT HOME (TELECOMMUTING)

How It Works

You work from home—all the time, or certain days each week, or from time to time depending on tasks. You may be connected to the office by computer modem, FAX, or telephone.

Considerations

Advantages
- Keeping full pay and benefits.
- Saving travel time and expenses, as well as lunch and wardrobe costs.
- Having less stress.
- Being able to concentrate on some tasks better out of office.

Disadvantages

- Incurring hidden expenses, such as increased heating, lighting, and electricity costs.
- Finding needed work space.
- Having difficulty working when the children are home—especially toddlers—unless your home office has its own entrance.
- Losing networking opportunities.
- Possibly not liking the isolation of working alone.

What You Need to Demonstrate

- How the work will get done.
- How communication with co-workers and supervisor will continue undisrupted.

What You Need to Negotiate

- Pay and benefits (should be equivalent to that of full-time employees in the office).
- How projects will be assigned.
- How much time, if any, you'll spend in the office.
- What equipment you'll need and who pays for it (employer should).
- How you'll be supervised.
- Evaluation.

Bargaining Points

- Telecommuting saves the company money. (It costs about $4,000 to equip an employee to work away from the office. Working in the office costs an average of $20,000 per worker each year for rent, security, cleaning services, and other costs.[3])
- Telecommuting helps retain valuable employees.

The Communications Workers of America developed these principles for working at home:

1. Equal pay for telecommuters and others doing the same work.
2. Telecommuters to be in the office at least two days a week.
3. Managers to visit telecommuters' homes no more than twice a month with at least 24-hours' notice.

4. Employer to furnish and install all equipment and supplies and pay all work-related expenses.

5. The union may inspect work stations for safety and ergonomics.

6. Telecommuters will be notified routinely of job openings and advancement opportunities.

7. Telecommuters will be told about the union and given time to consult with union stewards.

8. Training will be offered to keep telecommuters current with new technologies.

Alternative schedules, more than other policies, require individual negotiations. But as with all the other policies described in this book, the *right* to flexibility is more easily won when you work with others on behalf of everyone. Fight for the principles before you need them.

STEPS FOR ARRANGING A FLEXIBLE SCHEDULE

1. Figure out what you want and how much room you have to maneuver.

2. Decide on your ideal plan, an acceptable compromise, and your bottom line.

3. Find precedents.

4. Approach your supervisor.

5. Follow up in writing.

Tips:

Demonstrate how the plan you want can work to the company's advantage.

Prepare to negotiate for fair pay, benefits, and evaluation measures.

III

The Challenge at Home—Helpful Advice and Personal Choices

10

Finding Good Dependent Care

Making time for your family is one giant hurdle. The other is finding the best possible care for your child or parent while you are working.

CHILD CARE

In the past, most women who had to work outside the home relied on relatives to watch their children. But today, the relatives are likely to be holding jobs themselves. That means finding—and paying—someone, who may well be a stranger, to care for the children you cherish.

We all know the value to children of quality care and, conversely, the harm caused by neglect. According to psychologist Faye Crosby, good child care is also the most significant factor in relieving the stress of balancing work and family—more important than marital happiness or success at work.[1]

What constitutes quality care? Individual values vary and so will choices for who should mind the kids. The American Academy of Pediatrics recommends that child care provide the following:

- It should be *stimulating*, helping the child to ask questions and solve problems.

- It should promote the *mature self*, enabling a child to develop confidence, creativity, and curiosity.

- Child care should foster *social skills*, so that children learn to operate as part of a group.

Many parents continue to rely on relatives; 18 percent of pre-school children are cared for in this way. But a much larger number of parents turn to day-care providers—because suitable relatives are not available, because the parents want their child in a larger social setting, or because they prefer providers with special training in early child development.

Children can be cared for either in their own home or outside the home. If outside the home, they can go to a family day-care provider or to a day-care center.

Choices

Family Day-Care Provider   In family day care, a caregiver in a private home watches several children. Many states have licensing procedures for family day-care providers and guidelines for the number of day-care children that can be in the home at one time (they are covered in the next section).

If you are interested in family day care, you can call the National Association for Family Day Care, 800-424-2246, to get a number for the resource and referral agency nearest to you.

Day-Care Center   Day-care centers are set up in schools, in YMCAs, in churches or synagogues, in workplaces, or in their own buildings. They usually operate from early morning to early evening. Some care only for preschool children. Some include a licensed kindergarten so a child can stay there until he or she is ready for the first grade, and others have busing arrangements with schools that have a half-day kindergarten. Some centers are even being set up as sleep centers for parents who work at night.

Choosing a Day-Care Provider

Finding good care is a major challenge (and source of stress) for many working parents, especially for those who base their choice primarily on the cost or on the hours the center is open. What follows are some basic guidelines for choosing a day-care center or family-care provider, based on resources provided by the Child Care Action Campaign and the National Council of Jewish Women:

Visit   Visit for an extended period of time on more than one occasion. Visit at least once unannounced—if the provider doesn't allow this, choose someone else. Continue to visit after placing your child with the provider. Trust your observations and your child's reactions. Do the kids seem happy and active? Are the caregivers attentive and enthusiastic? Do they praise children more often than they correct them? Are they patient with accidents? Do the kids go to the caregiver for comfort and help? Are they treated as individuals?

Check Qualifications Choose a provider who is licensed and regularly inspected.

Determine Ratio of Staff to Children Make sure the ratio of staff to children meets or exceeds the following guidelines:

Family day care:

1 adult for 5 children (no more than 2 infants under one year)

Day-care centers:

1 adult for 3 or 4 infants or toddlers
1 adult for 4 to 6 two-year-olds
1 adult for 7 or 8 three-year-olds
1 adult for 8 or 9 four-year-olds
1 adult for 8 to 10 five-year-olds

After-school care:

1 adult for 10 to 12 children

Examine the Environment Look for an environment in which children can feel competent and can engage in meaningful activities, at least some of which are planned (like storytelling, art, and building). Toys in sufficient quantities should be available for each age group. Physical activity is important; there should be a safe outdoor area where children can play, weather permitting.

Ask about Relations with Parents Parents should receive regular reports of children's accomplishments and of any problem areas. Ideally, caregivers and parents function as partners who share information and work together to solve problems.

Check on Health and Safety At least one caregiver should know first aid and cardiopulmonary resuscitation (CPR). All caregivers must follow basic rules for cleanliness. Choose a provider who does background checks on all staff.

Know Your Child Different kinds of care work better for some children than for others: Not every child thrives in a highly structured environment, for instance. Look for a situation that matches your child's needs.

Find Out Policies   Ask what the center's policies are concerning fees, late pickups, administering medications, and other issues. Once you set hours for your child, can you change them? Will you be fined for arriving late?

Finding Care for Children with Special Needs

Children with special needs, whether physical, emotional, or behavioral, need child-care providers who understand those needs and have the appropriate training and resources. Bonnie Michaels and Elizabeth McCarty, directors of a consulting firm called Managing Work & Family, Inc., list these considerations:[2]

- Does the program have other children with special needs?
- Does the program communicate a caring and sensitive feeling?
- Has the environment been adapted to the special needs of your child?
- Does the program support you, the parent?
- Are necessary support services available (such as physical or speech therapists)?
- Does the caregiver have specialized training?

Be sure to consult an agency in your area that deals with your child's special needs. They often have lists of approved caregivers.

In-Home Care

Parents who can afford to may choose to hire someone to come to their own home. Some people feel this arrangement is less disruptive to the children and offers more reliable care. Magazine editor Priscilla Painton described her situation this way: "You get someone you can decide will be like a third parent. It gives you that peace of mind. It's another person the children adore and love. You end up paying much more; most women can't afford it. But for me, as much as it's a hardship financially, it's really worth it long-term."

Other parents like having their kids in a situation where they interact with other children. Again, your tastes—and income—will determine your choice. Some providers bring another child with them to your home. If you do hire in-home care, be familiar with what forms to fill out and taxes to pay. Federal taxes include Social Security and Medicare taxes (Form 942) and an annual unemployment tax (form 940 or 940-EZ). You're responsible for sending the

IRS a Wage and Tax Statement (W-2) at the end of the year for your caregiver, along with a Transmittal Income and Tax Statement (W-3). State requirements vary.[3]

Finding In-Home Care

Here are some steps for finding an in-home care provider:

Advertise   Place ads in the newspapers and with college placement offices. Include the vital information: number and ages of children, days and hours, experience required, whether the person must have a car.

Interview   You can screen people over the phone and then set up in-person interviews with those who seem most qualified. You'll want to ask not only about qualifications and experience, but also outlook: Does the provider's child-rearing approach work well with your own? How would the individual feel about following your guidelines? Pose a number of situations and ask for specific answers; for example, what if the children are squabbling, or what if the baby has been fed and changed and still cries? Get an idea of the person's favorite children's books, music, games. If you find a good candidate, arrange for the person to interact with your child while you do other things, and observe from time to time.

References   Ask for names and phone numbers of families the candidate worked for (as a provider or, if this is the first full-time job, as a baby-sitter). Call and ask detailed questions about the kind of care situation and the family's degree of satisfaction.

Follow Up   Once you've hired someone, you can arrange an unannounced visit just as you would at a day-care center. Pay attention to your child's responses when the caregiver arrives and leaves every day and when you talk about how the day went.

Sharing Shifts

Some couples solve the dilemma and expense of child care by working different shifts. This arrangement has the advantage of making sure one parent is always involved with the kids. It also saves money and increases the role for fathers. Many working-class families have been doing this for a long time. As James Levine, director of the Families and Work Institute's Fatherhood Project, put it, "It's not glitzy and role-reversing; it's necessary."[4]

A recent Census Bureau study found that the proportion of families paying for child care fell from 40 percent in 1988 to 35 percent in 1991, primarily because of the increase in care from fathers. In 1988, 15 percent of preschoolers whose mothers worked outside the home were cared for by their dads. That figure rose to 20 percent by 1991.

The drawback to this arrangement is that the couple barely see each other. Once the children are in school, the second-shift parent has very little time with them or the spouse. Poet Sue Doro captures the agony of such a choice in this verse from the poem "Turning a Bad Thing into Good":

> monday through friday
> she phones every night
> on her 8 o'clock break
> from the telephone
> in the warehouse
> that's the most quiet
>
> then for ten minutes
> she listens to her children
> grow.

Paying for Child Care

For most families, child care is a major expense—averaging 23 percent of income for families earning below $15,000 per year. The average payment for care is $3,500 per child per year. Day-care providers may require a sizable deposit, so the cost can begin even *before* a baby is born.

For millions of Americans, cost remains the biggest obstacle to arranging quality care. Some assistance is available if you qualify:

Public Funding Title XX is a program of federal funds made available to states to provide child-care assistance for low-income families. The 1990 Child Care and Development Block Grant was intended to help parents pay for child care and increase the supply and quality of care. Unfortunately, these funds are woefully inadequate.Some proposed welfare reform legislation would allocate more money to child care both for women moving off welfare and for the working poor. To find out if you're eligible for public funds, call your local Department of Social Services (listed in the phone book under County).

Head Start Low-income parents are eligible for Head Start, which provides part- or full-day child care. Unlike some centers for the poor, which have been criticized for simply warehousing kids, many Head Start programs have been singled out as providing exceptional care.

Dependent Care Tax Credits If you're paying someone to watch your children (age 12 or younger), you may be able to claim a credit against your federal income tax for part of your child care expenses. Both single parents and two-parent families in which at least one parent works full- or part-time and the other either works or is a full-time student are eligible for dependent care tax credits. As of 1994, you're allowed to claim a percentage of your actual costs up to $2,400 for one child, $4,800 for two or more, depending on your income. To claim the credit, you must list the Social Security number of the provider and keep records of all costs incurred.

Dependent Care Assistance Program Many employers offer this program, known as DCAP, which allows employees to set aside pretax dollars for dependent care purposes (including elder care). At the beginning of the year, you declare how much money should be allocated for this purpose, up to a maximum amount of $5,000. You don't pay taxes on this sum—and neither does the employer. The program requires that you "use it or lose it," so set aside the amount you know you will spend. As with the federal tax credit, you must be willing to list the child-care provider's Social Security number. DCAP is a *substitute* for the federal tax credit—you can use one or the other, but not both. DCAP works better for parents with a family income over a certain amount (roughly $23,500 in 1994); lower income families, who pay fewer taxes, benefit more from the federal tax credit.

Earned Income Tax Credit Parents whose annual family income is less than $23,755 in 1994 are eligible for the earned income tax credit (EITC) if at least one parent is employed and at least one child under age 19 lives at home for more than half the year. (Workers with two or more children may earn up to $25,295.) The credit can add to a family's income as much as $2,038 for one child and $2,528 for two or more children to help pay for child care or any other expense. To find out how to apply for the EITC, ask your employer or call the IRS hotline, 1-800-829-1040.

Sliding Scale Fees   Some child-care centers allow parents to pay varying fees according to income. Be sure to ask if a sliding scale is available.

Guidelines for Latchkey Kids

Finding care for school-age children presents another challenge. Many parents scramble to find some dependable arrangement for before and/or after school. Use the suggestions that were given for finding a family day-care provider or for interviewing someone in your home. Make sure the provider can handle children who are restless and hungry after a day inside at school. Leave clear guidelines on what snacks and activities are allowed, when homework has to start, what happens if siblings fight, and whether or not the kids can play outside or have friends come over.

Most parents agonize over when it's okay to leave a child alone after school. Unfortunately, many simply can't afford to pay for after-school care. Flexible hours that allow a parent to be home when school ends can help, as can after-school programs and adequate wages. (See Chapter 16.) Deciding when your child is old enough to be left alone will depend a lot on your circumstances and the child's maturity. (Most states have legal guidelines, often age 13; these are usually enforced only in cases of outright neglect.) For those whose kids are home alone, here are some guidelines to reduce risk and fear or loneliness:

• If you are not allowed to receive a phone call from your children when they get home, arrange for someone with whom they can—and must—check in every day.

• Have clear rules about what your child can and can't do regarding using the stove, watching TV, having friends in, going outside, answering the door, and so on.

• Find out what services are available in your community to help latchkey kids. Some cities have a hotline where staffers help with homework questions or just provide conversation.

• Decide on special projects or activities to liven up this time.

• List emergency numbers and procedures in a readily visible place.

• Have a family telephone book available with numbers cross-referenced; e.g., Aunt Mary Smith should be under Smith and Aunt Mary. Children rarely remember relatives' last names. Do the same with friends.

- Practice safety routines with your child—how to call 911, how to escape if there's a fire, which neighbors can be relied on, how to answer the phone without revealing that they might be alone, and so on. Often children are frightened because they're unsure of how they'd handle certain situations; once they know the plan, they are less likely to worry.

- Encourage the child to talk to you about being alone. Together, look for any aspects of the situation that you can improve.

- Leave notes or small surprises for your child. You can begin a story or picture that the child then works on and gives you when you get home. Eventually you can collect these into a booklet.

Several handbooks have been written on latchkey care with safety tips, ideas for activities, and recommendations for good communication with your child. (See the resource list in Appendix A.) Your local library may have additional resources.

ELDER CARE AND SERVICES

According to Andrew F. Scharlach, a gerontology expert at the University of California at Berkeley, care for the elderly will soon be a bigger problem than child care for most working people. The issues involved in elder care are complicated, says Scharlach, because of the variety of needs faced by older people and often the distance involved between the caregiver and the elder relative.[5]

Many senior citizens want independence. They don't want to go to a nursing home or to move in with an adult child. But they may not be able to care for themselves. Even if they live with or near their children, their needs may be greater than an adult child can easily cope with.

You may need a brief leave to *arrange* care—time without other preoccupations to assess resources, and decide what kind of care is needed and where to find it.

When Sidney's mother had a stroke, he was frantic about how she would manage when she left the hospital. Neither her finances nor his permitted full-time care, and he knew his mother didn't want to go to a nursing home. Sidney was able to take two weeks off to investigate available services. He found a number of low-cost and even some free programs to help his mother. He was able to arrange a van to take her to physical therapy four times a week, a Meals on Wheels program to bring her lunch and dinner, and a housekeeper to come in twice a week to clean and do laundry. Sidney then changed his schedule slightly to be able to stop by his mother's home every morning to help her get up and make breakfast. Buoyed by being able to stay in her home, his mother made solid progress—and Sidney was able to return to work with a minimum of anxiety.

Range of Services

If you are faced with elder-caregiving responsibilities, figure out what help the person needs, what's affordable, what's reasonable for your family members to do, and what you can delegate to others. Many people are unaware of the wide array of services available. These originated in large part with the Older Americans Act of 1965 and the federal agency it established, the U.S. Administration on Aging, which then set up a network of state units and area agencies. Services include:

- Senior centers
- Daily meal delivery
- Housekeepers to clean, shop, and accompany the person to the doctor or other appointments
- Respite care workers to relieve the primary caretaker
- Phone check-in or companion services
- Carrier alert program (a decal on the mailbox tells the mail carrier whom to alert if mail is accumulating or anything else seems out of order; a similar program is offered by many local utility companies)
- Volunteer programs through schools and community or religious groups that help with repairs and shopping
- Adult day-care centers
- Social workers to make sure the person's receiving all the aid she or he is eligible for and that the programs are working well
- Home-health-care providers
- Transportation services
- Assisted-living situations
- Support groups for caregivers

Choosing Adult Day Care

One area that's seen big growth in recent years is adult day care. This option allows the elderly person to live at home or with a relative while still having stimulation, activities, and professional care during the day. Unfortunately, supply lags behind need. And most states still lack certification programs. The American Association of Retired Persons (AARP) gives these suggestions for what to look for in an adult day-care facility:[6]

- Is it clean? Do participants seem comfortable?
- Is it licensed or certified?
- Does the staff treat patients with dignity? What are staff qualifications?
- Does each patient have a care plan? If so, how is it monitored?
- Is transportation available?
- Do the hours and activities meet your relative's needs?
- What are the fees? Is public or private funding available?

Getting Help

Many private services have sprung up to help the caregiver evaluate their relative's needs, locate resources, and follow up to make sure they're satisfactory. More than 550 providers belong to the National Association of Professional Geriatric Care Managers, based in Tucson, Arizona. The organization began with thirty members in 1985. "They go from the small, home-based business to major corporations, companies who have everything in house," said Jihane Rohrbacher, an association spokeswoman.[7] For fees ranging from $40 to $150 an hour, the agencies provide a case manager to assess, coordinate, and/or provide services.

For the many people who can't afford private management, the U.S. Administration on Aging has a toll-free information and referral line known as Eldercare Locator. Every month, about 4,000 people call the number: 1-800-677-1116. You can also look in the yellow pages of your local telephone directory under Family Services, Information and Referral Services, Seniors, or Hotlines. Often, the local United Way office has a list of services as well. Organizations such as AARP and agencies set up to deal with specific health conditions, such as the Alzheimer's Association, can also provide useful information.

Before you call a clearinghouse—an agency that has gathered information on available services—know what your needs are. Then get as many specifics as possible from staff about location, hours, and fees for a variety of services, along with the name of the person to ask for. Make sure you know what paperwork they need, and bring that with you.

Emotional Costs

Even when services are available, they're often expensive and difficult to oversee. Your elderly relative may be confused and frightened by strangers taking charge of daily routines. Some become ill and recover, but most are in a process of decline.

"It's a lot easier to manage the lives of little kids who live under your roof and are healthy than to care for people who are adults, live elsewhere, and have a whole household that must be dealt with—groceries, bills, mail, taxes," summed up one woman. "Even if you meet their physical needs, they're lonely and scared. You feel you just can't do enough." At such a difficult time, flexibility and understanding from your employer can make an enormous difference.

When a parent is dying or has suffered a serious illness or injury, you may need time off—period. Then, it's not a question of finding a capable professional who can provide the service instead of you—you want to be there, and you should be able to arrange it. A decent employer will make every attempt to allow the necessary leave.

WHAT TO LOOK FOR IN DEPENDENT CARE

Child care should stimulate children, promote their curiosity, and foster social skills.

Be sure the child-care provider allows unannounced visits—and make them.

Ask candidates for in-home child care how they'd deal with specific situations.

Make choices for your child based on the individual child, your values, and your income.

Research ways to get financial assistance for care if possible.

Latchkey kids need clear rules, safety routines, and appropriate activities.

Use national and local clearinghouses to get information on elder-care services.

11

Balancing on the Home Front: Getting the Whole Family to Share the Load

---

While this book is definitely not for women only, working women's double duty is a common occurrence. After working a full day on the job, many mothers are still expected to manage the load at home, as was shown in this scene from the TV show "Roseanne:"

After a rough day at work, Roseanne comes home to find her children fighting and needing attention. The house is a mess and dinner isn't ready. "I'll make dinner," offers husband Dan. "Oh, but honey," Roseanne replies, "you just made dinner three years ago!"

What Roseanne and many other working mothers need are working fathers—men who are also preoccupied with what to make for dinner and how many clean clothes are in the drawers. Research shows that men today are more interested than previously in spending time with their families and more open to doing tasks historically seen as women's work. But the reality in the home is still nowhere near equality.

SHARING HOUSEWORK EQUALLY

More men today say they'd like additional time at home. In 1992, DuPont surveyed 8,500 employees. Some 57 percent of the men wanted flexibility at work in order to spend more time with their families—up from only 37 percent five years earlier.[1]

Some men discover the value of spending time with their families late in their careers. Governor Lowell Weicker, Jr. of Connecticut announced he wouldn't run for reelection because he wanted to spend more time with his second family than he had with the first.

Even some very conventional institutions are beginning to recognize the value of men expanding their roles in the family. In 1993, the National Conference of Catholic Bishops unanimously approved a statement urging men to share fully in child rearing and household duties. The bishops advised men to view "their traditional role as 'provider' for a family in more than an economic sense. Physical care of children, discipline, training in religious values and practices, helping with school work and other activities—all these and more can be provided by fathers as well as mothers."[2]

Men *are* doing more work in the home—but still not as much as they think they're doing.[3] Even when men and women share household tasks equally, women are often responsible for identifying and assigning tasks, as if they generate the work and other family members help them. Women do more housework even if their male partner is unemployed.

If you are a woman who doesn't get enough help from your partner, here are some ideas to improve the situation.

Start with Agreement on Principles

Establish the principles first with your partner, then at a family meeting including everyone old enough to sit still. Make it clear that having a family and a job means having a life, being fulfilled, being normal—for women as well as for men. It's okay for either men or women to choose life without kids or for one partner to choose to stay home if the family can afford it. But for those who choose to raise children and have jobs, the expectations for both partners should be the same.

This means that the job/family challenge is a common problem for all family members to tackle. Sharing the work includes responsibility for figuring out what needs to be done as well as for doing it. Here's the bottom line: Everyone needs to agree that mom is equal to other family members. That means her time is as important as that of anyone else in the family. When tasks are simply left to mom, her time objectively is valued *less* than everyone else's.

One ground rule is that kids can start helping at a very early age: Guide babies to put toys in a box or basket. Teach toddlers to put dishes in the sink, pick up toys, help pick up papers and other items, and put dirty clothes in the hamper. Encourage young children to help dust and sweep, use a hand vacuum, set and clear the table, keep their rooms neat, help rake and shovel. Happily, younger children *like* helping with chores, so you can easily make a game of it. What starts as fun can become a good habit.

Make a Family Plan for Housework

Once your family accepts the principle of everyone sharing the work, you need a plan on how to proceed. Brainstorm ways to handle chores. You want your family to buy into the plan, rather than be given assignments. Tasks can be divided up in a variety of ways: You can make a list together; then whoever gets up first on Saturday morning chooses a chore, and whoever wakes up last gets what's left. You can rotate chores, or leave them to the luck of the draw or "spin" (some families make a chore wheel). Or family members can choose certain jobs they like best, as long as everyone is satisfied with the division of labor.

When you draw up your plan, adhere to these guidelines:

• Include standards and regular evaluations, with *consequences* if a person doesn't do his or her share or doesn't do it well. The standards should be reasonable—living in a pigsty may be okay with some family members, but that doesn't make it okay. Similarly, those who've had very strict standards may have to relax them. Remember: It's more important to have your *life* in order than your closets (but you should be able to get to the closet).

• Whenever possible, make chores *fun,* or at least less burdensome. Add music; work together as a family; build in a reward or special activity when the chores are done. (Our family cleans best when we're having company and have to whip the house into shape. Sometimes we *pretend* someone's coming in order to get in gear.)

• Include training if necessary. At 9to5, we believe in equality of opportunity: Men and kids can learn if given the chance.

> Psychologist and author Lawrence Kutner tells about the time he was up during the night with his two-month-old son, who had spit up on each of eight successive changes of clothing. His wife gave him this essential tip: "Why don't you try a bib?"

• If someone doesn't do his job, no one else should do it for him. Carry out what the family agreed on as consequences (e.g., a lost privilege or an additional chore).

• Celebrate success at each step. Have a special family outing or meal to congratulate yourselves for chores well-done and well-shared. Recognize improvement as well as excellence. Frequent praise and mutual appreciation will help your system work.

HOW OTHERS HAVE DONE IT

Women I have interviewed use a wide range of approaches to involve male partners and kids in housework. Here are some examples:

Kathy's husband, Jim, took early retirement when his employer downsized. For the first two weeks at home, he expected his wife and son to do all the work—until they went on strike. The two of them wrote a mission statement and goals they wanted Jim to meet. Pitch in or you won't get fed, they said. Now Jim does the laundry and grocery shopping, visits Kathy's elderly mother, and negotiates with her caregivers. He's found he's much happier staying busy than sitting around.

Mary Alice's family agreed to a dinnertime system that worked for years: Mary Alice cooked. John, the younger son, set the table. Mary Alice's husband cleared and cleaned the table. Mark, the older son, did the dishes. When Mark reached his late teens, he complained that dish washing was interfering with his social life. "My job interferes with my social life," said Mary Alice. "We all do what we have to do." So Mark hired John to do the dishwashing. John recently told Mary Alice he needed more money. "I'm not your employer," she told him. "Negotiate with Mark." John did—and got a raise.

Denise, who's divorced, has taught her four children that housework is for everyone who lives in the house. Beginning at age seven, each child is assigned chores. Anyone who has a grievance about how chores are performed or about any other family issue can raise the concern at the weekly Family Forum. If the grievance is critical, an emergency Family Forum can be called. Denise finds this method saves time and aggravation mediating kids' quarrels. When her daughter wore her son's T-shirt without his permission, for example, he brought his complaint to the Family Forum. The group decided on ground rules—no getting into each other's things without permission—and a punishment: The culprit had to wash that T-shirt and some others for her brother.

When Donna first talked to her husband, Steve, about sharing the work, he agreed in principle and began to take on various tasks. But problems quickly developed. Steve washed a red shirt with the whites and turned them all pink. He volunteered to do the grocery shopping, then brought back a number of extra items that were both expensive and high-calorie. After Donna criticized Steve for leaving crumbs on the counter, he complained that her standards were too high. Donna's initial response was to do most chores herself. Resentment mounted to the point where the couple sought help from a counselor. As a result, they sat down and took a hard look at the patterns they'd developed. They asked themselves how much of Steve's sloppiness was resistance, what standards were reasonable, and what support Steve needed. Donna stopped worrying about the grocery items; Steve agreed to follow directions about separating clothes and to keep the counters clean. They built in monthly check-ins. Ten years later, they're doing fine—and have enlisted their two children, both born in the interim.

MANAGING TROUBLE SPOTS

If your household seems filled with tension, try to identify the worst time of day and set goals to make improvements there. Once you've built in some relief, you can move on to other problem areas. It may be helpful to keep a log for a week or two and see exactly how each family member is spending his or her time. This will identify disparities (the kid who complains "I always have to do everything!" may be surprised at how little she really does). The log can also be useful for analyzing trouble spots and comparing goals to what really happens.

Here are some typical trouble spots with tips on improving each:

Early Morning

Lots of families find themselves rushing to get ready for day care or school and work. When my older son was two years old, he used to say "Harry, Harry, Harry" all the time. I was puzzled because we didn't know anyone by that name. Then one day, I realized he was imitating me saying "hurry"—that's how I knew we had to reorganize. These steps may help you streamline your morning:

• Get as much ready as possible the night before. Kids can get their backpacks together and leave them at the door. Make sure all homework assignments and any parental signature forms are included. Shoes, jackets, mittens, and so on, can be lined up as well. Kids can pack the nonperishable items for their lunch. They can also choose their clothes the night before and help collect the necessary pieces for any special outfit. There's nothing like finding out at the last minute that your child needs to wear a white shirt to school and the one he has is dirty.

• As a family, choose a special calendar to keep track of important events and appointments. Along with the activity, list any special requirements—"Sherri's field trip, pack lunch"; "Robert's dentist appointment, needs note the day before." Include the dates that fees or forms are due, as well as dates for a big test or project completion (and don't forget birthdays, anniversaries, first day of spring, etc.). On Sunday, review the calendar for the coming week.

• Don't let breakfast become a battleground. The kids can help select what they like for breakfast—and prepare it. Have available quick nutritious substitutes (bananas and other fruit, bagels, breakfast bars) for the times someone might have to rush. To limit those occasions, make sure everyone gets up with plenty of time to get ready; that may mean earlier bedtimes, but cutting down on the rush is more than worth it.

• Be clear on ground rules—who makes breakfast for whom, who clears the table, whether the TV can be on.

• Lots of people have low energy in the morning. Build in fun anywhere you can. This could be simply an affectionate wake-up ritual. Music can help.

After Work

The kids want attention, maybe help with homework; everyone's hungry; you need to unwind. These suggestions may help:

• Plan the menus ahead of time, so that all the necessary food and supplies are on hand. Let the kids each have a night to choose the menu (and help prepare it).

• Prepare some meals in advance—casseroles, soups, and other dishes can be frozen and stored; some dishes can be left to cook in a slow cooker; vegetables can be cut up in advance for a stir fry. If you're making something that takes work and freezes well, make a double or triple recipe and save the rest for later.

• Decide how many take-out meals you can afford, and build these into your budget and planning. Some parents worry about the trade-off between convenience and nutrition; investigate what's available and make choices you feel comfortable with.

• Mealtime is a great time to communicate and build your identity as a family. Sometimes conflicting schedules make it virtually impossible for everyone to eat together. Try to coordinate some time together, such as having dessert with the latecomers.

• Try to avoid errands immediately after work. Stock up on staples like milk. Having extra time may be worth the expense of deliveries.

• Make a brief quiet time for everyone when you come home. This can include music or TV, an acknowledged period for everyone to relax. Include a healthy snack so the person cooking dinner doesn't have to rush.

• Develop a system for each person to take turns summing up the day. If you have a baby or a small child too young to participate, explain to the others that you'll deal with this child first to avoid interruptions.

• Make sure everyone has a place to do homework, even if it's the kitchen table. That area should be respected and kept or made clear. Others who have business in the area (phone, TV) need guidelines on respecting the need for quiet. Any child without homework can have a range of activities, such as drawing, reading, or quiet play, to keep from disturbing the others.

• Keep a supply of homework-related materials, such as glue, markers, paper, and pencils.

• Make sure your children get phone numbers of classmates so they can call if they forget or miss a homework assignment.

Bedtime

Ending the day with shouting and tears is one of the most stressful situations for working parents and their children. To avoid that:

• Have clear rules on the time for going to bed.

• Don't wait until the last minute to round everyone up for slowdown or preparing for bed.

• Include something each child likes as a ritual so they don't see going to bed as a punishment. This might be a story or music or a private talk.

• Have consequences for getting out of bed, continuing to talk after bedtime, and other infractions.

Getting a Grip on Chores

In order to manage your time more efficiently—and leave more of it for your family and yourself—try the following:

• Batch errands, and plan them out in some reasonable order (according to location, items that need refrigerating, etc.).

• Do a load of laundry every day rather than letting it accumulate. Folding and putting away clothes is something even young children can help with. Older children can do their own laundry or take turns being responsible for the family laundry.

• Make lists. Avoid repeat trips to the store to pick up things you forgot during the main shopping excursion. One method is to make a master list including all the items the family uses, even only occasionally. Put a copy on the refrigerator or some other convenient place during the week, so family members can check off things they need and things that ran out. (If your family saves money by using manufacturer's coupons, keep them organized by category in an accordion folder. Whoever writes something on the shopping list can check the coupon folder and put any coupons in an envelope kept by the shopping list.)

• Choose a shopping time (such as a late weekday evening) when the store is less crowded than on weekends or right after work.

• Expect the unexpected. Assume your kids will get sick at inconvenient times. Be clear about how much flexibility will be allowed at work and who to contact in case of emergency. Have contingency plans: Is there a relative or friend who can help? If your child gets sick while you're at work and you can't leave, can a colleague or neighbor pick up the child? Make sure the children and your caregiver or school are familiar with these backup plans and are comfortable with the individuals who will fill in.

• Some of the biggest strains on working families are after-school activities, especially sports or other projects that require transportation. Carpooling may help—if you have a car and can leave work early when it's your turn to drive. You may be able to trade some other service, like preparing team snacks or making phone calls, in exchange for not driving. Schools and clubs need to assume that some people will not be able to participate without help and discuss ways to make that help available.

Dealing with Travel

My younger son developed a fear of plane crashes after seeing *La Bamba* when he was seven. Each time I had to travel, he prepared an elaborate good-bye. We took him to a therapist twice who helped him learn relaxation techniques to reduce the fear to a scale he could manage. One day as I was leaving, he told me, "I'm not afraid of plane crashes anymore, Mom. I'm really okay. There's just one thing I'm a little afraid of." "What's that?" I asked. "Killer bees."

It's hard to be away from your family under any circumstances, but especially if a family member is going through a difficult time. These steps can help:

• Prepare well in advance. Mark on the family calendar the dates you'll be away, information about travel plans, and where you can be reached in case of emergency. Think ahead to what needs to be done while you're gone and plan ways to fill in. If your mate is resentful about shouldering all the responsibility during your absence, name the problem and try to work it out ahead of time.

• Involve family members in the trip as much as possible. Use a map to show the kids where you'll be. Let them know why you're going, and share how things went when you get back.

• Build in regular communication. A daily phone call is a good investment to find out how everyone's doing and to reassure the kids that you're not out of touch. Encourage them to share problems as well as triumphs. Be sure to call when you arrive at your destination to let them know you had a safe trip. (My older son would greet these calls with his own antidote to his brother's fears: "It's Mom. She made it! She's alive!")

• If you have to miss anything important—a performance or athletic event, a big test or term paper, a special day at work for your partner, a birthday or anniversary—find a way to be present in spirit. This can be as elaborate as a delivery of flowers or balloons by a store (or by a relative or friend) or as simple as hiding a note before you leave.

• Build in a special ritual or celebration when you get back.

• Some hotels are beginning to offer child care as an attraction to parents who have to travel on business. Think about the pros and cons of having a child with you. Is networking outside of the business meetings an important part of the experience? Do you need some downtime on your own? Can you add on a day or two to make the trip a family adventure? If you accumulate frequent flyer miles, calculate if any trip can be combined with family time.

• Extra child-care expenses that you incur as a result of the travel should be paid for by your employer. Get clear on this policy before you agree to travel as part of your job.

TIPS FOR SINGLE PARENTS

All of the issues discussed in the preceding sections hit single parents harder. Shopping with small children and no car, for example, may require several trips a week (and to a more expensive corner store), eating up valuable time and money. Single parenthood usually means fewer resources as well as fewer hands and ears—it's hard to afford or transport a helper at the very time you need one most. These tips may be useful:

• Make sure you have a support system in place, and use it. Develop a network of relatives, friends, groups like Parents Without Partners. Even if all you get is the opportunity to sound off, that can help.

> Ellen Priewe, mother of three children ages two, four, and eight, told a reporter how she survives long days of trying to finish her college degree. Every morning before waking the children, she talks on the phone with her best friend, also a single mother and classmate: "We cry and complain and wail and gripe and say things like 'Why are we *doing* this to ourselves?' and 'I can't *do* this any more.' And by the time we say good-bye, we're ready to face another day."

• Many single parents do "kiddie exchanges" with friends, taking someone else's kids for a while in order to have some time off in return. Friends and neighbors can also share such tasks as running errands or picking up something at the store. You can all chip in for a mutual baby-sitter for a major shopping expedition. You may have to initiate the exchange and monitor closely to make sure it's fair, but this can be a big help.

• Local YMCAs or municipal recreation departments often offer baby-sitting classes and certification. Call them for names and phone numbers of reliable sitters who live in your neighborhood to cut down on travel time.

• If you're planning to go out with friends, have the kids at one location and share the sitter's costs.

• Get your religious congregation to sponsor activities for single parents and their children. Make sure the planning committee arranges car pools or other forms of transportation.

• If you can afford a helper, think about having a high school student come occasionally after you get home from work to play with younger kids while you help with homework or just have some time to catch up on errands and housework. Or provide your own helper: your voice on tape.

Victoria recalls how her mother recorded her voice on tape for the young children to listen to while she cooked or cleaned and the older kids did homework. The little ones were fascinated *and* quiet!

• Build an element of fun into chores; turn housework into a family time. Listen to music or play a game (such as pretending a celebrity is coming over and acting out the visit, or coordinating a dance routine while doing the vacuuming and dusting).

• Make time to do physical activity together, even if it's just taking a walk or playing catch.

• Try for a special bedtime ritual with each child.

• Make the children's bedtime early enough to save some time for yourself.

• Give yourself credit. The fact is, single parents should give efficiency and financial management tips to corporate executives. Many are extraordinarily resourceful with little public support.

MAKING TIME FOR YOURSELF

In addition to doing her job and raising two children, Sandra takes classes at night. When she pulls her car into her garage at the end of a long day and turns off the engine, she sometimes closes the car windows, locks the doors and sits inside for ten minutes or so. "It's the only time I have to myself," Sandra explains.

Surveys differ about how much time parents think they're spending with their children. But here's something studies agree on: Most people don't feel they have enough time with their spouse. And the overwhelming majority of mothers say they don't have enough time alone.[4]

In its *National Study on the Changing Workforce*, the Families and Work Institute concluded that many parents cut back on time for themselves as the only way to manage all the demands on their time. But the findings suggest that carving out some time for yourself represents an important investment in mental health and well-being.[5]

AVOIDING GUILT

Once, after a particularly stressful day, I snapped at my older son, who was then eight years old. "I'm sorry, honey," I said, "I had a bad day and I shouldn't have taken it out on you." "That's okay, Mom," he replied. "Don't take it out on yourself either."

Many people today are tormented about the decisions they feel forced to make in balancing work and family. They feel guilty for leaving their children with someone else. If they stay home for an extended period of time, a woman may worry she's abandoning what women all over the country are striving for, or a man may fear he's not a real man. And what mother hasn't blown a fuse with a family member and then beaten herself up for it?

Throwing out guilt is easier said than done. But at least you need to recognize messages that manipulate the guilt. Consider this ad for Partnership for a Drug-Free America:

> A mother leaves a message on the answering machine for her son. "I won't be home until late again. Do the usual"—meaning toss something in the microwave. "I left you some money," the neglectful mother adds. "Use it however you want." She ends with this note: "Dad won't be home 'til Tuesday. He says hi." The teenager, of course, uses the money to buy drugs.

Toss out this kind of message. Having to work late is hardly equivalent to neglect. And many stay-at-home parents also have to deal with a teen's drug or alcohol problems.

Know the facts about child care: According to psychologist Faye Crosby, studies show that no one form of child care, including mom staying home, is better for kids than any other. The key is having a caregiver who provides love, stimulation, and safety.[6]

Know the evidence about women who have chosen to continue to be in the workforce (keeping in mind that a majority are there out of necessity). Crosby again: "My findings show that women with jobs liked their home life better than women who stayed at home; and at the workplace, women and men who had families liked their jobs better than men and women who were single."[7]

Similar findings come from Marilyn Heins, pediatrician, and Anne M. Seiden, psychiatrist, in *Child Care/Parent Care*: "Parents cannot effectively give to children what they do not have to give. When parents are too stressed, or too unfulfilled, or too guilty to take their own needs into account, the children suffer."[8]

Guilt is a bigger problem for women than it is for men. Garry Trudeau hit the nail on the head in a Doonesbury cartoon on the subject. "Why don't you seem as torn up [as I am] about not being able to spend time with [our son]?" the wife asks her husband. "Well," he replies. "it may be because I'm spending a whole lot more time on family than my father did, and you're spending far less time than your mother did. Consequently, you feel incredibly guilty, while I naturally feel pretty proud of myself."

Working parents are still measuring themselves against an old—and double—standard. Men get lots of praise for being involved in any way with their kids; women are judged more by what they *fail* to do. A man who leaves a meeting early for a child's activity may hear, "What a good dad!" The message to a woman in the same situation may well be, "You call yourself a professional?"

Part of the solution is to stop framing the job/family dilemma as a women's problem. Over and over, we see articles on women struggling with the choices; workshops on juggling are more common at women's conferences than at circus school. Figuring out how to have a family *and* a job is an issue for men *and* women, for families, for business, and for society as a whole. That's the only real way to end the guilt—and stress—that's tearing women up.

In the meantime, whether you're home or employed, learn to embrace the choice you're making and enjoy the best parts of it, even while you work for broader choices for yourself and others.

PRINCIPLES FOR SHARING HOUSEWORK

Having a family *and* a job is a normal life, for women as well as for men.

Family members need to share responsibility for identifying household chores—and for doing them.

Children can start helping at an early age.

Get organized to streamline tasks and reduce tension.

Build fun into chores.

Expect—and prepare for—the unexpected.

Single parents with limited resources can build a strong support system.

To be a better parent and partner, make time for yourself.

12

How Would You Handle These Job/Family Conflicts?

The following scenarios are based on real-life stories of conflicts between job and family responsibilities. Think about how you would handle each situation if you found yourself in it. Then look at our approach. (These situations involve interactions with co-workers or assume a nonunionized workplace. See Chapter 15 for using union channels.) The purpose here is to *anticipate* such conflicts so that you have an action plan when they arise—because they happen even to the most organized among us.

Scenario 1

You scheduled an important early morning meeting with your boss, who's been out of the office a lot and hard to catch up with. That morning your young child wakes up sick.

Because you have to expect the unexpected, the best way to deal with this situation is to be prepared ahead of time. That means taking care of two areas: emergency child care, if possible (from a relative or trusted friend); and lines of communication with your boss for the times when no one but you is available—or no one but you will do. If you have a partner, of course, he or she should be prepared to step in if possible. Many couples take turns using their own sick days to care for sick children.

In the event that no one else can care for the sick child, see if you can schedule a telephone meeting with your boss during a time when your child is napping or engaged in quiet activity. If this isn't possible, reschedule the meeting. What happened is inconvenient, but you are not to blame—and your boss ought to realize that, especially if the steps you've taken are clear.

Scenario 2

You've negotiated to work part time. But you've quickly realized you're being expected to carry a full-time load.

Your negotiations should have included a realistic assessment of what you'd be able to accomplish in the reduced schedule and should have been summed up in writing. If that's the case, refer to that discussion and document in a meeting with your manager.

If there was no discussion or document, have the talk now. Tell your manager you're happy to work full time every hour on the job, but since you're working fewer hours, you obviously have to decrease your work load. Review your duties, carefully estimating how much time each normally takes. Then make a specific proposal for how to restructure the job. Be prepared with a Plan B. If your manager agrees to the adjustment, build in a regular evaluation procedure to make sure the new schedule is working.

If the manager refuses to make any changes despite your reasonable arguments, go to the next level or as high as you need to for a reconsideration. Appeal to any statement the employer has ever made about helping employees balance work and family. Should that commitment prove hollow, you may have to make a choice between returning to full-time hours (and full pay, of course) or finding another job.

Scenario 3

You're pregnant. A male co-worker keeps making annoying jokes: "When my wife was preggers, she couldn't keep her eyes open. How are you going to finish that report?" and "Soon we'll have to widen the hall." When you ask him to stop, he says, "*Oops*, those prego hormones must be really out of control." You don't want to cause trouble, but his attitude is beginning to get to you.

The best situation would be for someone else to take your co-worker aside and raise his consciousness. It's helpful if the person most affected by biased behavior doesn't always have to be the one to explain what's wrong with it.

If that's not possible, ask this co-worker to meet with you or send him a memo. Use whatever tone feels comfortable. Your argument can go something like this: "You may not mean to offend, but when you make those jokes, I feel that I'm not being seen as a serious worker. I'm sure you realize that many pregnant women still have a hard time being treated fairly on the job. I'm asking you to stop." If your attempt is unsuccessful, ask your manager to intervene.

Scenario 4

Your company allows employees to bring a child to work in a pinch. You support this policy; but when your co-worker's three-year-old runs up and down the hall, you have a hard time concentrating.

Helping working parents doesn't mean ignoring the needs of other employees. Let your co-worker know your feelings and ask for help in solving the problem together: "How can we make it possible for your child to be here and still get our work done?" If there's no office (or play area) that is more secluded, it may make sense for the parent to take work home.

Scenario 5

You're the parent whose three-year-old has to come to work with you because of an emergency. You don't want her to bother your co-workers, but you have some work that can only be done in the office.

Ask for a discussion of some guidelines—should there be areas that are off-limits to kids, for example? Is there an office or other area that can become a makeshift play area if necessary? Use the discussion to express your appreciation for the company's flexibility and your thanks to your co-workers for putting up with the inconvenience. Encourage the others to come to you with any suggestions or specific concerns.

Scenario 6

Your father has Alzheimer's disease. You want to rearrange your schedule in order to give your mother some relief. Specifically, you ask to come in early and take a longer lunch hour, during which you'll briefly visit your parents. The company leaves these decisions to managers' discretion. Your manager says no, on the grounds that lunchtime coverage is already difficult to handle.

Before asking for a change in schedule, do your homework. Know how coverage works and how your absence can be accommodated. Make a case for the advantages of coming in early—increased concentration, access to certain office machines, and so on. See if any co-workers are willing to adjust their lunchtime in a way to work out the coverage issue.

If there's no way to alleviate the crunch, see if there's another time of day when you could help your mother, and propose that. Be persistent, and ask for any refusal in writing in case you need to appeal the decision. A good manager should help you come up with an alternative, rather than just dismissing your request. If your manager won't budge, appeal to that person's manager or to someone in personnel.

Scenario 7

> You're a new father who wants to be involved with your baby. When you go to your manager to make arrangements for leave, he encourages you to limit your leave to your vacation time.

How strong a position you take depends, of course, on your personal circumstances and the risks involved. But you certainly have the *right* to object to the manager's suggestion. Typically, supervisors get away with this kind of intimidation because no one challenges them.

Ask the manager if he would make the same suggestion to your female co-workers. If so, is it company policy to treat men differently and to discourage men from being good dads? Or is it just the policy of his department? Tell him you'd like his suggestion in writing. Even if he backs off, ask for assurances that your taking the leave won't be used against you in the future.

Be sure to make your own record of the meeting. If you don't receive any confirmation of the discussion from your manager in writing, send him or her a memo with your understanding of the meeting and its resolution.

Backing down and limiting your leave to vacation time when you don't have to will make it more difficult for other male employees, as well as leaving you with too little time with your baby.

Scenario 8

> The director of the agency where you work requires you to attend weekend meetings and workshops that sharply cut into the time you have with your kids. These were not the terms when you were hired.

If other staff also resent weekend meetings, appeal to the director. Make the case that the meetings could be held during regular work time. Point out that many staff feel inconvenienced and that an alternative would boost morale and attendance. Stress the importance of family time. Even if you're the only one who minds, the agency should respect your family responsibilities. You may need to appeal to the Board of Directors. If changing the schedule is impossible, negotiate for paid time off on days when your children are home, if you so choose.

Should you fail, decide whether your job is worth the conflict with your family time. And if you leave, be sure to let the agency know that the inability to resolve this conflict was a contributing factor.

Scenario 9

In the past, you haven't minded weekend and evening meetings at work. But now that you're a parent, your attitude has changed.

If you feel your job can be done on a 9-to-5 schedule, approach your supervisor. Acknowledge that you did agree to the hours you've been working, but point out that parenthood has changed your situation. Make the case for fulfilling your job responsibilities during daytime hours. If you need to redefine your job, propose how to do that in a way that meets the organization's needs as well as your own.

Scenario 10

Your employer has an on-site child-care center, but you know that some employees can't afford the fees.

Volunteer to put a group together to study this issue and make recommendations. Some companies use a sliding scale to determine fees: Parents with higher household incomes pay higher fees, and those with lower incomes pay less. There may also be foundation or nonprofit funding available to help subsidize the cost of the center. A third alternative would be corporate vouchers or a scholarship fund for eligible workers.

In addition to identifying alternatives, the group can clarify how a center that's affordable to all employees better meets the mission of the company and improves its image in the community.

Scenario 11

You're part of a group working to extend benefits to unmarried partners. A contingent of employees has formed to oppose your efforts as immoral and contributing to the breakup of the family.

You have to expect this type of opposition. Your best approach is to organize discussion broadly among your co-workers and ask for support wherever you can from top management. Don't expect to win over those who have the most extreme views. But do try to neutralize their influence. Urge people who are open to your position to be vocal about it. The wider the range of supporters, the harder it will be for your opponents to dismiss the proposed policy as an extreme one.

Keep your arguments simple and focused: The United States has many different kinds of families. Strong family units, however defined, are good for society. To strengthen those units, partners need benefits just as married spouses do.

Scenario 12

You're up for a promotion. You want to have a second child but fear you might lose the promotion if you become pregnant, even though the company has a good leave policy.

Here's another example of the value of fighting for a change in corporate culture *before* you actually need it. Only when women are assured that they won't be penalized for having families will they feel confident about using policies that exist on paper.

You might have to wait for the promotion—or decide to wait to have a baby. But you may find that naming your fear to your supervisor is the best way to get the company to take a look at the issue. Tell the manager that you know you have the necessary qualifications and would love to have the opportunity to advance. Ask if a pregnancy would take you out of the running. Express your concern that attitudes about new mothers being less able to handle higher level positions is contributing to a glass ceiling in the company.

If your manager is open to your comments, the two of you can brainstorm how to bring up the topic for broader discussion.

Scenario 13

Your child's teacher calls to set up an urgent meeting with you and school officials regarding a problem your child is having, and you can't get off work.

First, make an accommodation with the teacher to meet over the phone or at a more convenient time. Then work on winning the right to expand family leave to include school functions (some state legislators have introduced measures to this effect; see Chapter 16).

Schools also need to make it possible for working parents to participate in the children's education. If the teacher or school officials are uncooperative, raise the issue with the local school board. Ask other parents to join you at a school board meeting at which you present a variety of scheduling options, keeping in mind that many teachers are working parents and need time off, too.

As for expanding the policy for leave at your workplace, follow the steps in Chapter 6.

Scenario 14

You're always rushing and feel so stressed when you get home from work that you can't enjoy being with your kids.

Analyze how you spend your time each day. Identify the chief trouble spots and make some small but dramatic changes. For each task you do, ask if it must be done, and if so, if it must be done by you. Then prioritize the ones that really fall in your domain. Look for ways to increase the support you receive from others. If your main problem is the number of hours you must be on the job, see if there's any way to reduce your work load. Talk with co-workers; they may have ideas or feel the same.

Something has to change. If it's not possible to redesign your job, you may need to look for another one. Pay attention to the warning signs your body is giving you. If possible, take a few days off to get a handle on the situation and make decisions. If nothing else, concentrate on improving time with your kids and making at least one change in your daily pattern, such as listening to music that you find soothing on your way home, adding some exercise or meditation, carving out some quiet time for yourself.

Scenario 15

You and your spouse work split shifts so that someone is always home with your young children. Weekends are filled with errands; Sunday is a family day. The situation is working out well for the kids, but you and your partner are feeling the strain of spending too little time with each other.

Many couples experience this problem. Try to take care of as many errands as possible during the week, bringing the children along where possible. Set aside one time slot over the weekend—such as Saturday morning or evening—just for each other. If relatives can't help by watching the children, it's worth hiring someone for this respite or arranging swaps with other families.

Look for other spots during the week as well. One of you may be able to get flexibility at least one day a week to overlap shifts. If that's not possible, try having a once-a-week wake-up ritual—you can switch off having the late shift person wake or be woken up by the early partner to spend some time together.

Many couples would love to have at least one person go on a reduced schedule without severe financial penalties. This longer-term reform would go a long way toward strengthening the family.

Scenario 16

Your department head often plans social activities for staff members on Friday night. As a single parent, you're not in a position to join them. You worry about missing out on valuable networking, not to mention enjoyable social time.

If you think your supervisor is basically supportive but just not tuned in to the needs of single parents, ask for a meeting and raise the issue. Explain that you appreciate the convenience of Friday night for most of the staff, but that you feel the arrangement puts you at a disadvantage. Other people may join the staff who are in a similar situation. See if together you can come up with an alternative, such as a longer staff lunch one Friday a month. You may also be able to arrange a sitter or "kiddie exchange" so you can attend a Friday evening get-together every now and then.

If you have misgivings about approaching the department head, talk to a co-worker you trust. That person may be willing to raise the issue and make the case. If the manager is insensitive and nonresponsive, higher management needs to know and intervene.

Scenario 17

Your colleague is pregnant. As a male employee, you want to be helpful but not offensive. What guidelines should you follow? Is it all right, for example, to open the door for a pregnant employee?

It's all right (and kind) to open the door for any employee, provided you get there first and don't stampede past people in order to beat the person to the door. Similarly, accept the kindness of someone who holds the door open for you. Pregnant women are like anyone else—they want to be treated fairly and respectfully and not be patronized. Pregnancy doesn't scramble the brains; assume your colleague can handle the same mental difficulty in assignments. But added weight concentrated in one area of the body can create physical discomfort. Keep meetings brief and to the point. Offer to get lunch or supplies for your colleague if you're going that way.

IV

Getting Support for the Family-Friendly Workplace

13

What Your Employer Should Do

> You can have all the machinery in the world, but without this thing called an employee, you aren't going to make money.
>
> *Claude Cox, information-service specialist, Tenneco Gas Co., commenting on why he okayed a flexible schedule for an employee whose partner was dying of AIDS*[1]

Family-friendly policies aren't just good business practices, they're good for business. How much can we reasonably ask employers to do? Where should employers start? This chapter will address the decision makers at all companies and examine what steps they can and should take in accordance with their organization's resources.

A FRAMEWORK FOR BECOMING FAMILY-FRIENDLY

Neither strict compliance with the law nor a few programs here and there make a company family-friendly. An *integrated approach* is best, in which top management views all aspects of the organization and asks: How can we make it easier for our employees to blend life outside work with their responsibilities at work, so that they can function better and have more peace of mind?

A comprehensive approach involves the following steps:

1. *Assess the current situation*, including the corporate culture. Find out what family needs your workers have and whether those needs are interfering with productivity. At the very least, take stock of how the company currently handles family conflicts (see Appendix B for sample assessment survey). If you have the resources, conduct focus groups to get employee feedback from every area of the company and at every staffing level.[2] Let employees know that

limited resources may not permit all suggestions to be implemented, but that their concerns will be taken seriously. This step can often save money and ensure that employees get what they really want and need. Susan Thomas, Director of Employment Policies and Programs for CIGNA Corporation, gives this example to illustrate the importance of employee involvement: Thomas was going to introduce a series of high-gloss brochures on the company's philosophical approach to job/family programs. Fortunately, she posed the suggestion to focus groups first. "We don't have time to read," the workers told her. During a period of cost reduction and expense control, the workers would have been offended by such a costly pamphlet. What they wanted instead was a simple piece of paper with a summary of all the company's job/family programs and a list of phone numbers for more information. Thanks to their input, that's what they got.

2. *Make sure top management is aware and committed.* US West CEO Richard McCormick worried about whether his ninety-year-old mother was eating regularly. To find out what to do, he called the company hotline on elder-care issues. A CEO "must champion these issues," says McCormick, "or quit taking family calls at work."[3]

3. *Sensitize all management and hold them accountable.* The attitude of managers is critical in implementing whatever policies the company adopts. Managers need adequate education and training on each policy and the rationale behind it. Appreciation of job/family issues should be one criterion in hiring and in evaluating supervisory staff. Ask workers for feedback on their managers. Make workers familiar with procedures for appealing what they consider to be an unfair decision.

4. Spread the word that the *company encourages balance between job and family responsibilities.* Policies on paper may not mean much. People need to know they won't be punished for using these policies—and the best way to do that is to make visible those who take advantage of flexibility and *succeed.* Particular attention should be paid to encouraging men to use whatever policies exist, since many cultures see family policies as for women only.

5. *Develop a partnership with workers* in devising family-friendly programs. The more input they have, the more likely the policies will reflect real needs and solve real problems. If the company has a union, make policy development a joint venture.

6. *Provide cross training*—teaching the skills and duties of one job to someone in another position—so no one is indispensable. Even small firms can benefit from this practice.

7. *Formalize the policies* by writing them down and establishing guidelines beyond "manager discretion," so that they'll apply across the board and be clear to everyone.

8. *Change the way the company defines success.* Leaders should be chosen because of creativity, performance, and ability to motivate, rather than the number of hours spent at the workplace. Employers need to value the ability to communicate rather than the ability to travel and commitment to goals rather than a commitment to dropping everything for a meeting. Decision making (and training) should be broadened to front-line workers.

9. *Support other companies that offer family-friendly policies.* Indicate a preference for vendors that have good job/family programs.

POLICIES EVERY COMPANY CAN ADAPT AT LITTLE OR NO EXPENSE

Many policies cost little or nothing to implement, but provide crucial relief to employees and send a message that the company values families. Every company, regardless of size or resources, can adapt these policies:

Flexible Scheduling

Flexibility can take many forms, including hours worked, use of leave, and consideration of the needs of pregnant women and nursing mothers.

1. Hours worked can be flexible in these ways:
   - Different daily start time/end time
   - Number of hours worked per week
   - Compressed work week (e.g., four 10-hour days)
   - Extra hours some days, shorter hours on other days
   - Ability to make up time if doctor's appointment for employee or employee's dependent has to be scheduled during working hours
2. The use of leave should include:
   - A clear leave policy at least as generous as the federal Family and Medical Leave Act, even if the company is not cov-

ered by the Act. The policy should be familiar to all employees, apply to men as well as women, and include time off for purposes of caring for a new or sick child, a sick spouse or parent, or a personal illness, with continuation of health benefits and guarantee of return to the same or equivalent job.

- A broad definition of family to include significant others and extended family members
- Use of sick time to care for sick family members
- Paid vacation days, available in half-day or even one-hour increments
- Leave for school conferences and events
- Flexible lunch hours to take care of personal business
- Brief calls to and from home

3. Pregnant workers and nursing mothers should have:
- A smoke-free workplace or work area
- Short breaks every two hours to stretch lower back muscles
- If possible, a separate room with a couch
- A private area (and sufficient time) for nursing mothers to pump milk

Holding Managers Accountable

For managers to take family-friendly policies seriously, the employer needs to provide:

- A clear message of the commitment of top managers
- Written policies and support, instead of relying on supervisor discretion
- Resources for managers who want help implementing the policies
- Sensitivity to job/family issues as a criterion in management selection and evaluation

Education and Information

Even employers with limited resources can organize various programs to support workers with family responsibilities, such as:

- Workshops on topics like parenting, elder care, and grief
- Education for male as well as female employees on the importance of prenatal care

- Peer support groups (e.g., caregivers, new parents)
- Community resource fairs
- Bulletin board (actual or computer) information exchange
- Wellness programs to reduce stress

The local Chamber of Commerce or other business associations may be able to sponsor these programs for clusters of small companies.

Awareness of Family Needs

Some efforts to help working families simply require that employers not interfere with family needs:

- Schedule meetings at convenient times.
- Make sure education benefits are accessible to working parents (classes scheduled after work, for example, may not be realistic for everyone; offering reimbursement to those who pass a course may be meaningless for single mothers or others who can't afford the upfront fees).
- Avoid requiring parents to work late or travel on short notice.
- If parents have to work outside of normal hours, provide child care or reimburse child-care expenses.
- Make sure policies such as snow days don't discriminate against parents.

POLICIES EVERY COMPANY SHOULD CONSIDER

The following are examples of programs that require some investment but not big expenditures. Every company should think seriously about its ability to enact these programs and the benefits the company will gain if they do. (For more information, see resources in Appendix A.)

- Job-sharing: If employees are interested, talk with them to see how work could be accomplished by two people sharing one position. Make sure the job-sharers don't sacrifice advancement opportunities. Help those who want to job-share find a partner. Educate employees about the program.
- Mentoring programs to provide role models and support, particularly for men who want to put more emphasis on family life

- Dependent Care Assistance Program, allowing use of pretax dollars for child or elder care (Since the employer saves taxes on this amount, the program is cost-effective, but it does require a fee to the IRS and bookkeeping adjustments.)
- Negotiating employee discounts with a child-care provider
- Allowing employees to work from home occasionally or for an extended period of time (Be sure anyone who works at home receives the same pay rate and does not miss out on networking opportunities.)
- Resource and referral for dependent care
- Financial assistance with sick-child care
- Screening for high-risk pregnancies
- Leave bank, where employees can donate unused paid leave to other employees who've run out
- Bereavement leave
- Specialized training for managers on job/family issues

If your company is thinking of enacting these programs, keep these guidelines in mind:

- Make sure that the programs are available to everyone—management and nonmanagement, men as well as women.
- Encourage, don't just allow, employees to choose flexible schedules or leave.
- Educate employees about the policies, so that people are not left to find out on their own.
- Have managers work with employees to develop clear work goals and criteria for success.
- Rely on employees to take initiative to make the flexible schedule work.
- Most important, make sure the alternative schedules are *voluntary* and *equitable* (part-time work, for example, should be at the same pay rate, with benefits prorated).

Whatever level of commitment your company can make, the programs should be available to all workers as a right, not only if it's convenient. Faith Wohl, former work/life coordinator at DuPont, pointed out how much easier it is for a company to plan for a maternity leave than it is for a heart attack.[4] Most companies figure out how to handle tasks resulting from such a medical emergency.

They could easily apply the same techniques to leave for family-care purposes.

WHAT COMPANIES WITH MORE RESOURCES CAN DO

The following programs are more expensive than those already listed and require more time to plan and implement. Firms may need the help of an outside consultant. Despite the extra planning needed, employers who have made the investment agree that the return on such programs is well worth the effort (see Chapter 7):

- Longer unpaid leave with job-back guarantee and continuation of benefits
- Help with co-payment expenses for expectant mothers
- Paid leave, either at full or partial salary
- Domestic-partner benefits
- On- or near-site child care, including a specially equipped room for children with mild illnesses
- Intergenerational care center
- A program, like the Doting Dads program at the Los Angeles Department of Water and Power, that encourages men to be involved fathers (see Chapter 5)
- Subsidies for dependent care
- Employer-sponsored child-care services, such as holiday and vacation programs or after-school care
- Special equipment (pumps, refrigerators) for nursing mothers
- Part-time work with full benefits
- Employee Assistance Program
- Long-term care insurance for employees and dependents
- Relocation assistance for family members, such as paying moving costs and helping the new hire's partner find a job
- Partial or full reimbursement of adoption costs to parallel hospital coverage for childbirth

Few companies can do everything, and most could benefit from more government help. In evaluating employer response to family needs, Families and Work Institute co-president Dana Friedman drew three conclusions: "(1) No one solution will meet all employee needs; (2) any support from the company can be helpful; and (3) business cannot solve the problems alone—they are too vast, diverse, and complex."[5] Government, says Friedman, needs to help develop a base of community services and assist those in greatest need and those who work for smaller companies.

Regardless of whether an employer is able to add a few programs or many, the key to becoming a family-friendly workplace is to see this change as integral to how business is done.

JUST DO IT!

Each employer has to evaluate the organization's particular situation and decide how extensive programs should be, how those programs can enhance overall company objectives, how quickly to try to reach those goals, and how to track the programs' effectiveness. But the first step is simply deciding to do something, then setting a time limit by which implementation should begin.

Employers taking the plunge should remind themselves that what they're doing isn't just helpful to employees, it's good business. As Stride Rite Chairman and CEO Arnold Hiatt said in comparing his company to those who haven't implemented job/family policies: "We're not visionaries. They're dumb. . . ."[6]

HOW EMPLOYERS CAN HELP EMPLOYEES—AND THEIR BUSINESS

Nearly every company, regardless of size and resources, can offer flexibility and support.

Successful family-friendly companies use an integrated approach, rather than adding on a few programs.

Policies should be formal and available to all on a voluntary and equitable basis.

Companies with greater resources can consider programs such as paid leave and support for child care.

Decide what makes sense for your company to do—and then *do* it.

14

What Managers Can Do: Handling Family Leave and Flexible Schedules

It's fine to say employees should have flexible schedules and generous leave provisions. But what if you're the manager who has to keep the work flow going? Even if you're sympathetic to workers with family responsibilities—or are struggling with those responsibilities yourself—how do you implement family-friendly policies without sacrificing productivity?

Here are several scenarios that address leave policies, flexible scheduling, and hiring and promotion practices. See how you would manage these situations; compare your thoughts to our suggestions. And ask yourself the tough questions.

MANAGING LEAVE

Scenario 1

> A male employee tells you he wants to be off every Friday for the next six months to care for his new baby. You suspect he really wants to go fishing and hunting. What should you do?

Check out what your suspicions are based on. A guy can like hunting and fishing and still be an involved father. Working families (and especially working women) desperately need men to take more responsibility at home. If you objectively think every Friday off would disrupt the work flow and set a bad precedent, see if the employee can schedule other days off instead. Consider assigning a mentor (not a cop) on the model of the Doting Dads program of the Los Angeles Department of Water and Power, which encourages men to be involved parents. In short, help the employee to be the father he says he wants to be.

(Q: Would you have the same problem if the employee were female?)

Scenario 2

A Native American employee has a nephew with a terminal illness. In his tribal culture, the employee tells you, there is no distinction between immediate family and extended family members. The employee would like to use family leave to help care for the nephew. Where do you draw the line?

Cultural differences are real and need to be acknowledged. Employers shouldn't just pay lip service to managing diversity. Let each employee define who's a family member. Most people won't choose to take time off (especially unpaid) for a nephew; if this employee does, respect the commitment and try to accommodate the request.

Scenario 3

An employee who is a big asset to the department has taken a four-month adoption leave. You don't want to bother the employee at home, but you could really use this person's advice on an important project.

Like many situations, it's best to discuss parameters before the leave. Encourage the employee to set clear boundaries and to feel free simply to be off. But also state your appreciation for the person's experience and your interest in some communication during the leave. The employee may be willing and able to be available on a limited basis and may like the idea of keeping in touch. Build in flexibility for the employee to back off once the adoption starts or at any point during the leave. Some parents underestimate beforehand what a new baby will involve.

(Q: Did you assume this employee is female? Would you have the same concerns if the employee were male?)

Scenario 4

After a generous and long-negotiated leave, an employee decides not to return to work. You find yourself resentful. How should this experience affect your decisions about other employees?

You can't generalize about other parents' behavior from the decision of one parent. Do check into the specifics of this employee's situation to see if anything could have been done differently. Did the employee have problems finding child care, for example? Could these problems be alleviated by referrals? Was a flexible schedule on return an option? Some parents do change their minds after they see the new baby or try to swing back into a work schedule without what feels like enough time at home. A number of firms allow employees to take a longer leave than usual, with a guarantee of return rights as soon as a position is available. Encourage your company to consider this. It doesn't make sense to lose an investment in a valuable employee if it can be avoided. See Scenario 11 for thoughts on the importance of cross-training so that the organization can manage during an employee's leave, even a long one.

(Q: Did the employee's gender affect your attitude toward others of the same sex?)

Scenario 5

The company allows men time off for family responsibilities, but so far none of the male employees has taken more than a week off. As a senior manager, how can you be sure men feel free to take the time they need?

Employees pay most attention not to formal policies, but to what the corporate culture rewards and punishes. The key to increasing men's role at home is the attitude of top management and the existence of role models. Get employee feedback (through an anonymous survey or, if you have the resources, focus groups conducted by an outside consultant) to find out what employees perceive the culture to be, and publicize the results. Then design an education/promotion campaign to encourage men to be more involved with their families. Look to benchmark companies for ideas. Use whatever method your organization relies on to communicate important information to all staff. Initiate lunchtime discussions to focus attention on the issue.

Scenario 6

An employee takes ten weeks leave for childbirth. Later, she uses up the rest of the twelve weeks leave allowable under the FMLA when her child falls ill. Now her mother has had a stroke, and she's requesting some additional time off. Should you grant it?

Obviously, it's inconvenient for someone to be out this much, but imagine how much more troubling the situation is for her. It's important to make unpaid time available on a flexible basis for emergencies. The more you respect this person's situation and can put yourself in her shoes, the more she'll give back in return. Agree to her taking a few additional days off, with the option of reduced hours for a while afterward. That will allow her to have some income in addition to time to help her mother, and you'll have the advantage of her experience at work at least on a part-time basis.

(Q: Would you feel any differently if the employee were male?)

Scenario 7

You want to be helpful to women returning from maternity leave, but you don't want to encourage the view that new mothers are less capable. Should you expect the same level of performance from them as from other employees?

If this employee were returning after a heart attack or gall bladder surgery, what would your expectations be? Chances are you'd assume the employee needed to ease back into work. You'd pay attention to the person's energy level, allow more breaks, and expect that some days might be harder than others. Although giving birth is not usually as debilitating as many other temporary disabilities, new mothers face a unique situation: They have to recuperate at the very time when they're least able to get uninterrupted sleep. Studies show that a supportive supervisor is as important as a supportive spouse in helping new mothers who work make a successful transition to parenthood.[1] Mothers are also much less likely to quit and are more loyal to their employer if they work for a flexible boss.[2]

Scenario 8

An employee who has no children resents the attention the company is giving to working parents. She feels other employees expect her not to take vacation time at Christmas so they can be off with their children. She'd like to spend the holidays with her parents, who live far away.

This employee has a legitimate request. If the company's family policy is framed only in terms of children, it should be expanded. At a department meeting, talk about the importance of valuing everyone's life outside of work. Encourage this woman to talk about her feelings in a nonaccusatory way, and give her support. Most likely, other staff haven't thought much about her situation. Be sure she's given credit for the times she's filled in for someone on leave or stayed late when someone else couldn't—and make clear that her time shouldn't be taken for granted. At the same time, explain to her that at some point she may need extra consideration to deal with a personal or family illness and should support the company's efforts to help parents of young children.

Scenario 9

You manage a small branch office. Because it's less than 75 miles from company headquarters, your staff is covered by the FMLA. The chief salesperson wants to take twelve weeks off when her baby is born. You feel resentful because the extra work will fall on you, but you don't want to pressure her to come back early.

Your resentment is understandable. Headquarters should help, either by adjusting the goals for your office during this period or by sending someone to fill in. This could be a person in a similar job at headquarters or a temporary employee. If the employee on leave can't be replaced by a temp, consider shifting some responsibilities. Cross-training could build morale for another employee, whose own duties might be more easily performed by a temp.

Leave can be inconvenient. But remember, hiring and training a permanent replacement would be even more trouble in the long run.

Scenario 10

A client complains to you because the employee who usually handles her account is out on parental leave. She doesn't believe anyone else is familiar enough with her needs to do a satisfactory job.

Before going on leave, the staff person should have gotten in touch with the client and introduced her to the person who would be handling the account in her absence. The three of them should have met more than once before the leave began. The client should realize that a temporary shift to another staff person is better than starting over with another firm. Be sympathetic to the client's concerns, but emphasize your commitment to helping employees have a family and a job. Some employers have moved toward a team approach to account management, in part to deal with employee leave or turnover.

MANAGING FLEXIBLE SCHEDULES

Scenario 11

> The department is implementing flexible hours. Because of the service you provide, some evening and weekend work is necessary. How should you decide who does what?

Give this problem to the workers to solve. Encourage volunteers to organize the discussion, and solicit feedback on what each employee is willing and would most like to do. Your job is to oversee and coordinate the process; as a good coach, you'll make sure employees have the skills they need to make the assessment efficiently. Make clear what the needs of the department are and your willingness to adjust as much as possible as long as those needs are met. Offer incentives for the least desirable time slots. If the employees cannot come to a resolution, choose some fair way of sharing the burden.

Scenario 12

> An employee from another department comes to you for help. He wants to work part-time. The company policy says this decision is up to the discretion of the manager, and his manager has said no.

Your long-term goal should be to work to make policies less subjective and guidelines more clear—and evaluations of management more closely linked to success in helping staff balance job/ family obligations. In the meantime, you can help the employee draft an appeal to the manager or to that manager's supervisor. Depending on the atmosphere at the company, it may be best for you to limit your involvement to that of a behind-the-scenes supporter. Or it may be appropriate for you to approach the manager in person to urge flexibility, drawing on your knowledge of positive experiences in your department and others.

Scenario 13

> You have a number of employees who want to use flex time. This means you won't always be on-site to supervise them, yet you'll be responsible for their output. How can you be sure they'll do their best job if no one is there to oversee them?

Companies that use flex time find that productivity *increases* overall because of the improved morale—and, typically, because of fewer interruptions for employees in off hours. Good management techniques of coaching and motivating should help keep output up. Use whatever methods you currently employ to keep track of productivity. If you have concerns about any individual, focus on that person. Raise your concerns with the employee and set specific goals for improvement. Make any necessary adjustments; for example, this person may be one who needs more structured assignments during the unsupervised time. Let this employee know you want to continue to make flex time available, but that the agreed-upon goals will have to be met.

Scenario 14

An employee wants to skip lunch every day in order to leave one hour early to be home when the kids get off from school. You believe a lunch break is important for employee productivity.

Affirm the employee's desire to be home with the kids, but point out why you think a lunch break is important for personal health and productivity. Then together look for alternatives; for example, could the employee take a half hour instead of an hour for lunch and come in a half hour earlier? If the children's schedule doesn't permit an earlier start time, it may make sense to reduce total weekly hours by two and a half for a while. Or the employee might want to leave early four days a week and work an extra two and a half hours the other day, with a high school student coming in that afternoon to watch the kids after school. Be flexible and helpful in identifying options.

(Q: Would the employee's gender play any role in your approach?)

MANAGING HIRING AND PROMOTION POLICIES

Scenario 15

You're in charge of choosing someone to coordinate a high-priority project that will last for two years. Given the duration of the project and the intensity of the work, you'd like to make sure the individual will not miss any stretch of time. Is that concern legitimate? What questions can you ask candidates for the job?

As you interview candidates, describe the project, why it's important to finish it in two years, and why the work will be intense. Ask each candidate if she or he can make this kind of commitment.

Do not ask personal questions. Do not speculate on any individual's circumstances (e.g., she's recently married so she's probably trying to get pregnant). It's understandable that you want a stable staffing situation for this project, but you should recognize that anyone can become ill or have an accident. Design the project so no one is indispensable.

(Q: Ask yourself honestly if you would have the same concern regardless of whether the candidate is male or female.)

Scenario 16

You're invited to a meeting with the highest level managers. During a discussion of a new position that is opening up, one of the vice presidents says a particular employee can't be considered for the job because she has young children. No one disagrees. Should you say anything? If so, to whom and how?

The more statements like this one go unchallenged, the harder it is to change the corporate culture. You have to judge the risks and consequences of speaking up or staying silent. If you work in an environment where raising concerns is strictly forbidden, you'll have to weigh whether you want to stay at the company. On the other hand, a comment like this made about women but not men is not only inappropriate but illegal. You're actually doing the employer a favor by questioning it. You may want to start by talking to your supervisor or to someone you trust for advice on how to proceed. Was anyone else in the meeting troubled by the remark? It's helpful if you're not alone in bringing this to someone's attention. The tone you use can make a big difference; appeal to good sense and relevant statements the employer has made about being an equal opportunity employer, rather than being overly accusatory.

SETTING THE TONE

The Families and Work Institute's *National Study of the Changing Workforce* found that the deciding factor in a supervisor's responsiveness to job/family issues wasn't the manager's gender but the ability to "put oneself in the shoes" of those one supervises. Employees who were asked to rate their supervisors judged those who were juggling work and family demands to be managing both work and people more effectively than those who were not. This runs counter to the view that those with family responsibilities make inferior managers.[3]

Individual managers can do much to help workers balance work and family responsibilities. Consider these examples:

• *Shari Kaplan, Vice President, Corporate Services Development, United Health, Inc., Milwaukee, Wisconsin:* The daughter of Kaplan's secretary needed a series of operations after a bad car accident. The secretary told Kaplan she'd reschedule an upcoming surgery because it would coincide with a big meeting. "I know you need me to take minutes," the woman said. "Don't even think about it," Kaplan replied. "I'll get a vice president to take minutes." And she did.

• *Raydean Alcevado, President and CEO of Research Management Consultants, McLean, Virginia:* When her personnel manager had trouble finding child-care for the baby she was about to deliver, Alcevado suggested she bring the baby to work. She did, and so have others. "People can't get cranky when there's a baby around," said Alcevado.[4] "Now people take 'baby breaks' instead of coffee breaks." Alcevado believes this policy has helped attract some valuable employees. One candidate viewing the company saw Alcevado wheeling an employee's baby in a carriage. "That's the president," she was told. The candidate took the job.

WHAT MANAGERS CAN DO

State guidelines for family policies clearly, in writing.
Apply the same principles to everyone.

Encourage men as well as women to be responsible family members.

Respect cultural differences.

Establish good communication to help employees identify and share expectations about leave.

Make flexibility a reality whenever possible—not just when it's convenient.

Involve employees directly in working out arrangements for flexible schedules.

Work for strong company policies rather than leaving most decisions to managerial discretion.

Ask top management for sufficient resources to handle the work when an employee is on leave.

15

What Unions Can Do

Small art and love and beauty their drudging spirits
knew. Yes, it is bread we fight for, but we fight for roses,
too.

> From "Bread and Roses," song from 1912 textile strike
> in Lawrence, Massachusetts.

Often, enlightened management gets the credit for the development of family-friendly policies. In fact, unions have been in the
forefront of this fight for well over a century. Many of the best
practices were the result of years of collective bargaining. The
media may profile successful women executives, but some of the
most inspiring role models are among women union leaders.
Although unions are institutions affected by the dominant culture
and themselves in need of change, a number of unions also provide
models for policy reform and how to get there.

HELPING SHAPE THE JOB/FAMILY AGENDA

In some ways, the traditional agenda of labor—better wages, safer
working conditions, shorter hours, health care and pensions, job
security—has always been about improving life for families. Unions
explicitly described the fight for the eight-hour day, for example, as
a way to help workers have a life beyond laboring for someone else:
"eight hours for work, eight hours for rest, eight hours for what we
will."[1]

Originally, though, help for families meant help for male breadwinners. The craft unions and mainstream unions of the American
Federation of Labor (AFL) viewed women (and immigrants and
people of color) as competition. Their own advancement, they
believed, depended on restricting membership in the trades. While
the AFL did organize some women and upheld the principle of

equal pay for equal work, they spent more energy keeping women out of the workforce than fighting to upgrade their status. This statement by AFL leader Samuel Gompers in 1906 was typical: "It is the so-called competition of the unorganized defenseless woman worker, the girl and the wife, that often tends to reduce the wages of the father and husband."[2]

The craft unions advocated protective legislation for women because they knew such laws would reduce competition from women by making them unappealing to employers. In 1918, for instance, the New York street rail workers union lobbied for a state law to exclude women under age twenty from the jobs and to limit the number of hours women could work to a consecutive nine hours a day. Women members were so angry that they formed their own union. When the law went into effect in May 1919, 800 of 1,500 women lost their jobs.[3] The AFL at that time didn't fight for protection in low-paid job areas, such as laundry, domestic work, or teaching, where women were dominant.

History of Social Justice

At the same time, another trend within the trade union movement always championed social justice. The Knights of Labor welcomed women and people of color. The National Colored Labor Union promoted a woman to its first executive committee and set up a committee on women's labor at its first meeting in 1869. That committee, in a resolution adopted unanimously by the convention, urged the new union to benefit from "the mistakes heretofore made by our white fellow citizens in omitting women."[4] Later the Industrial Workers of the World, known as the Wobblies, inherited that tradition. They led the 1912 Lawrence, Massachusetts, textile strike in which Elizabeth Gurley Flynn emerged as a leader. Debates over protective law took place within the labor movement just as they did among women's groups; the craft unions' dominance began to wane.

After the depression, organizing campaigns led by the emergent Congress of Industrial Organizations (CIO) actively involved families and included women workers in textile, tobacco, and auto-related industries. In the 1960s, many unions worked closely with the civil rights movement and organized workers in health care, sanitation, and the public sector. More women came into the unions, bringing with them a greater awareness of the need for family-friendly policies.

Labor support for child care, for example, goes back fifty years. Unions fought for establishing child-care centers during World War II and argued against dismantling them after the war. Since they merged in 1955, the AFL-CIO has emphasized the need for federal funding and standards to create a national child-care system, which it argued should be universal, not two-tiered. Unions helped develop the Comprehensive Child Care Act of 1971 and were active in the coalition to win the Act for Better Child Care (ABC) in the 1980s. In 1983, given the opposition from Reagan's administration, the AFL-CIO developed a detailed program for bargaining for child care. Fifteen years earlier, they had worked to amend the Taft-Hartley Act to make child care a permissible issue for labor-management negotiations.[5]

In addition to early bargaining for child care, some unions took the lead in setting up day-care facilities. The Amalgamated Clothing and Textile Workers (ACTWU), for instance, developed child-care centers in Baltimore, Chicago, and other cities in the early 1960s, providing care for more than 1,800 children of union members—more than any other private institution in the United States at the time.[6]

The overwhelming majority of large, public-sector employers where the workforce is unionized provided parental leave with a job guarantee before passage of the FMLA. Even most low-wage service workers had such leaves before FMLA if they were in unions.[7] A report by the National Council of Jewish Women found that 55 percent of union members surveyed had job-protected leaves of eight weeks or more, compared to 33 percent of nonunion workers. By 1991, union contracts for four months or more of job-guaranteed leave were common.[8]

And the union movement was one of the major partners in the coalition that helped win the Pregnancy Discrimination Act in 1978. Since most unions had won disability policies for their members, insisting that pregnancy be treated the same as other short-term disabilities meant women union members, far more than their unorganized sisters, were able to take paid maternity leaves.

Women Unionists

Organizations of women unionists date back to 1845 and the creation of the Lowell Labor Reform Organization. From the start, these groups saw the importance of legislative action. The Lowell

Female Labor Reform Association successfully pressured the Massachusetts legislature to hold the nation's first public hearings on factory conditions; mill women testified about the burden of long hours.

Carrying on that tradition in modern times has been the Coalition of Labor Union Women (CLUW), formed in 1974. The group's most comprehensive effort to create a job/family agenda and make it a priority for the labor movement came in 1988 as part of an event they called the American Family Celebration. CLUW brought 40,000 unionists and their children to Washington, DC, in May of that year. Rather than limiting family policy to any particular legislation for child care or family leave, CLUW's American Family Bill of Rights included the right to a job and economic security, to health care and quality education, and to equal opportunity.[9] The group upheld a broad view of family, including single parents, same-sex partnerships, and families without children.

UNIONS AND FAMILY-FRIENDLY POLICIES

Labor unions' support for balancing work and family led to some of the earliest and most comprehensive models of workplace support for child care, family leave, flexible schedules, and other family-friendly policies. Here are some examples of the kind of policies unions can fight for.

Child Care

Union bargaining on child care has won resource and referral services, Dependent Care Assistant Programs (DCAP), establishment of on-site or near-site centers, direct financial assistance, and increased supply of quality, affordable care. The union role in these policies often represents long-term work on the part of dedicated local leaders. The extensive child-care fund negotiated by the Communications Workers of America (CWA) and the International Brotherhood of Electrical Workers (IBEW) with AT&T (described in Chapter 4) was made possible by years of organizing on the part of CWA.[10] Examples of what unions can bargain on child care include the following:

• *On-site centers:* One of the most ambitious programs unions helped win is the Empire State Child Care Network, which by March 1991 included fifty on-site centers serving the children of New York state employees. Run by a Labor-Management Child

Care Advisory Committee, including representatives of the state and its six public employee unions, the committee provides grants of $40,000 and technical assistance to workplaces that want to set up new centers. Fees are on a sliding scale. This network took nearly two decades of work to develop.[11]

• *Resource and referral services:* Since 1984, the United Auto Workers (UAW) negotiated a growing number of these services with the Big Three automakers (Chrysler, Ford, and General Motors). Coordinated by national labor-management committees and funded by the employers, the program involves trained local child care specialists who provide individual assistance to workers.

• *Before- and after-school care:* The Service Employees International Union (SEIU) Local 715 and Santa Clara County, California, collaborated with a local school district experiencing falling enrollment and funds. A number of union members transferred to that school district. Beginning in 1983, a school close to two large county buildings provided free space for an inexpensive program run by the YWCA and paid for by parents. Children can arrive from 6:30 A.M. and stay after school to 6:00 P.M.; they also have full-day activities during summer and on any other days schools are closed.

• *Child care subsidies:* The first contract of the Harvard Union of Clerical and Technical Workers/American Federation of State, County and Municipal Workers (HUCTW/AFSCME) and Harvard University included provisions for a $50,000 annual fund for child-care subsidies, in accordance with financial need. Effective January 1, 1990, the employer agreed to a monthly allowance of $50 per child for costs of preschool care.

• *Prorated subsidies for part-time employees:* District 65-UAW and *Village Voice* agreed that the employer would pay up to $750 per year toward child-care expenses for preschoolers, $500 per year for other children through age twelve, to a maximum of $750 per family. Part-timers are entitled to amounts prorated to the number of hours they work.

• *Center open during nontraditional hours:* In 1988, the State of New York agreed to fund three pilot programs for the Empire State Child Care Network (see *On-site centers*) aimed to help employees who worked shifts earlier or later than traditional hours.

• *Reimbursing the cost of sick-child care:* Alameda County Employees Labor Coalition/SEIU Local 616 and Alameda County, California, agreed that employees will be reimbursed 90 percent (up to $80 a day) of the cost of sick-child care, to a maximum of $350 per employee per year.

• *Well-baby care:* SEIU Local 31M bargained with the State of Michigan to expand health insurance to pay for well-baby care office visits from birth to eighteen months; annual physical check-ups from twenty-four months to age nineteen; and immunizations and laboratory tests from birth to age nineteen.

Family Leave

Unions worked to expand leave for new babies and to include time to care for sick family members. Examples of contract language include the following:

• *Unpaid child-care leave of up to forty-eight months:* AFSCME District Council 37 and the City of New York agreed to allow one instance of a leave forty-eight months long, thirty-six months for all other child-care leaves. Those who elect a shorter time off may extend the leave by up to two extensions of a minimum of six months each.

• *Paid parental leave:* The Amalgamated Clothing and Textile Workers Union (ACTWU) Local 36 bargained with Cedar Riverside People's Center in Minneapolis, Minnesota, to allow employees with one or more years of seniority up to two months of parental leave with pay for new babies. Employees also may use sick days to care for a sick spouse or significant other or for a child, in case of an emergency.

• *Returning from leave part-time:* The contract of SEIU Local 235 and the City of Boston permits employees to return from leave part-time in the same or equivalent position with four weeks' notice.

• *Paid personal days:* The International Union of Electrical Workers (IUE) Local 444 at Sperry Corporation in Lake Success, New York, arranged for their members to have up to ten paid personal days per year out of recognition that they have "from time to time, valid personal reasons for absenting themselves from work."

Flexible Schedules

Unions with large female memberships have often negotiated flextime clauses built around a core period of work every day. Several also negotiated job-sharing provisions, benefits for part-timers, and limits to mandatory overtime and to arbitrary trans-fers. Examples include:

• *Flexible hours:* District 65 UAW and Barnard College, New York City, agreed employees may arrange flexible hours for reasons including school needs, medical needs, or daytime classes not available outside regular working hours.

• *Job-sharing:* The contract of AFSCME Local 2505 with the Executive Department of the State of Oregon specifies that job-sharing employees accrue vacation leave and sick and holiday pay on a prorated basis; they also share the insurance benefits based on the percentage of time worked.

• *Benefits for part-timers:* ACTWU Local 36 won the right for part-timers at Cedar Riverside People's Center to receive prorated pay for holidays and vacation; those working twenty hours or more also receive paid health insurance.

• *Limiting mandatory overtime:* In 1985, the National Association of Letter Carriers (NALC) got an agreement from the U.S. Postal Service that employees who wished to could place their names on an "Overtime Desired" list. Others are not required to work overtime unless all those on the list have worked up to twelve hours in a day or sixty hours in a week. Auto workers at Buick City, a General Motors complex in Flint, Michigan, went on strike in 1994 over health and safety concerns associated with excessive overtime at that plant. As a result, the company agreed to hire nearly 800 additional permanent employees to cut down on the need for overtime.

• *Taking family responsibilities into account in transfers and promotions:* The United Food and Commercial Workers (UFCW) Affirmative Action Language reads: "Every effort will be made to take family responsibilities into account in transfers and promotions regarding store preferences."

Other Areas

Union efforts to win family-friendly policies include other areas as well:

• *Long-term-care insurance:* The UAW secured an agreement from Ford to institute an experimental policy for long-term care. The company would pay costs of nonmedical custodial care at home or in a nursing home for employees and their dependents.

• *Shorter work week:* Faced with the possibility of major layoffs at the Unit Drop Forge Company in Milwaukee, Wisconsin, the UAW negotiated a four-day week for all employees at 80 percent pay.

(The union's counterpart in Germany was able to negotiate with Volkswagen for a similar reduction in hours but only a 10 percent reduction in pay.)

• *Higher pay:* One of the most important ways unions help workers have a family *and* a job is higher pay and greater benefits. Overall, workers who are union members have a wage advantage of 6 percent over nonunion workers with the same education and types of jobs.[12] The union advantage is even greater for women and people of color—12 percent for women, 13 percent for women of color, 18 percent for men of color.[13] Likewise, workers in unions are much more likely to have health insurance, pensions, paid vacations, sick leave, and other benefits. Leave and flexibility are crucial to balancing work and family. But first you have to be able to afford the time off. Peace of mind comes from having the opportunity to be with a sick family member—but also from being able to pay for the expenses of their illness.

• *Union staff:* Many unions have developed strong internal policies to support members' family responsibilities. Some allow organizers working away from home to return on the weekend at union expense. Almost all unions offer paid leave and excellent health care. And unions are far ahead of the corporate world in supporting nontraditional families. The United Food and Commercial Workers, for example, includes domestic partners not only in health care but in pensions as well.

PROVIDING ROLE MODELS

The movie *Norma Rae* portrayed the title character neglecting her husband and children as she became active in the fight to unionize the southern textile mill where she worked. In fact, hundreds of unsung women union leaders have successfully combined raising a family with union activity (like other women, often neglecting themselves in the process).

Consider the example of Delores Huerta, a teacher and mother of six when she got involved with the United Farmworkers Union back in the 1950s. "A lot of people thought I had gone completely bananas," recalls Huerta,[14] who was pregnant with her seventh child when Caesar Chavez first contacted her.

Huerta was a picket captain during the initial strike in 1955. After the growers got injunctions, all the picketers started getting arrested. Huerta was one of the first people to go to jail. "Having women and children on the picket line made it easier to keep our nonviolence stance," says Huerta. "Men liked women on line—they kept up the 'anima.' I think this is what made the farmworkers movement strong. It's a family movement."

Huerta later had four more children. She described being torn about her involvement: "I knew a lot of people were depending on me. I asked God to give me a sign if I should stop what I was doing and pay more attention to my children."

Huerta functioned as first vice president and principal negotiator for the union. This forced men to deal with the reality of what it means to be a working mother. Says Huerta, "When I had my younger children and I was still negotiating, I had to take nursing breaks. . . . Everybody would have to wait while the baby ate and then we'd come back to the table and start negotiating again. That was kind of fun. It also made the employer sensitive to the fact that when we were talking about benefits and the terms of the contract, we were talking about families, children." The union's work meant that wages went up, housing improved, fewer children were working in the field.

"I'm very grateful that I was given this chance during my lifetime to help people, to organize them," Huerta concluded. "As far as my children are concerned, they've turned out well. They know how to fight for people and how to fight for themselves." Several of her children work in the legal or medical field with low-income people. "My whole ideal has been for my children to be in a position where they can also serve others. That is my reward."

Role models among union women exist especially on the local level, where the women's work is less visible but directly touches the lives of many people.

MOBILIZING SUPPORT WITHIN THE UNION

In order to make contract gains like the ones just described, union activists have to start by organizing *inside* the union. Before going to management, the union has to know what members need and want. That means listening to the members and involving them in formulating policy. It also means having some formal structure, with appropriate resources and legitimacy to make things happen.

Some unions have created a "work and family" committee. CLUW points to the example of the Oil, Chemical and Atomic Workers (OCAW) Local 8-149 in Rahway, New Jersey, which published a leaflet on developing such committees. The local used the successful model of the health and safety committee, built on these principles:

- The committee relies on an educated rank and file to identify problems and come up with solutions.

- It seeks to build an alliance among workers, their families, and the community.

- It aims to become a "permanent presence" within the union, rather than having a single-issue focus.

- It negotiates with management to achieve formal recognition, becoming the body to which management is accountable in this area and that reports to union members.

- It develops a long-term strategy with winnable goals.[15]

At times, the union leadership may resist such efforts. If you use good organizing tactics, you can help move these issues onto the agenda. Some tips are:

- Form a core group.

- Get support from someone in leadership, even if that person isn't a key decision maker, to see whom to approach and how.

- Articulate the benefits to the union, to male as well as female members, older as well as younger workers, and demonstrate how failure to act creates an unfair burden on women.

- Go as high up as needed until someone listens.

Listen to Members

OCAW Local 8-149 held a day-long workshop attended by spouses and children to draw up its work-and-family agenda. Unions can also discuss the issue at union meetings (with union-sponsored child care), in newsletter articles, or at social events. A useful tool is a survey to assess member needs, asking specific questions about how people deal with child care and elder care, how current arrangements affect their ability to perform on the job, and what sort of assistance would be most useful. CLUW advocates professional help to design the questionnaire; its booklet has some samples.

Unions often get a good response if they have members fill out the survey at a special meeting or have stewards distribute surveys and follow up to make sure they're returned. Then they publicize the results—which may be surprising. SEIU Local 715, for example, had intended to bargain with Santa Clara County officials for an on-site child-care center. Their internal survey showed members in one large complex were mainly concerned about before- and after-school care. Those findings led to the unique arrangement described earlier.

Work with the Community

Many resources and experts exist. The union can use them both to provide information to members on what's available and to devise solutions for expanding the supply of affordable, quality care. Unions can form alliances with these organizations to work for greater funding and other public policy changes.

Use Multiple Strategies

Collective bargaining is the union's main tool to win family-friendly policies. But some areas require changes in the law. Traditionally, unions have worked hard to pass *legislation* establishing minimum labor standards and general social welfare guarantees. The union can work to convince management to be an ally in this effort—or at least to neutralize other business opposition—by showing the advantage of a more level playing field. If all companies have to offer leave, for example, or contribute to a fund to replace income for people on leave, management doesn't have to worry about being at a competitive disadvantage.

Unions often expand rights for workers through the *grievance procedure*. In the day-to-day administration of the contract, the union maintains the rights of workers but also begins to break new ground. It may take cases to arbitration to set precedents and begin to expand workers' rights.

The best way for unions to expand family-friendly policies is to *organize* more workers into unions. For many women in particular, the ability to have some say over leave, scheduling, and benefits for part-time work makes unionizing very attractive. While union membership overall has declined, the number of women in unions has continued to increase since 1980.[16] (See the resource list in Appendix A for information on how you can join a union.)

THE CHALLENGE TO CHANGE UNION CULTURE

Like any other institution, unions reflect the culture of the times. Historically, women faced open opposition from male union members on many occasions; the majority of international unions in the nineteenth century had constitutions that banned female membership.[17] Listen to Elizabeth Gurley Flynn, a well-known organizer, describing the Gastonia textile strike in 1929:

> The women worked in the mill for lower pay and in addition had all the housework and the care of the children. The old world attitude of man as lord and master was strong. At the end of the day's work, now strike duty, the man went home and sat at ease while his wife did all the work preparing the meal, cleaning the house. There was considerable male opposition to women going to meetings and marching on the picket lines. We set out to combat these notions. The women wanted to picket. They were strikers as well as wives and valiant fighters.[18]

Today, while the hostility is much less common (although by no means absent), barriers to women's involvement are multiple. Labor educator Ruth Needleman describes four main areas of concern regarding balancing work and family:[19]

- *Time:* Union activity on top of a full-time job and a family is hard for anyone, but especially for women.

- *Responsibility:* Even if the union makes accommodations for child care, women still bear chief responsibility for the home front.

- *Values:* The skills and qualifications that are valued in union work often omit or discount the kinds of tasks women do— behind-the-scenes work, taking care of relationships and events. Women may have a great deal of experience from a religious or community group, not to mention from running a family. Yet such skills and experience, says Needleman, are "devalued in unions as in life."

- *Models:* Because labor is at such a critical stage, unionists find it almost impossible to think of any model other than the 24-hour-a-day activist. In the past, most union leaders were men whose wives took care of family and household responsibilities. This is less true today, but the model remains the same.[20] In fact, combining work, family, and union responsibilities takes exceptional skills, which should be highly valued and rewarded and serve as a new kind of model.

Pamela Roby and Lynet Uttal interviewed union stewards, both male and female, to see how they balance work and family demands. Two-thirds of the male stewards lived with a partner and children, as compared to one-fourth of the women. Those men had higher participation rates in union activities than male stewards who were single; the opposite was true for women. While male stewards placed work above family (missing occasions like birthday parties), female stewards put family first (often the birthday party wouldn't happen if they didn't make it happen). Female stewards do much more housework than male stewards, even those males with an employed partner.[21]

Roby and Uttal found that these practices help the most:

1. Meetings:
   - Schedule meetings at convenient times. (CWA and UFCW locals hold monthly membership meetings at two different times on the same day to accommodate varying schedules.)
   - Give plenty of advance notice of meetings.
   - Hold meetings at convenient sites.
   - Keep meetings short or at least to the length of time advertised.

2. Arrange for paid release time for union work and meetings. UAW stewards at the New United Motors Manufacturing (NUMMI) plant in California have two hours a week of company-paid time for union work. CWA pays for its stewards' release time.

3. Child care:
   - Provide child care and hot meals for members and their children during union meetings.
   - Reimburse members for child care and other expenses incurred while doing union business.

New Ways of Doing Business

Ruth Needleman supports these ideas, but goes further to argue for a change in *union culture*. Just as in the corporate world, unions have to change the way they do business. This means trying collective forms of leadership, sharing jobs like handling grievances and negotiating contracts, and rotating leadership responsibilities.

Needleman interviewed women union leaders who felt they couldn't be a part-time president or handle a strike or contract negotiations half-time. But they *could* handle six months on, six off. Certain periods of work can be high intensity. But, says Needleman, "if knowledge is shared, if no one is indispensable, if time is spent planning, delegating, and sharing responsibilities so that there's a group of knowledgeable people instead of one, then people can leave and return" or share a union position.

Needleman's model would require more money in the short run. But above all it requires more people, more involvement, and more democracy—the very things unions need in order to survive and grow. "When the masses of workers look at union activists, they say, 'I like that person—but I don't want to live that life,'" says Needleman. A new model can draw in more people who'll equate union activism with community and skills-building without having to sacrifice one's family.

Unions must also take leadership in encouraging men to share responsibility at home—and rewarding those who do. "Recognition completes the circle," Needleman maintains. "Now, many unions tell you it's okay to take time off, then criticize you if you do. There has to be a turnaround. People have to get rewarded for having an integrated life."

WHAT UNIONS CAN DO

The historical agenda of unions for better wages, hours, and working conditions has helped improve life for families.

Union bargaining on child care has won referral services, financial assistance, on-site centers, and increased supply of quality, affordable care.

To win change from management, unions need to organize internally.

Unions need to schedule meetings at convenient times, get release time for union work, and make accommodations for child care.

Unions need to change their own culture to make job/family balance possible.

16

What Your Elected Officials Can Do: Public Policy Solutions

Chapters 13 and 14 described what employers and managers need to do to ease the conflict between job and family. But they can't carry out all the necessary changes on their own. What role should government play?

Your elected officials are an important part of the solution. They can use their position to educate businesses and the public about the need for change. And they can use public funds as leverage to bring about that change. Government can also help by passing laws to ensure that having a family *and* a job is a basic right guaranteed to all. They're most likely to do these things if they hear from you about what's needed. This chapter covers specific areas where government can help. It also provides information on how you can let your officials know what you want them to do.

ENLIGHTENMENT AND EDUCATION

Those who have access to public forums have an excellent opportunity to raise awareness of the conflicts that exist for many working families. Government officials can state strongly that no one should lose a job because of responsibilities at home, nor should they jeopardize the well-being of family members because of responsibilities at work.

To educate business leaders and the public, elected officials can use several avenues:

1. Government officials at the federal and state levels can fund efforts to educate employees about their legal rights and to get information into the hands of employers about their responsibilities—and about the advantages of family-friendly policies.

2. Officials can recognize and reward family-friendly practices in small as well as large firms. Any awards should reflect actual practices, not written policies. That means checking with employees as well as management and finding out usage, not just availability of programs.

3. Enforcement agencies can sum up complaints and circulate this information broadly to employer groups. The information would clarify what practices are not allowed under the law and serve to warn employers that violations will be dealt with.

4. The agencies can also publicize certain employment practices that may be problematic; for instance, many employers use absence control (or no-fault absentee) policies. Under these policies, employees who miss more than a prescribed number of days for any reason are subject to discipline. But any employee eligible for the FMLA is entitled to take that time without being punished for doing so. The very existence of such absentee policies often serves to deter workers from using their rights out of fear of being fired.

ENCOURAGEMENT

Government can devise programs to help businesses enact family-friendly programs. Some of these are described here:

Financial Incentives

Today, many state and local governments offer tax breaks and outright financial gifts to companies that locate in their area. Sometimes these incentives reward practices that hurt families. Milwaukee-based Briggs & Stratton, for example, received more than $200,000 in Community Development Block Grant Funds from Poplar Bluff, Missouri, for switching 2,000 jobs from Milwaukee to a plant there. But those jobs were taken from workers in Milwaukee—workers who have families to support.

The use of public dollars needs to be refocused so that government resources help working families. The following practices should be adopted:

1. Make a company's job/family policies one criterion for awarding government contracts (as the Office of Federal Contract Compliance and Procedures does with affirmative action).

2. Develop subsidies and/or tax credits to help small businesses with fewer resources offer family-friendly policies.

3. Prohibit the use of government funds to help businesses take jobs from one area to another.

Consortia

Government can do much to facilitate collaboration among small businesses that lack sufficient resources to establish a full range of family-friendly policies on their own:

1. Help small businesses create networks to ease job/family conflicts. The networks could help participating firms combine resources to set up a child-care center or to provide resource and referral services for dependent care. They could offer technical assistance to help participating employers set up programs like DCAP and flexible work schedules. And through the networks, employees from all participating businesses could have access to workshops or resource fairs.

2. Make it possible for groups of small businesses to share a pool of temps at decent pay and benefits to fill in for employees on leave or reduced schedules. Government resources could help provide job training and coordination.

Wage and Job Creation Policies

Government officials have been reluctant to adjust the minimum wage and have focused instead on ways to supplement low wages through the Earned Income Tax Credit (EITC—see Chapter 10). Those who live in poverty despite working should get help to raise their income. But the problem with the EITC as a strategic approach, rather than a stopgap measure, is that it institutionalizes low pay and an artificially low minimum wage, making it difficult for many working families to survive. It also rewards employers who have the ability to pay but who rely on low wages rather than investing in their employees.

Government should consider, instead, outright subsidies or tax breaks to small businesses that need help covering the costs of bona fide job/family policies, while raising the minimum wage until it is fair and equitable. This means:

• Developing clearly stated eligibility criteria for businesses to qualify for subsidies.

• Adjusting the minimum wage to make up for inflation, and

indexing it to increase automatically according to the cost of living or some other reasonable standard.

- Requiring equal pay and benefits for part-time and temporary workers—everyone doing the same job for the same company would receive the same base hourly pay regardless of total hours worked or status as permanent or temporary employee. Part-time workers would also receive benefits on a prorated basis. Such a measure would allow more people to work reduced hours and have more time for their families.

EXPANSION OF RIGHTS

When President Clinton signed the Family and Medical Leave Act on February 5, 1993, he praised the new law for providing Americans with "what they need most—peace of mind. Never again will parents have to fear losing their jobs because of their families." Sadly, many parents still have this fear. Only an estimated 43 percent of women and 48 percent of men are covered by the FMLA.[1] Every worker in the United States needs to be guaranteed the right to be a responsible family member *and* a good employee.

The following legislative changes are needed:

Strengthen Existing Law on Leave

- *Require that companies with fewer than 50 employees be covered under the FMLA.* As was done with the Americans with Disabilities Act (ADA), the threshold can be lowered gradually so that employers of 15 or more employees are included, making the law consistent with the ADA and with Title VII of the Civil Rights Act. Some provision also has to be made to protect employees in the very smallest firms (40 percent of the workforce would still not be covered even with a threshold of 15).[2]

- *Include other part-time employees.* Part-timers who work fewer than 1,250 hours a year (about 25 hours a week) are not covered by the FMLA. Yet they, too, have family needs and should be eligible for the same benefits.

- *Remove the exemption for branch offices.* Limiting coverage for smaller branch offices more than 75 miles from another work site unnecessarily excludes people from FMLA protection. Many state laws do not have this exception and have been easy to administer. The restriction should simply be removed.

• *Make substitution of accrued paid leave voluntary*. Under the FMLA, employers may require the employee to use up accrued paid leave, such as vacation or sick leave, during the FMLA leave. This could leave the worker in a vulnerable position of returning from leave and having to wait a year before having any vacation or of having a new baby and no sick days. Employees should be able to use any accrued paid leave at their discretion, not the employer's.

• *Revise the definition of "immediate family."* Significant family members not covered by FMLA include siblings, domestic partners, grandparents and grandchildren, and parents-in-law. For some cultural groups, as appropriate, family members should include aunts, uncles, nieces, and nephews as well.

• *Expand leave purposes to cover school functions*. Today, few parents are able to participate in their children's activities at school. Having the right to do so would surely pay off in greater parental involvement in education and stronger families.

• *Provide income replacement during leave*. Five states and Puerto Rico provide temporary disability insurance (TDI) funds so that those who are unable to work because of a medical condition originating outside of work may draw up to two-thirds of their wages during the period of leave. These programs, which have been in place for more than fifty years in some states, have been very successful at helping people remain employed and provide a model for funding family leave. A Carnegie Corporation task force called for expanding the TDI model, to be funded by modest contributions from both employees and employers.[3]

• *All employers should be required to distribute written documents to employees on how the company will implement the FMLA*. Employees need to know the details of company policy.

• *Guarantee sick leave to all workers, prorated for part-timers, and allow it to be used for a dependent's illness as well as for a personal illness*. Whether a medical condition is "serious," as the FMLA requires, or routine, a child with a 24-hour bug can't go to school, and a parent with a bad head cold shouldn't be at work.

• *Require men to take leave*. In Sweden, allowing men as well as women to take parental leave and providing income during the leave has resulted in more men caring for children (39 percent took leave in 1991, up from 22 percent in the early 1980s). Still, women continue to bear the major responsibility. On June 1, 1994, the

Swedish government passed a law requiring fathers to take a month of government paid leave or the family loses a month of benefits.[4]

Guarantee Other Employment Practices to Help Families

Both men and women might choose reduced schedules for certain periods of time if they could do so without jeopardizing the well-being of their families. The following public policies would help:

- *Pay and benefit parity for contingent workers* (see "Wage and Job Creation Policies" on page 197).
- *Universal health care.*
- *A shorter work week/work year.* Most other countries have significantly longer vacations than workers in the United States and work fewer hours per week. Harvard economist Juliet Schor points out that, since 1960, the number of an individual's work hours in the United States has grown by about 160 hours a year.[5] For working women, the increase has been *241 hours*.[6] There is nothing sacred about the 40-hour week; throughout the industrial period, the hours of work were reduced several times. Shortening the work week would have several advantages:
  - Jobs for more people, including mothers on welfare
  - More time for family members
  - Increase in productivity and morale
  - More jobs in vital areas such as education, child care, and infrastructure development

- *Labor law reform.* Workers in unions tend to earn higher wages and benefits than those who are not. While some nonunion workplaces have instituted generous family policies, most union workers are far ahead of their unorganized counterparts in leave and flexibility. The many obstacles to unionization need to be removed by such means as allowing card checks rather than elections (the signing of a certain percentage of union cards would suffice); first contracts negotiated within six months; sectoral bargaining (contracts by line of work rather than individual workplaces); and stronger (and swifter) penalties for employers who violate the National Labor Relations Act.

- *Consideration of the impact of regulations on family members.* The Clean Air Act is a good example. While the intentions of this legislation are excellent, incentives for car pools could end up discriminating against single mothers with small children who need to drive in order to pick up children at day care.

Other Support for Parents Taking Time Off

Some people advocate a "young child allowance" from the government as a means of allowing more parents to stay home with preschool children. Congress should study the pros and cons of such a provision, how it works in other countries, and what it would take to encourage men as well as women to use it.

Help with Dependent Care

The current child-care situation in this country can best be characterized as chaos and conflict. Parents can't afford what they have to pay, and child-care workers can't afford to live on what they earn. The resulting turnover is bad for workers, for parents, and especially for children.

The benefits of good child care are well-known. Trained, adequately compensated child-care providers with sufficient numbers and supplies can do a great job for kids—and for business. Yet businesses can't—and won't—take care of the problem on their own. As Stride Rite CEO Arnold Hiatt put it, "Frankly, I don't think corporate day care is the final answer. Can you imagine how many first graders would be educated if we depended upon corporate initiative?"[7] Solving the problem will take the following:

• *Understanding:* Americans have to recognize that care of young children is a social good and a universal public responsibility. They also have to weigh the long-term costs of failure to accept this responsibility.

• *Funds:* We need to expand the funds available for child care, to help parents pay for costs, and to increase availability and quality. The National Center for the Early Childhood Work Force is exploring various ways to see child care as a public service and connect the cost to the tax base—the income tax, an employer tax, payroll tax, or local property taxes. One model the organization is looking at is the Australian system of "Universal Fee Relief." There, parents pay for day care based on a sliding fee scale according to their income, and public funds make up the difference in cost. As a result, child-care workers receive a living wage—a "worthy wage"—and are able to provide more stability in care for young children than occurs in the United States.

• *Tax incentives for companies offering child-care assistance:* Since 1989, Connecticut has allowed businesses to deduct up to 50 percent of their child-care expenses from their taxes. *Prime Publications, Inc.*, a newspaper publisher in Southbury, Connecticut, established a child-care subsidy in 1987 to help employees to increase productivity and morale, and to reduce absenteeism and turnover. Any employee working at least 17.5 hours is eligible to receive up to $25 a day in reimbursement for licensed child-care costs for one child, up to $35 a day for more than one child. In 1990, the company spent $21,000 on child-care subsidies. "The dividends [of the child-care subsidy] have been tremendous," said one company official. "We have enthusiastic staff that praises us—this gives us great publicity. People want to work for us because of our benefit; we can selectively hire qualified staff. In addition, productivity has improved, newspapers are circulated in a more timely manner, and there is less turnover and absenteeism."[8]

• *Linking land use to child care:* In 1985, the city of San Francisco revised the city planning code to require office developers either to provide space for child-care centers or to pay a fee to a citywide fund used to establish affordable child-care. The State of Maryland requires space for child-care facilities in public buildings. Seattle allows developers who include free space for child-care to have more square footage than otherwise allowed.[9]

• *Loan forgiveness:* Marian Wright Edelman, director of the Children's Defense Fund, recommends the government forgive loans to students who study child development and work in the field of early childhood education.

• *Federal funds to improve child-care-worker wages:* Nine states are using Child Development Block Grant money to explore ways to improve salaries and benefits for child-care workers.

• *Improving the rights of foreign-born home-care workers:* Given the shortage of trained caregivers, many people have relied on immigrants. When Zoe Baird was nominated for attorney general, her failure to pay taxes on a foreign-born nanny brought to light the shortage, as well as the dilemma of many workers who can't get legal status in this country. The Task Force on Quality Legal Child Care of the New York Women's Bar Association calls for the following changes in the Immigration Act of 1990:[10]

- Set up a new temporary visa category for foreign workers whose employers have received certification from the Labor Department that they've made a good-faith effort to find a native-born employee.
- Reclassify home-care workers as skilled rather than unskilled, as they are now. Most visas are designated for professional or technically skilled workers.
- Require employers of home-care workers to comply with all laws and to pay the prevailing regional wage.

• *Long-term care*: Dependent care isn't only about children. Many employees struggle with how to pay for long-term care for their parents. Health care reform should include this provision.

• *Funds for in-home services*: Today, most insurance will not cover in-home care. Yet many elders in need of assistance would gladly stay at home or at the home of a relative if the services could be underwritten by Medicaid. In the long run, covering in-home care would lower health costs and provide a nurturing situation for significant numbers of people.

ENFORCEMENT

If the law is expanded to enable more people to balance job and family, enforcement must be strengthened. Today, even with strong commitment on the part of agency leaders and staff, inadequate funding hampers enforcement. Here is what's needed:

• *More funds for the Equal Employment Opportunity Commission and the Wage and Hour Division:* The funds should allow for increased staffing and training and should be accompanied by stricter turnaround times for handling complaints.

• *Increased penalties under the FMLA:* Companies found to be in violation of the FMLA should be given an opportunity to come into compliance and then fined if they do not. Such a mechanism, known as civil money penalties of up to $10,000, is in place for repeat violations of the minimum wage or child labor laws. The money collected through these fines could be put into a fund for public education about the law.

• *More diligent enforcement of the FMLA by the Wage and Hour Division to cut down on the need for civil suits:* The Division should change its practice and investigate cases whether or not the complainant has an attorney.

HOW YOU CAN INFLUENCE ELECTED OFFICIALS

Lawmakers need to hear directly from their constituents. Here are some ways to get their attention:

• *Write a letter about your experience.* If you can't afford dependent care or can't get the time you need for your family, say so; and describe the impact on your family and yourself. Encourage a friend to do the same. A personal letter, even if it's handwritten, is more compelling than a petition or preprinted postcard.

• *Join a group like 9to5,* which will keep you informed of new legislation being introduced or the status of pending bills. Pass the information on to friends and co-workers.

• *Take time to visit your elected officials at their home office.* If you don't know who your representatives are, call a nonpartisan group like the League of Women Voters or a local government office (such as the City Council) to get a list of local, state, and federal representatives. Most elected officials will arrange a meeting if you call first.

• *Look for opportunities like public hearings*—or work within an organization to plan your own—where you can testify about your personal experience.

• *Ask candidates about their support* for specific family-friendly policies and vote accordingly.

WAYS YOUR ELECTED OFFICIALS CAN HELP

Increase funds to educate workers about their legal rights and employers about their responsibilities.

Use the awarding of contracts and the use of tax credits and subsidies to encourage family-friendly policies.

Expand the FMLA to cover part-time workers and firms with fifteen or more employees.

Create a public fund to provide partial wage replacement during family leave to help make leave affordable for low-wage workers.

Legislate favorable employment policies, such as guaranteed pay parity for part-time work and a shorter work week. Provide additional funds for enforcement to help strengthen family leave legislation.

Conclusion: We Can Win the Job/Family Challenge

Recently, I asked a group of women workers what words they associate with the phrase "job and family." You know their responses: "dilemma," "conflict," "balancing act," "juggle," "stress"—and, of course, "guilt." Some tension between job and family responsibilities is inevitable. But we could reduce the problems enormously with solutions that have already been proven to work.

Most people would love to have someone home full-time to take care of the details of daily life. In reality, few people will. But we can get relief—by changing the way business does business, by winning more public support for families, and by having those who share the house share the work. That will take initiatives by business leaders, by employee groups, by elected officials, and by each of us individually.

To win the job/family challenge, we have to have flexibility at work and access to quality dependent care—and the ability to afford both. We need a new vision of success, where you don't have to sacrifice your family in order to contribute or to advance. Imagine the results if people running companies—or countries, for that matter—resembled more closely the people they serve. Chances are we wouldn't have a $700 billion deficit or 38 million people without health insurance. Individual businesses and our nation as a whole stand to gain from the ability of workers to be both good employees and good family members.

Change won't happen easily or on its own. You'll have to get involved and convince others that they should, too. But together, we can reach the point where having a family *and* a job is a blessing, not a burden.

APPENDIX A: RESOURCES FOR MORE INFORMATION

Your Rights Under the Law

9to5 National Association of
Working Women
238 West Wisconsin Avenue,
Suite 700
Milwaukee, WI 53203-2308
Toll-free Job Problem Hotline:
1-800-522-0925

Women's Legal Defense Fund
1875 Connecticut Avenue NW,
Suite 710
Washington, DC 20009
202-986-2600

Robert Stumberg, Janice
Steinschneider, and George
Elser, *State Legislative
Sourcebook on Family and
Medical Leave* (Washington,
DC: Center for Policy
Alternatives, 1989).

Adoption

Adoptive Families of America
3333 Highway 100 North
Minneapolis, MN 55422
612-535-4829

Aid to Adoption of Special Kids
657 Mission Street, Suite 601
San Francisco, CA 94105
415-543-2275

Association of Black Social
Workers
271 W. 125th Street, Room 414
New York, NY 10027
212-222-5200

Hispanic Advocacy and Resource
Center
2488 Grand Concourse, Suite 413
New York, NY 10459
212-733-1200

Balancing on the Home Front

Arlie Hochschild with Anne
Machung, *The Second Shift:
Working Parents and the
Revolution at Home* (New York:
Viking Press, 1989).

Bonnie Michaels and Elizabeth
McCarty, *Solving the Work/
Family Puzzle* (Homewood, IL:
Business One Irwin, 1992).
This book has a number of
useful charts and lists.

Child Care

Child Aware Information Line
815 15th Street NW, Suite 928
Washington, DC 20005
1-800-424-2246

Child Care Action Campaign
330 Seventh Avenue, 17th Floor
New York, NY 10001
212-239-0138
(CCAC has a number of useful
publications, including *Not Too
Small to Care: Small Business
and Child Care*, and *Speaking
With Your Employer About
Child Care Assistance*.)

Children's Defense Fund
122 C Street NW
Washington, DC 20001
202-628-8787

National Association of Child
Care Resource and Referral
Agencies
PO Box 402-46
Washington, DC 20016
1-800-424-2246 or 202-333-4194

National Center for the Early
Childhood Work Force
737 15th Street NW, Suite 1037
Washington, DC 20005
202-737-7700

IRS booklet No. 926: *Employment
Taxes for Household Employees*.

Some latchkey-children guides
include:
Ann Banks, *Alone at Home: A
Kid's Guide to Being in Charge*
(New York: Puffin Books,
1989).
Lynette and Thomas Long,
*Handbook for Latchkey
Children and Their Parents*
(New York: Arbor House,
1983).
Helen L. Swan, *Alone after School:
A Self-Care Guide for Latchkey
Children & Their Parents*
(Englewood Cliffs, NJ: Prentice
Hall, 1985).

Elder Care

Alzheimer's Disease and Related
Disorders Association, Inc.
919 N. Michigan Avenue, Suite
1000
Chicago, IL 60601
1-800-621-0379 or 312-335-8700

American Association of Retired
Persons (AARP)
601 E Street NW
Washington, DC 20049
202-434-2277

Association Nacional pro
Personas Mayores
3325 Wilshire Boulevard, Suite
800
Los Angeles, CA 90010
213-487-1922

Older Women's League
666 11th Street NW, Suite 700
Washington, DC 20001
202-783-6686

Family-Friendly Policies

Catalyst
250 Park Avenue South
New York, NY 10003
212-777-8900

Conference Board, Inc.
Work and Family Information
Center
845 Third Avenue
New York, NY 10022
212-759-0900

Families and Work Institute
330 Seventh Avenue, 14th floor
New York, NY 10001
212-465-2044

Work/Family Directions
930 Commonwealth Avenue
Brookline, MA 02215
617-566-1800

Work in America Institute, Inc.
700 White Plains Road
Scarsdale, NY 10583
914-472-9600

Carnegie Corporation, *Starting
Points: Meeting the Needs of
Our Youngest Children* (New
York: Carnegie Corporation,
1994).

C. Eichman and B. Reisman,
"How Small Employers Are
Benefiting from Offering Child
Care Assistance," *Employment
Relations Today*, Spring 1992.

Katharine Esty and Jame
Bermont, "Changing the
Corporate Culture to Support
Work & Family Programs"
(Washington, DC: The Bureau
of National Affairs, Special
Report No. 42, June 1991).

Dana E. Friedman, Ellen
Galinsky, and Veronica
Plowden, eds., *Parental Leave
and Productivity: Current
Research* (New York: Families
and Work Institute, 1992).

Ellen Galinsky, James T. Bond,
and Dana E. Friedman, *The
Changing Workforce: Highlights
of the National Study* (New
York: Families and Work
Institute, 1991).

Michele Lord and Margaret King,
*The State Reference Guide to
Work-Family Programs for State
Employees* (New York: Families
and Work Institute, 1991).

Karol L. Rose, *Work and Family:
Program Models and Policies*
(New York: John Wiley & Sons,
1993).

Felice Schwartz, *Breaking with
Tradition* (New York: Warner
Books, 1992).

Flexible Work Schedules

Association of Part-Time
Professionals
7700 Leesburg Pike, Suite 216
Falls Church, VA 22043
703-734-7975

New Ways to Work
785 Market Street, Suite 950
San Francisco, CA 94103
415-995-9860

Catalyst, *Flexible Work
Arrangements: Establishing
Options for Managers and
Professionals* (New York:
Catalyst, 1990).

Barney Olmstead and Suzanne
Smith, *Creating a Flexible
Workplace: How to Select and
Manage Alternative Work
Options* (New York: American
Management Association,
1989).

Gay, Lesbian, and Bisexual Rights

National Gay and Lesbian Task
Force
2320 17th Street NW
Washington, DC 20009
202-332-6483

National Center for Lesbian
Rights
870 Market Street, Suite 570
San Francisco, CA 94102
415-392-6257

National Gay and Lesbian Task
Force, "Lesbian, Gay and
Bisexual Civil Rights in the
U.S." and "Listing of
Corporations, Organizations,
Unions and Educational
Institutions Offering Domestic
Partner Benefits" (Washington,
DC: NGLTF, 1994).

Public Policy

Edward E. Zigler and Meryl
Frank, eds., *The Parental Leave
Crisis: Toward a National Policy*
(New Haven: Yale University
Press, 1988).

Janet Shibley Hyde and Marilyn J. Essex, eds., *Parental Leave and Child Care: Setting a Research and Policy Agenda* (Philadelphia: Temple University Press, 1991).

Starting Your Own Business

Jolene Godfrey, Our Wildest Dreams: Women Entrepreneurs Making Money (New York: Harper Collins Publishers, 1992).

Daryl Allen Hall, 1001 Businesses You Can Start From Home (New York, John Wiley & Sons, Inc., 1992).

Unions

Coalition of Labor Union Women
15 Union Square
New York, NY 10003
212-242-0700

Coalition of Labor Union Women, *Bargaining for Family Benefits: A Union Member's Guide* (New York: CLUW, 1991).

For information on organizing a union, call one of the following regional AFL-CIO offices:

Region 1 (Illinois, Indiana, Michigan, Wisconsin)
708-255-4747

Region II (Arkansas, Kansas, Missouri, Oklahoma)
918-622-0742

Region III (Delaware, Maryland, Pennsylvania, Virginia, West Virginia, Washington, DC)
414-644-1010

Region IV (Louisiana, Mississippi, Texas)
512-477-1811

Region V (Alabama, Florida, Georgia, North Carolina, South Carolina)
404-766-5050 or 407-896-9621

Region VI (California, Hawaii, Nevada)
213-387-1974 or 415-396-7152

Region VII (New Jersey, New York, Puerto Rico, U.S. Virgin Islands)
212-661-1555

Region VIII (Connecticut, Maine, Massachusetts, New Hampshire, Rhode Island, Vermont)
617-261-4840

Region IX (Alaska, Idaho, Montana, Oregon, Washington)
206-431-1343

Region X (Kentucky, Ohio, Tennessee)
615-333-9891

Region XI (Arizona, Colorado, New Mexico, Utah, Wyoming)
303-831-1311

Region XII (Iowa, Minnesota, Nebraska, North Dakota, South Dakota)
612-893-9282

General

Bureau of National Affairs, Inc.
1231 25th Street NW
Washington, DC 20049
202-472-4700

Institute for Women's Policy
Research
1400 20th Street NW
Washington, DC 20036
202-785-5100

National Council of Jewish
Women
53 West 23rd Street
New York, NY 10010
212-645-4048

Cathy Feldman, *Two Years
Without Sleep: Working Moms
Talk About Having a Baby and a
Job* (Santa Barbara, CA: Blue
Point Books, 1993).

Anne C. Weisberg and Carol A.
Buckler, *everything a working
mother needs to know* (New
York: Doubleday, 1994).

Government Agencies

U.S. Equal Employment
Opportunity Commission
1801 L Street NW
Washington, DC 20507
1-800-669-EEOC or 202-663-4900
202-634-7057 for the hearing
impaired

U.S. Administration on Aging
Department of Health and Human
Services
330 Independence Avenue SW,
Room 4760
Washington, DC 20201
202-619-0724

Congressional Caucus on
Women's Issues
2471 Rayburn House Office
Building
Washington, DC 10515
202-225-6740

Wage and Hour Division
200 Constitution Avenue NW
Washington, DC 20210
202-219-8727

Women's Bureau, U.S.
Department of Labor
Work and Family Clearinghouse
200 Constitution Avenue NW
Washington DC 20210
1-800-827-5335
To order publications:
202-219-6652

APPENDIX B: ASSESSMENT TOOL FOR EMPLOYERS AND EMPLOYEES: HOW FAMILY-FRIENDLY IS THIS ORGANIZATION?

Policy

What is the formal company policy in each of the following areas:

Leave	No. of Weeks	Paid?	Job Guar.?	Benefits Cont'd?
Leave for birth mothers				
Leave for birth fathers				
Leave for adoptive parents				
Sick leave				

	No. of Weeks	Use Sick Leave?	Job Guar.?	Benefits Cont'd?
Leave to care for sick child				
Leave to care for sick parent				
Leave to care for sick spouse				

	Yes	No
Includes domestic partners		
Parent equivalents		
Stepchildren		

Flexible Schedules	Yes	No
Start and end time		
Make up time (e.g., for school functions)		
Compressed work week		
Telecommuting		
Job-share		

	Yes	No	Same Hourly Rate?	Benefits Prorated?
Part-time work				

Assistance with Dependent Care   Yes   No
    Resource and referral workshops
    Pretax spending account
    Subsidies
    Discount at nearby center
    On-site or near-site center
    Sick-child care
    Programs for school-aged children
    Family calls allowed

Practice   Yes   No

(Ask these questions for each policy.)

1. Is it available for all employees?

2. Is the policy more generous for managers? If so, why?

3. Is access to the leave or flexibility determined by manager discretion? Why?

4. Is there a grievance procedure if the manager denies an employee's request?

Usage/Impact   Yes   No

1. Are policies clearly defined and familiar to all employees?

2. Does the employer know the number of employees who leave each year because they couldn't get the time off or flexibility they wanted?

3. Does the employer know the number of missed days because of problems arranging child care? elder care?

4. If there is an on-site or near-site child care center, are there any eligible employees who don't use the center because they can't afford it?

5. Does the employer track usage rates by those eligible? If so, what do they indicate? _____

6. How many men took leave
   For a birth or adoption in the past year? _____
   To care for a sick child? _____
   To care for a sick parent? _____
   Of these, how many are managers? _____
   How many are senior executives? _____

Advancement

1. What percentage of senior executives are
   females with children in school?_____
   males with wives who work outside the home
   and have children in school?_____
   How does the employer rate the results?

2. What are the figures on advancement for
   those who've used leave or flexible schedules
   compared to those who have not?_____

	Yes	No

3. Has the company encouraged men to take
   leave?
   If yes, how? _____

4. Are travel, moving, and long hours requirements for advancement?
   If so, has the employer studied the relationship between those requirements and
   skills needed for executive positions?

Oversight

	Yes	No

1. Does the employer have a mechanism to
   get regular feedback from employees on
   how they're dealing with the job/family
   challenge?

2. Is there a person in charge of job/family
   issues?
   If yes, how much authority does she/he
   have?_____

3. Are managers trained in how to help employees achieve job/family balance?

	Yes	No

4. Are managers held accountable for how well they accomplish job/family balance?

5. Has the employer identified areas that need improvement and set concrete goals to do so?

(If you have the luxury to choose where to work, this list can help you determine a family-friendly employer.)

APPENDIX C: POLICIES IN OTHER COUNTRIES

Country	Maternity Leave (in weeks)	Pay for Maternity Leave (as % earnings)	Paternity Leave	Pay for Paternity Leave (as % earnings)
Belgium	15 Before birth: 7 After: 8	82% first month 75% remaining leave (up to maximum amt.)	3 days	100%
Canada	17	Wks. 1–2 unpaid Wks. 3–17, 60% pay to a max. of $384/wk.	5 days	100%
Denmark	18 Before birth: 4 After: 14 (same for adoption)	Flat rate ($396*)	10 days	Same as maternity
France	16 Before birth: 6 After: 10 (18 for multiple birth, 26 if 3rd or later birth)	84% (not taxed)	3 days	Same as maternity
Germany	14 Before birth: 6 After: 8 (Mothers must take)	100%	No statute	—
Japan	12	60%	No statute	—
Kenya	8.5	100%	5 days	100%
Netherlands	16	100%	No statute	—
Sweden	15 months	90% for 12 mos. Fixed rate of $8.22 per day for last 3 mos.	10 days; 20 days for twins	90%
U.K.	40 Before birth: 11 After: 29	90% for 6 wks. Flat rate for 12 wks. Unpaid for 22 wks.	No statute	—

*All amounts based on 1992 figures.

Parental Leave	Pay for Parental Leave	Sick Child Leave	Pay for Child Leave
No statute. Local govt. pays if worker replaced by unemployed.	—	No statute	—
10 wks; 5 additional wks. if adopted child is ill or 6 mos. or older.	Unpaid	No statute	—
10 wks; either parent, 13–36 wks. sabbatical for child under 8—replace with unemployed.	Same as maternity 80% of highest unemp. rate	No statute	—
1 yr. full- or part-time until child is 3. Parents can share, work 16–18 hrs./wk. Companies of 100+.	Unpaid unless 3 or more kids, then $519/mo.	No statute	—
3 yrs. full- or part-time.	Mos. 1–18, flat rate Mos. 19–24, related to income Mos. 25–36, unpaid	2 parents–10 days ea. (25 total if 2 or more kids). Single parent, 20 days/1 kid, 50 days more.	100%
No statute	—	No statute	—
No statute	—	7 days	100%
Each parent 6 mos. part time until child is 4, work at least 20 hrs./wk. Includes adopted, stepkids.	Unpaid	No statute	—
450 days	90%	60 days per child per year up to child's 8th birthday.	90%
No statute	—	No statute	—

Source: *The Family-Friendly Employer: Examples from Europe.* (New York: Daycare Trust in association with Families and Work Institute, 1992); *Equal Worth* (Sweden: Swedish Institute, the Equality Affairs Division of the Ministry of Health and Social Affairs, 1993); Eileen Trzcinski and William T. Alpert, "Pregnancy and Parental Leave Benefits in the United States and Canada," *The Journal of Human Resources* XXIX (2), 1992.

NOTES AND SOURCES

Introduction

1. Institute for Women's Policy Research, "The Increasing Responsibility of Women Workers for Family Financial Needs" (Washington, DC: Institute for Women's Policy Research, 1994). Traditional couples accounted for 22 percent of all families with children in 1993, down from 44 percent in 1975. Dual-earner couples, who made up 37 percent of all families in 1975, accounted for 47 percent in 1993.

2. Joseph Pleck [a researcher at Wellesley College Center for Research on Women who has studied attitudes toward fatherhood], quoted in Susan Chira, "Obstacles for Men Who Want Family Time," *The New York Times*, October 21, 1993.

Chapter 1

1. Joint Economic Committee, "Families on a Treadmill: Work and Income in the 1980s," (Washington, DC: U.S. Congress, January 1992). In the last 15 years, wives' income have kept families above water. On average, wives worked 32 percent more hours in 1989 than in 1979. Without the increased hours and wages of wives, incomes for 60 percent of American families would have been lower in 1989 than in 1979.

2. According to the Bureau of Labor Statistics, families headed by women accounted for 18.1 percent of all families in 1993, compared to 13.6 percent in 1975.

3. Ellen Galinsky, James T. Bond, and Dana E. Friedman, *The Changing Workforce: Highlights of the National Study* (New York: Families and Work Institute, 1993), 44.

4. Ibid., 58. According to the study, women spend a total of 19.9 hours a week taking care of elderly relatives; men spend 11.8 hours. Among caregivers of the elderly, 23 percent have responsibility for two or more elders, most of whom live near the person with caregiving responsibility.

5. Ellen Galinsky and James T. Bond, "Parental Leave Benefits for American Families," (New York: Families and Work Institute, 1993), 3.

6. Eileen Trzcinski, "Employers' Parental Leave Policies: Does the Labor Market Provide Parental Leave?" in Janet Shibley Hyde and Marilyn J. Essex, eds., *Parental Leave and Child Care: Setting a*

Research and Policy Agenda (Philadelphia: Temple University Press, 1991), 215–16. Trczinski analyzed two surveys, one conducted in Minnesota and one in Connecticut, covering firms of all sizes. Overall, the survey found that fewer than 10 percent of Minnesota firms provided time off to new parents to care for newborn children, as opposed to disability leave. The Connecticut survey echoed these findings. Even among the largest firms, only 13.9 percent offer job-protected infant-care leave. This figure decreases with firm size: only 7.2 percent for companies of 50 to 99 employees, 3.6 percent for the smallest firms.

7. "Pregnancy Discrimination," *Lifetime Magazine*, Lifetime Cable TV, February 22, 1994.

8. Ibid.

9. Harriet Brown, "Beyond the Mommy Track," *Vogue*, September 1991, 506.

10. "Pregnancy Discrimination."

11. Bureau of National Affairs, *Pregnancy and Employment Handbook* (Washington, DC: BNA, 1987), 5.

12. James T. Bond, Ellen Galinsky, et al., *Beyond the Parental Leave Debate: The Impact of Laws in Four States* (New York: Families and Work Institute, 1991), vi. In Rhode Island, which has a statewide Temporary Disability Insurance program, none of the low-income mothers took fewer than six weeks leave. This compared with up to 19 percent of low-income mothers in the other three states studied who went back to work before six weeks.

13. Sheila Kammerman, "Parental Leave and Infant Care," in Hyde and Essex, *Parental Leave and Child Care*, 15–16. Private group insurance policies are more likely to include maternity leave, but fewer workers—and fewer women workers in particular—are included under those policies today than in 1980. Women are also concentrated in smaller firms, which are less likely to provide sick leave. And women make up two-thirds of part-time workers, who often have no benefits at all. Kammerman and Kahn concluded that there's been no meaningful increase in the percentage of women workers with paid maternity disability leaves since 1981. Vacation and personal leave policies also haven't increased during that time.

14. Roberta Spalter-Roth and Heidi Hartmann, *Unnecessary Losses: Costs to Americans of the Lack of Family and Medical Leave* (Washington, DC: Institute for Women's Policy Research, 1990), 25, 30.

15. Deborah J. Swiss and Judith P. Walker, *Women and the Work/Family Dilemma* (New York: John Wiley & Sons, Inc., 1993), 197. This book was based on an in-depth survey of 902 women who had graduated from Harvard professional schools over a 10–year period. The authors found that the vast majority of the women ran into a "maternal wall." The women felt virtually no recognition in the workplace for their role as parents.

16. Galinsky and Bond, "Parental Leave Benefits for American Families," 5.

17. Ford Foundation Women's Program Forum, "Men and Women: At Home and in the Workplace" (New York: Ford Foundation, May 1991), 5.

18. 9to5 National Association of Working Women, "1994–95 Profile of Working Women" (Cleveland: 9to5 NAWW, 1994), 3.

19. Ibid.

20. Galinsky, Bond, and Friedman, *The Changing Workforce*, 79.

21. Jonathan R. Veum and Philip M. Gleason, "Child care: Arrangements and costs," *Monthly Labor Review*, October 1991, 10–11.

22. Ellen Galinsky et al., *Work and Family Life Study Pinpoints Sources of Stress for Corporate Workers*, 5 Family Resource Coalition Rep. 7, No. 2 (1986).

23. Economic Policy Institute, Washington, DC.

24. The Conference Board, *Flexible Staffing and Scheduling in U.S. Corporations* (New York: The Conference Board, 1990), 12. A 1994 study by Linda K. Stroh and Karen S. Kush (which they summarize in "Flextime: The Imaginary Innovation," *The New York Times*, November 27, 1994) asked how many companies have "formal, permanent flextime programs that are available to a significant portion of the work force." Only 14 percent of responding companies answered yes. Of the remainder, 92 percent said it was "unlikely" or "very unlikely" that they would ever adopt flextime.

25. Barbara Presley Noble, "The Work-Family Bottom Line," *The New York Times*, November 20, 1994, F25. According to a survey by Massachusetts Mutual released in mid-November 1994, 41 percent of employees say their employers expect them to perform an unreasonable amount of overtime.

26. Robert Reich, Secretary, U.S. Department of Labor, and Karen Nussbaum, Director, Women's Bureau, "Working Women Count!

A Report to the Nation" (Washington, DC: U.S. Department of Labor, 1994), 3.

27. Women's Legal Defense Fund, "Most Employers Do Not Currently Have Job-Guaranteed Family and Medical Leave" (Washington, DC: Women's Legal Defense Fund, 1991).

28. Galinsky, Bond, and Friedman, *The Changing Workforce*, 90. Of those who earn less than $7 an hour, 32 percent have no health insurance, even for themselves; 36 percent in that wage group lack pensions.

29. Arlie Hochschild with Anne Machung, *The Second Shift: Working Parents and the Revolution at Home* (New York: Viking Penguin, Inc., 1989), 1.

30. Donna Britt, "So women can 'have it all'? Don't bet on it." *Milwaukee Journal*, September 26, 1994, A7.

31. Hochschild, The Second Shift, 40.

32. Britt, "So women can 'have it all'?"

Chapter 2

1. Mary Francis Berry, *The Politics of Parenthood* (New York: Penguin Books, 1993), 42–64. Berry points out that because men in colonial times labored close to family members, and because women were considered untrustworthy, fathers were seen as better suited to oversee their children's development. The author illustrates men's involvement not just in children's education and labor, but in their emotional lives as well. The shift from father care to mother care, says Berry, came with the growth of cities and manufacturing and commercial activities. By the Civil War, responsibility for children had become the special sphere of women.

2. Nancy F. Cott, "Divorce and the Changing Status of Women in Eighteenth Century Massachusetts," in M. Gordon, ed., *The American Family in Social Historical Perspective*, 2d ed. (New York: St. Martin's Press, 1978), 129.

3. Alice Clark, *The Working Life of Women in the Seventeenth Century* (New York: Harcourt Brace, 1920), cited in Alice Kessler-Harris, *Out to Work: A History of Wage-Earning Women in the United States* (Oxford: Oxford University Press, 1982), 7.

4. Harriet A. Jacobs, *Incidents in the Life of a Slave Girl, Written by Herself* (Cambridge, MA: Harvard University Press, 1987), 87.

5. Ibid., 89.

6. Kessler-Harris, *Out to Work*, 9.

7. Ibid., 17.

8. Ibid., 18.

9. Ibid., 71.

10. Nancy Cott, *Root of Bitterness: Documents in the Social History of American Women* (New York: Dutton, 1972), 328.

11. Quoted in "A Century of Women, Part I, Work and Family," Turner Broadcasting System, June 7, 1994.

12. Kessler-Harris, *Out to Work*, 122.

13. Ibid.

14. Rheta Childe Door, *A Woman of Fifty* (New York: Funk & Wagnalls, 1924), excerpted in Anne Firor Scott, ed., *The American Woman: Who Was She?* (Englewood Cliffs, NJ: Prentice Hall, 1971), 19–20.

15. "Women on the Night Shift," *Life and Labor* 6 (December 1914), cited in Rosalyn Baxandall, Linda Gordon, and Susan Reverby, eds., *America's Working Women: A Documentary* (New York: Vintage Books, 1976), 159.

16. Ibid., 159–160.

17. Ibid., 160.

18. Baxandall, Gordon, and Reverby, *America's Working Women*, 263.

19. Mary Van Kleeck, "Artificial Flower Makers" (New York: Survey Association, 1913), cited in Baxandall, Gordon, and Reverby, 162.

20. Report No. 103 (Washington, DC: U.S. Government Printing Office, 1914), cited in Baxandall, Gordon, and Reverby, 153–154.

21. Dick Gregory with Robert Lipsyte, *Nigger: An Autobiography* (New York: E.P. Dutton & Co., Inc., 1964), excerpted in Scott, *The American Woman*, 33–34.

22. Ibid., 35.

23. Kessler-Harris, *Out to Work*, 296.

24. Quoted in "A Century of Women."

25. "First Report of the Advisory Council on Disability Benefits," State of New Jersey Department of Labor and Industry, Division of Employment Security, Disability Insurance Service, Trenton, NJ, February 9, 1951.

26. Baxandall, Gordon, and Reverby, 291.

27. Caroline Zinsser, *Raised in East Urban: Child Care Changes in a*

Working Class Community (New York: Teachers College Press, 1991), 93.

28. Ibid., 94.

29. Ibid., 100.

30. Women's Bureau No. 246, *Employed Mothers and Child Care* (Washington, DC: U.S. Government Printing Office, 1953), cited in Baxandall, Gordon, and Reverby, 293.

31. Baxandall, Gordon, and Reverby, 291.

32. Ibid., 295.

33. Alice and Staunton Lynd, eds., *Rank and File, Personal Histories by Working Class Organizers* (Boston: Beacon Press, 1979), quoted in Baxandall, Gordon, and Reverby, 273.

34. CLUW, *Bargaining for Family Benefits: A Union Member's Guide* (New York: CLUW, 1991), 26. A survey of garment workers in New York City found that many were bringing their children to work or leaving them home alone because of lack of available child care.

Chapter 3

1. The Supreme Court upheld such laws on the grounds that women's maternal function is unique. "Differentiated by these matters from the other sex, she is properly placed in a class by herself," it claimed, "and legislation designed for her protection may be sustained, even when like legislation is not necessary for men and could not be sustained" (*Muller v. Oregon*, 108 U.S. 412 [1908]). Excluded from protective laws were large categories of women such as domestics and agricultural workers; almost all women of color fell into these categories until World War II.

2. Alice Kessler-Harris, *Out to Work: A History of Wage-Earning Women in the United States* (Oxford: Oxford University Press, 1982), 245–246.

3. Ibid., 247.

4. Barbara Bergmann, *The Economic Emergence of Women* (New York: Basic Books Inc., 1986), 156.

5. Susan Deller Ross, "Legal Aspects of Parental Leave: At the Crossroads," in Janet Shibley Hyde and Marilyn J. Essex, eds., *Parental Leave and Child Care: Setting a Research and Policy Agenda* (Philadelphia: Temple University Press, 1991), 94.

6. The five states with Temporary Disability Insurance (TDI) funds are Rhode Island (1942), California (1946), New Jersey (1948),

New York (1952), and Hawaii (1969). Employees in these states may draw up to two-thirds of their wages while they are out of work due to a non-work-related illness or injury. Rhode Island began to limit benefits for pregnancy in 1946, cutting them off at a maximum of 15 weeks, compared to a maximum of 26 weeks for other disabilities. Later the limit was reduced to 12 consecutive weeks, 6 weeks before and 6 weeks after delivery, except in cases of unusual complications. California at first included pregnancy only if there were complications. New Jersey lumped pregnancy with injuries that were "willfully self-inflicted or incurred in the perpetration of a high misdemeanor" and denied coverage. New York limited benefits to women who became disabled 2 weeks *after* returning to work following the end of the pregnancy. For more on TDI, see 9to5 Working Women Education Fund, "Wage Replacement for Family Leave: Is It Necessary? Is It Feasible?" (Cleveland: 9to5 WWEF, 1991).

7. "A Century of Women, Part I, Work and Family," Turner Broadcasting System (TBS), June 7, 1994.

8. Ibid. According to the TBS broadcast, Rep. Martha Griffiths helped sway the vote. She castigated her colleagues for laughing at the suggestion that sex discrimination should be outlawed: "We've sat here for four days discussing the rights of blacks and other minorities, and there has been no laughter, not even a smile. But when you suggest you shouldn't discriminate against your own wives, your own mothers, your own daughters, your own granddaughters, or your own sisters, then you laugh." Her remarks were followed by absolute silence.

9. Ibid.

10. *Phillips v. Martin Marietta Corp.*, 400 U.S. 542 (1971).

11. Employers who opposed seeing pregnancy as a disability made the following arguments for their position: Pregnancy is a natural function, private and usually voluntary; Rhode Island's TDI experience showed it cost too much to treat pregnancy as a disability; unlike people with other short-term disabilities, women don't go back to work after pregnancy; though pregnancy may disable, excluding it doesn't amount to sex or class discrimination.

12. According to Kessler-Harris (*Out to Work*, 313) the Women's Bureau began to see pregnancy as a temporary disability during the 1940s as part of their efforts to encourage women to join the workforce. In 1955, the Women's Bureau supported proposals to offer women paid maternity leave. Director Freida Miller testified

in favor of a Senate bill to give married federal civil service employees up to two months paid leave (*Out to Work*, 304).

13. Three cases were key. In 1971, Jo Carol LeFleur sued the Cleveland School Board after they ordered her to leave in the middle of the year and not come back before her baby was three months old. LeFleur told TBS she was shocked: "We could put up with you if you had a tumor, but we can't put up with you having a baby." When she complained to her union rep, he replied, "Mrs. LeFleur, this is not a big deal. Just go home. Just have the baby." Instead, LeFleur sued. By a 7-to-2 vote in *Cleveland Board of Education v. La Fleur* (414 U.S. 632 [1973]), the Supreme Court ruled that employers can't set an arbitrary time when a pregnant woman has to give up her job. Five years later, in *Crawford v. Cushman* (531 F.2d 114, 2d Cir. [1976]), a federal circuit court said mandatory discharge of pregnant women from the military was a violation of the Fifth Amendment. The seniority case, *Nashville Gas Co. v. Satty* (434 U.S. 136 [1977]), was decided the following year.

14. *General Electric Co. v. Gilbert* (429 U.S. 125 [1976]). This case was based on Title VII. An earlier case, *Geduldig v. Aiello* (1974), dealt with the Fourteenth Amendment argument.

15. The "voluntariness" argument continues to plague us today. In a 1987 case, *Winberly v. Labor and Industrial Relations Commission of Missouri* (479 U.S. 511, 107 S. Ct. 821 [1987]), the Supreme Court said a woman who was out of work because her employer didn't offer job-protected maternity leave was not eligible for unemployment. Since all workers who "voluntarily" leave for non-job-related reasons were treated the same, no discrimination was involved.

16. Dorothy McBride Stetson, "The Political History of Parental Leave Policy," in Hyde and Essex, *Parental Leave and Child Care*, 413. Stetson points out that law concerning leave in the United States went through three periods. First was maternity protection (1890s to 1950s): Women were defined as being primarily mothers who needed protections from the hazards of work. Then came the period of pregnancy as disability (1950s to 1970s): Women were defined as workers who needed the same disability rights as men. More recently (1980s), the focus changed to maternity/parental leave. Increasingly, this last category is being recognized as family and medical leave, to help women and men balance job and family responsibilities.

17. *Miller-Wohl v. Commissioner of Labor and Industry of Montana*, 515 F. Supp. 1266–67 (D. Mont. 1981).

18. These fears were understandable. Consider the examples of companies who forced women to prove they were sterile in order to take certain jobs. Because of the danger of exposing pregnant women to substances such as lead, companies like American Cyanmid and Johnson Controls barred all women who could become pregnant—even if they were not pregnant or had no plans to become pregnant—from certain jobs (which often paid better) that might expose them to hazards. Known as "fetal protection policies," these were challenged in a series of court cases. The position of the women suing and of their unions was: Make the jobs safe. If they're not safe for pregnant women, chances are they're not safe for other women or for men either. In 1991, the Supreme Court struck down such policies in *United Auto Workers v. Johnson Controls, Inc.* (59 United States Law Week 4209–4219 [1991]).

19. *California Federal Savings & Loan Association v. Guerra*, 479 U.S. 272 (1987).

20. United States General Accounting Office, Human Resources Division, *Parental Leave: Estimated Cost of Revised Parental and Medical Leave Act Proposal* (GAO/HRD 88–132) September 1988. The GAO estimated that an 18-week unpaid leave to care for a new or sick child would cost employers less than $478 million—far less than the $2.6 billion figure put out by the Chamber of Commerce (originally they projected the cost at $16.2 billion, but later conceded that estimate presumed a worst-case scenario—Martha Brannigan, "Laws on Parental-Leave Benefits Draw Opposition from Employers," *Wall Street Journal*, October 12, 1987). Only one in three workers on leave is actually replaced, found the GAO, and that cost is similar or less than the cost of those replaced. The GAO's reckoning didn't take into account any *savings* to employers from lower absenteeism and turnover, which other studies have found to be significant (see Chapter 12).

21. Ross, "Legal Aspects of Parental Leave," 107.

22. James T. Bond, "Who Is Eligible for Leave Benefits Under the Family and Medical Leave Act of 1993?" (New York: Families and Work Institute, 1994), 4.

23. Some states allowed leave only for birth parents, or only for birth or adoption. A few allowed leave to care for sick children but only in very limited cases—in Rhode Island, for instance, the child had to be on the edge of death or face a very serious medical problem, such as an organ transplant or limb amputation. Even after the Cal Fed decision, which specified that statutes for women were per-

missible only for the period of disability, Tennessee's law permitted a four-month leave for pregnancy, childbirth, or nursing with no reference to disability. Legal expert Susan Deller Ross argues that this discriminated against men: "Fathers who want to bottlefeed their babies or just spend time with them get no help from the statute." ("Legal Aspects of Parental Leave," 99). Ross points out that the California model also allows discrimination against pregnant women. Small employers (5 to 14 employees) were specifically authorized to exclude pregnancy coverage from medical insurance, to cap paid disability benefits at 6 weeks, and to exclude pregnant women from training programs if they could not finish at least 3 months prior to their due date. Louisiana's law copied all these—and passed in 1987.

Chapter 5

1. Cathy Feldman, *Two Years Without Sleep: Working Moms Talk About Having a Baby and a Job* (Santa Barbara, CA: Blue Point Books, 1993), 49.

2. Michele Galen, "Work and Family," *Business Week*, June 28, 1993, 88.

3. Sue Shellenbarger, "More Companies Experiment with Workers' Schedules," *Wall Street Journal*, January 13, 1994, B1.

4. Galen, "Work and Family," 86.

5. New Ways to Work, *Work Times*, 11, no. 4 (San Francisco, CA: New Ways to Work) October 1993, 4.

6. Shellenbarger, "More Companies Experiment," B6.

7. Interview in San Diego, California, June 29, 1994.

8. New Ways to Work in Partnership with DuPont, *Flexibility: Compelling Strategies for a Competitive Workplace* (San Francisco: New Ways to Work), 9.

9. "Labor Letter," *Wall Street Journal*, January 11, 1994, 1.

10. "Mommy Track," *Lifetime Magazine*, Lifetime Cable TV, February 22, 1994.

11. New Ways to Work/DuPont, 1.

12. Rhino Foods, Inc., "Co(mpany)-Creating Solutions to Overcapacity in Staffing" (Burlington, VT: Rhino Foods, 1993).

13. New Ways to Work/DuPont, 8.

14. Kathi Marshall and Carol Kramer, "Work-site Prenatal Programs Cut Costs," *Personnel Journal*, October 1993, 46.

15. Comment at February 10, 1994, press conference hosted by 9to5 in Milwaukee, Wisconsin.

16. Karol L. Rose, *Work and Family: Program Models and Policies* (New York: John Wiley & Sons, 1993), 10–81.

17. NBC Evening News, May 25, 1994, "Families in Crisis."

18. Elizabeth Harris Pope, "A Friend of the Family," in *Special Report on Family* (Knoxville, TN: Whittle Communications, November 1989), 28.

19. Esther B. Fein, "Looking Beyond Family to Aid the Elderly," *The New York Times*, April 6, 1994, A11.

20. *Business Ethics*, May/June 1993, 9.

21. Anne C. Weisberg and Carol A. Buckler, *everything a working mother needs to know about pregnancy rights, maternity leave and making her career work for her* (New York: Doubleday, 1994), 53.

22. New Ways to Work, *Work Times* 12, no. 2, April 1994, 6.

23. Galen, "Work and Family," 82.

24. Rose, *Work and Family*, I–4.

25. Julie Amparano Lopez, "The Enforcers," *Wall Street Journal Reports*, June 21, 1993, R7.

26. Sue Shellenbarger, "So Much Talk, So Little Action," *Wall Street Journal Reports*, June 21, 1993, R4.

27. Sue Shellenbarger, "Family Feud," *Wall Street Journal Reports*, June 21, 1993, R9.

28. Galen, "Work and Family," 83.

29. Shellenbarger, "So Much Talk, R4.

30. Ibid.

31. *Kansas City Star*, October 5, 1993, D14.

32. Sprint Employee Network press release, September 27, 1993.

33. Sue Shellenbarger, "Work and Family" column, *Wall Street Journal*, November 19, 1993.

34. Galen, "Work and Family," 84.

35. Feldman, *Two Years Without Sleep*, 46.

36. Weisberg and Buckler, *everything a working mother needs to know*, 142.

37. Deborah L. Jacobs, "Back From the Mommy Track," *The New York*

Times, October 9, 1994, F1. The study, conducted by business professors Joy Schneer and Frieda Reiton, compared 128 women MBAs who had never taken a break with 63 who had taken some leave and gone back full time by 1987.

38. Armin A. Brott, "Values Collide on the 'Daddy Track,'" *Washington Post*, August 19, 1993.

39. Ibid.

40. Susan Chira, "Obstacles for Men Who Want Family Time," *The New York Times*, October 21, 1993.

41. Ibid.

42. "Labor Letter," *Wall Street Journal*, August 24, 1993, 1.

43. Galen, "Work and Family," 84.

44. Robert L. Rose, "Small Steps," *Wall Street Journal Reports*, June 21, 1994, R10.

45. Feldman, *Two Years Without Sleep*, 78.

46. Susan Bacon Dynerman and Lynn O'Rourke Hayes, *The Best Jobs in America for Parents Who Want Careers and Time for Children Too* (New York: Rawson Associates, 1991), 27.

47. Lopez, "The Enforcers," R7.

48. Laura Leete-Guy and Juliet B. Schor in report for Economic Policy Institute, cited in "Nothing Leisurely About Time Off," *Los Angeles Times*, March 22, 1992.

49. Dianne Solis, "Labor Letter," *Wall Street Journal*, November 16, 1993, 1.

50. Steven Greenhouse, "If the French Can Do It, Why Can't We?" *New York Times Magazine*, November 14, 1993, 59–62.

Chapter 6

1. Interview in San Diego, California, June 28, 1994.

Chapter 7

1. Michele Galen, "Work and Family," *Business Week*, June 28, 1993, 82.

2. Ibid., 86.

3. National Council on Jewish Women's National Center for the Child, "Accommodating Pregnancy in the Workplace" (New York: NCJW, 1987).

4. Sherry Herchenroether, "Family Leave without Labor Pains," *Working Woman*, January 1992, 27.

5. Carol Kleiman, "Companies Tackling Work/Family Issues," *Chicago Tribune*, July 12, 1993, 8: 1.

6. Sue Shellenbarger, "More Companies Experiment with Workers' Schedules," *Wall Street Journal*, January 13, 1994, B6.

7. Galen, "Work and Family," 82.

8. Ibid.

9. Ibid.

10. Catalyst, *Flexible Work Arrangements: Establishing Options for Managers and Professionals* (New York: Catalyst, 1989).

11. Galen, "Work and Family."

12. "Labor Letter," *Wall Street Journal*, August 24, 1993, 1.

13. Southport Institute for Policy Analysis, "Caring Too Much? American Women and the National's Caregiving Crisis," cited in Women's Legal Defense Fund, "Americans Need Leave for Elder and Spousal Care" (Washington, DC: Women's Legal Defense Fund, 1991).

14. Robert Weisenberg, Testimony before the Wisconsin Senate Agriculture, Health and Human Services Committee, Milwaukee, September 23, 1987.

15. Michelle Lord, *It's a Matter of Time, the Report of the Governor's Project on Family Leave* (New York: New York State Industrial Cooperation Council, 1990), 27.

16. Eileen Trzcinski and William Alpert, *Leave Policies in Small Business: Findings from the U.S. Small Business Administration Employee Leave Survey*, October 1990.

17. James T. Bond, Ellen Galinsky, et al., *Beyond the Parental Leave Debate: The Impact of Laws in Four States* (New York: Families and Work Institute, 1991), iv.

18. Karol Rose, *Work and Family: Program Models and Policies* (New York: John Wiley & Sons, 1993), 12–16.

Chapter 8

1. "The Good News About Pregnancy and Work," *Working Woman*, September 1991, 105. This study looked at 1,283 pregnant medical residents. (See also Perri Klass, "Having Healthy Babies," *Cosmopolitan*, April 1992).

2. Kathleen Hughes, "Pregnant Professionals Face Pressures at Work as Attitudes Toward Them Shift," *Wall Street Journal*, February 6, 1991, B1:4.

3. "Pregnancy Discrimination," *Dateline NBC*, May 10, 1994.

4. Dana Friedman, "Linking Work-Family Issues to the Bottom Line" (New York: The Conference Board Report Number 962, 1991), 7.

5. Anne C. Weisberg and Carol A. Buckler, *everything a working mother needs to know about pregnancy rights, maternity leave and making her career work for her* (New York: Doubleday, 1994), 19. This book otherwise contains much useful advice and information.

6. Keith Epstein, "How We Countered the 'Family-Time Famine,'" *Washington Post*, April 11, 1994, B5.

7. For more information, see National Center for Lesbian Rights, *Recognizing Lesbian and Gay Families: Strategies for Obtaining Domestic Partner Benefits* (San Francisco: NCLR, 1992).

Chapter 9

1. 9to5, National Association of Working Women, "1994–95 Profile of Working Women" (Cleveland: 9to5 NAWW, 1994), 2.

2. Felice Schwartz, *Breaking with Tradition* (New York: Warner Books, 1992), 78.

3. Work in America Institute, Inc., *Work in America* (Scarsdale, NY: Work in America Institute, September 1992).

Chapter 10

1. Faye Crosby, *Juggling: The Unexpected Advantages of Balancing Career and Home for Women and Their Families* (New York: The Free Press, 1991), 8.

2. Bonnie Michaels and Elizabeth McCarty, *Solving the Work/Family Puzzle* (Homewood, IL: Business One Irwin, 1992), 114–115.

3. In 1994, Congress changed the regulations for paying taxes on household help. Taxes are now due annually instead of quarterly, on amounts of $1,000 or more a year, rather than $50 a quarter (some states still require quarterly filing). The law excludes students under age 18.

4. Barbara Vobejda and D'Vera Cohn, "More fathers take over day-

care duties," reprinted in the *Milwaukee Journal* from the *Washington Post*, May 20, 1994.

5. Esther B. Fein, "Looking Beyond Family to Aid the Elderly," *The New York Times*, April 6, 1994, A11.

6. Mary Beth Franklin, "Finding Options," *AARP Bulletin* 35, November 1994 (Washington, DC: AARP), 13.

7. Fein, "Looking Beyond Family."

Chapter 11

1. Armin A. Brott, "Values Collide on the 'Daddy Track,'" *Washington Post*, August 19, 1993.

2. Peter Steinfels, "U.S. Bishops Issue Message on Family," *The New York Times*, November 17, 1993, A1.

3. Ellen Galinsky, James T. Bond, and Dana E. Friedman, *The Changing Workforce: Highlights of the National Study* (New York: Families and Work Institute, 1993), 54. The study showed 43 percent of men in dual-earner families reported sharing the work 50/50; only 19 percent of the women in those families agreed. Although men are contributing significantly more, few take primary or equal responsibility; 71 percent of women have major responsibility for household and children, compared to only 5 percent of men.

4. "Parents say they find plenty of time for children," *Milwaukee Journal*, December 2, 1993, A6. A parenting survey conducted for Massachusetts Mutual Life Insurance Co. and *Family Fun* magazine found 75 percent of mothers working outside home, 65 percent of those remaining home, and one-third of fathers said they didn't have enough time alone.

5. Galinsky, Bond, and Friedman, *The Changing Workforce*, 76.

6. Faye Crosby, cited in "Juggling: The Unexpected Advantages of Balancing Career and Home for Women and Their Families," *Los Angeles Times*, October 22, 1991.

7. Ibid.

8. Susan Chira, "Still Guilty After All These Years: A Bouquet of Advice Books for the Working Mom," *New York Times Book Review*, May 8, 1994, 11. The book is now out of print.

Chapter 13

1. Michele Galen, "Work and Family," *Business Week*, June 28, 1993, 88.

2. For sample employee surveys, see Karol Rose, *Work and Family: Program Models and Policies* (New York: John Wiley & Sons, 1993), 7–60 – 7–71.

3. Robert L. Rose, "Small Steps," *Wall Street Journal Reports*, June 21, 1993, R10.

4. Julie Amparano Lopez, "The Enforcers," *Wall Street Journal Reports*, June 21, 1993, R7.

5. Dana Friedman, "Work vs. Family: War of the Worlds," in *Personnel Administrator*, October 1987, 38.

6. Elizabeth Harris Pope, "A Friend of the Family," in *Special Report on Family* (Knoxville, TN: Whittle Communications, November 1989), 28.

Chapter 14

1. Ellen Galinsky and James T. Bond, "Parental Leave Benefits for American Families," (New York: Families and Work Institute, 1993), 5.

2. Dana Friedman, *Linking Work-Family Issues to the Bottom Line* (New York: The Conference Board Report Number 962, 1991), 18. A study by Families and Work Institute showed that, compared to women who work for inflexible bosses, mothers who work for flexible bosses are seven times less likely to want to quit and nearly four times as likely to say they love their jobs.

3. Ellen Galinsky, James T. Bond, and Dana E. Friedman, *The Changing Workforce: Highlights of the National Study* (New York: Families and Work Institute, 1993), 30.

4. Interview, January 28, 1994, at Women's Economic Summit, Leesburg, VA.

Chapter 15

1. Roy Rosenzweig, *Eight Hours for What We Will: Workers and Leisure in an Industrial City, 1870–1920* (New York: Cambridge University Press, 1983).

2. Samuel Gompers, "Should the Wife Help Support the Family?" AF 13 (January 1906), 36.

3. Alice Kessler-Harris, *Out to Work: A History of Wage-Earning Women in the United States* (Oxford: Oxford University Press, 1982), 194. Many of the women preferred working swing shift, which included the desirable short stretch of 5–6 hours after day and before night shifts.

4. Philip Foner, *Organized Labor and the Black Worker, 1619–1973* (New York: Praeger, 1974), 34.

5. Susan Cowell, "Family Policy," in Dorothy Sue Cobble, ed., *Women and Unions* (Ithaca, NY: ILR Press, 1993), 120. For sample contract language, read the excellent booklet by the Coalition of Labor Union Women, *Bargaining for Family Benefits: A Union Member's Guide* (New York: CLUW, 1991). See Appendix A for address to order. Most contract examples in this chapter are drawn from this booklet.

6. Joyce Miller, "Comments," in Cobble, *Women and Unions*, 144.

7. Carolyn York, "Bargaining for Work and Family Benefits," in Cobble, *Women and Unions*, 129.

8. Ibid., 130. A survey by the American Federation of State, County and Municipal Employees (AFSCME) of larger public service worksites showed 85 percent of contracts allowed for leave; 70 percent of these were for four months or more. A similar SEIU survey found 84 percent of public-sector contracts provide six months or more of job-guaranteed leave, almost all with continuing health benefits. Even in the private sector, two-thirds of Service Employees International Union's surveyed contracts gave job-guaranteed leave of three months or more; 45 percent of those continued health benefits.

9. The American Family Bill of Rights called for:
   1. The right to a job and economic security.
   2. The right to health care.
   3. The right to child and elder care.
   4. The right to family leave.
   5. The right to services for the elderly.
   6. The right to quality education.
   7. The right to equal opportunity.
   8. The right to equal pay for work of equal value.
   9. The right to permanent housing.
   10. The right to live and work in a safe and accessible environment.

10. York, in Cobble, *Women and Unions*, 138–140.

11. Ibid., 133–136. The largest of these unions, the Civil Service Employees Association (CSEA), has many members who can't afford to send their children to the state centers. CSEA has made bargaining for subsidies a priority.

12. Roberta Spalter-Roth, Heidi Hartmann, and Nancy Collins, "What Do Unions Do for Women? Final Report to the Women's Bureau, U.S. Department of Labor" (Washington, DC: Institute for Women's Policy Research, 1994), 15.

13. Ibid., 23.

14. "A Century of Women, Part I, Work and Family," TBS, June 7, 1994. All comments from Huerta quoted here are from this documentary.

15. CLUW, *Bargaining For Family Benefits: A Union Member's Guide* (New York: CLUW, 1991), 2. See also "Building Work and Family Committees: A Union-Based Approach," available from OCAW Local 8–149, 90 Lewis Street, Rahway, NJ 07065.

16. Spalter-Roth et al., "What Do Unions Do for Women?," 3.

17. Dorothy Sue Cobble, "Remaking Unions for the New Majority," in Cobble, *Women and Unions*, 4.

18. "A Century of Women, Part I, Work and Family," TBS, June 7, 1994.

19. Interview with Ruth Needleman, July 30, 1994. Unless otherwise noted, all comments from Needleman are from this interview. See also her "Comments" and those of Roberta Lynch in Cobble, *Women and Unions*, 406–421.

20. Pamela Roby and Lynet Uttal, "Putting It All Together: The Dilemmas of Rank-and-File Union Leaders," in Cobble, *Women and Unions*, 363–377.

21. Ibid.

Chapter 16

1. James T. Bond, "Who is Eligible for Leave Benefits Under the Family and Medical Leave Act of 1993" (New York: Families and Work Institute, 1994), 4. The percentages are particularly low in a number of female-dominated occupations—wholesale and retail trade (only 34 percent of the workers are covered), business or professional service (40.5 percent), and personal service (25.6 percent).

2. Ibid., 6.

3. For more information, see 9to5 Working Women Education Fund, *Wage Replacement: Is It Necessary? Is It Feasible? Is It Winnable?* (Cleveland: 9to5, WWEF, 1992).

4. New Ways to Work, *Work Times*, Vol. 12, No. 3 (San Francisco, CA: New Ways to Work), July 1994, 7. For more information on what other countries do, see Appendix C.

5. Erik Gunn, "The time-poor American," *Milwaukee Journal*, April 19, 1994, C7.

6. "Women are more likely to have sleep problems," *Milwaukee Journal*, March 27, 1994, G5.

7. Elizabeth Harris Pope, "A Friend of the Family," in *Special Report on Family* (Knoxville, TN: Whittle Communications, November 1989), 30.

8. C. Eichman and B. Reisman, "How Small Employers Are Benefiting from Offering Child Care Assistance," *Employment Relations Today*, Spring 1992, 59.

9. Lucinda M. Finley, "Legal Aspects of Child Care: The Policy Debate over the Appropriate Amount of Public Responsibility," in Janet Shibley Hyde and Marilyn J. Essex, eds., *Parental Leave and Child Care: Setting a Research and Policy Agenda* (Philadelphia: Temple University Press, 1991), 130.

10. "Solving the Zoe Baird Problem," *The New York Times*, July 3, 1994.

Index

ABOUT 9to5

If you're having any kind of problem on the job—sexual harassment, concerns about pregnancy or family leave, discrimination, wages and hours, health and safety—call the 9to5 Job Problem Hotline. Our trained counselors can give you the advice and support you need.

9to5 JOB PROBLEM HOTLINE
1-800-522-0925

— —

9to5, National Association of Working Women, would welcome you as a member. Complete this form and mail it to:

> 9to5, National Association of Working Women
> 238 W. Wisconsin Avenue
> Milwaukee, WI 53203

_____ I would like to join 9to5. Enclosed please find my check for $25 made out to 9to5.

_____ Enclosed is my tax-deductible contribution to 9to5, Working Women Education Fund, the research and education arm of 9to5.

_____ I will designate my payroll deduction to 9to5, Working Women Education Fund. Please send me a reminder.

Charge my dues/contribution to my:

_____ Visa _____ Mastercard Expiration Date _____

Credit Card # _____ Signature _____

_____ My dues are enclosed. Please send me information on starting a 9to5 chapter or becoming a local 9to5 representative.

_____ Please send me more information on 9to5.

Name _____

Address _____

City/State/Zip _____

Phone (home) _____ (work) _____

Job title _____ Industry _____